Psychology
A Self-Teaching Guide

Psychology
A Self-Teaching Guide

Frank J. Bruno, Ph.D.

John Wiley & Sons, Inc.

Published by John Wiley & Sons, Inc., Hoboken, New Jersey
Published simultaneously in Canada

For general information about our other products and services, please contact our Customer Care Department within the United States at (800) 762-
2974, outside the United States at (317) 572-3993 or fax (317) 572-4002.

Wiley also publishes its books in a variety of electronic formats. Some content that appears in print may not be available in electronic books.

ISBN 0-471-44395-6

Printed in the United States of America

10 9 8 7 6 5 4 3 2 1

To those who seek a greater
understanding of human behavior

Contents

Preface

To help you learn psychology on your own, *Psychology: A Self-Teaching Guide* employs the following distinctive features:

- Each chapter begins with a five-question true-or-false preview quiz; answers can be found near the end of a given chapter.

- Immediately following the quiz there is a short list of chapter objectives.

- Following each section there are one or several questions pertaining to the material in the section. The questions are of the fill-in-the-blank variety. Answers are provided immediately following the questions.

- A ten-question multiple-choice self-test appears toward the end of each chapter. Answers to the self-test immediately follow.

- A list of key terms appears at the end of each chapter.

How Do You Use the Book?

I hope that you will use the book by being an active, not a passive, learner. You can accomplish this by following a step-by-step process for each chapter:

1. Take the five-question true-or-false quiz. Even if you don't know an answer, make a guess. This will get you involved in the material. Turn to the answer key at the end of the chapter. Score the test. You should, of course, be pleased if you get four or five questions correct. On the other hand, don't be concerned if you only get two or three correct. Obviously, you haven't studied the material yet. The purpose of the quiz is to break the ice, verify what you already know, and give you a preview of what is to come in the chapter.
2. Review the chapter objectives. Their aim is to give you some idea of what you need to pay attention to in the chapter. The objectives help to give your study focus and direct you to what is of particular importance in the chapter.
3. Read each section and pay particular attention to the emphasized terms and their meanings.
4. Respond to the fill-in-the-blank sentences at the end of each section before moving on to the next one. Attempt the answers through the use of mental

recall. It is a good idea to actually write down, not just think about, your answers. If necessary, cover the answers at the bottom of the questions. Then check your responses against the answers provided. Look back at the relevant section if there is anything you don't understand.

5. Take the ten-question multiple-choice test at the end of the chapter. If you're not sure of an answer, take a guess. Your guess is likely to be an educated, not a random, guess. After all, you have been studying the material. On most college multiple-choice tests there is no penalty for guessing. Only correct answers are scored, and nothing is taken away for missing a question.

6. Score the test using the answers that immediately follow it. On an absolute scale, a score of 10 or 9 correct equals an A. A score of 8 correct equals a B. A score of 7 correct equals a C. A score of 6 correct equals a D. A score of 5 correct equals an F. Refer back to the material associated with questions you missed, and evaluate why you made an error.

7. Review the key terms at the end of the chapter. The terms are listed in alphabetical order. Look up any terms you don't recognize or that have little meaning for you.

I believe that you will find psychology to be an interesting subject. Also, you will discover that it has relevance in terms of everyday life. I have made every effort to write a book that will make it possible for you to readily grasp psychology's key concepts. I hope you find the process of learning more about behavior a meaningful and valuable experience.

A number of people have helped me make *Psychology: A Self-Teaching Guide* a reality. My thanks are expressed to:

Jeff Golick, editor at John Wiley & Sons, for recognizing the merits of the book.

Mark Steven Long for carefully supervising production.

Karen Fraley for excellent copy editing.

Bert Holtje, agent with James Peter Associates, for his confidence in my ability.

Gene Brissie, agent with James Peter Associates, for his support and assistance.

Jeanne, my wife, for our many meaningful discussions about human behavior.

Franklin, my son, for our frequent conversations about words, language, and meaning.

Josephine Bruno, my mother, for listening to my ideas.

George K. Zaharopoulos, a true teaching colleague, for his steadfast encouragement of my writing projects.

David W. Yang for his help in preparing the manuscript.

1 Introduction: The Foundations of Psychology

True or False

1. T F Modern psychology is defined as the science of the mind.
2. T F The goals of scientific psychology are to (1) describe, (2) explain, (3) predict, and (4) control behavior.
3. T F Sigmund Freud was the principal founding personality of psychoanalysis.
4. T F The biological viewpoint assumes that most behavior is learned.
5. T F Clinical psychology, a field that stresses psychotherapy and psychological testing, is the single largest field of psychology.

(Answers can be found on page 15.)

Objectives

After completing this chapter, you will be able to

- define psychology;
- state the goals of scientific psychology;

- identify the five classical schools of psychology and their founding personalities;
- name and describe the six principal viewpoints used to explain behavior;
- name and describe seven important fields of psychology.

Looking at the Word *Psychology:* From Ancient to Modern Meanings

The word **psychology** has had several different meanings from ancient to modern times. Here is its present definition: *Psychology is the science that studies the behavior of organisms.* This definition should guide you throughout your study of this book.

Three words in the definition merit special attention: (1) science, (2) behavior, and (3) organisms. Modern psychology is considered a *science* because it bases its conclusions on **data,** information obtained by systematic observations. The research methods used by psychology are covered in chapter 2.

Behavior has three aspects: (1) cognitive processes, (2) emotional states, and (3) actions. **Cognitive processes** refer to what an individual thinks. **Emotional states** refer to what an individual feels. **Actions** refer to what an individual does.

An **organism** is any living creature. Consequently, the behavior of dogs, rats, pigeons, and monkeys can be legitimately included in the study of psychology. Such organisms have indeed been subjects in psychology experiments. However, traditionally the principal focus of psychology has been humans. When animals are used in experiments, the implicit goal is often to explore how such basic processes as learning and motivation, as studied in animals, can cast a light on our understanding of human behavior.

(a) What does psychology study? _____

(b) What are the three aspects of behavior? _____

   Answers: (a) The behavior of organisms; (b) Cognitive processes, emotional states, and actions.

Although you now know the modern definition of psychology, it is important to realize that the word *psychology* has its roots in ancient meanings associated with philosophy. The Greek word **psyche** means soul. Consequently, to philosophers living 400 to 300 B.C., psychology was the "study of the soul." This was the meaning given by Socrates, Plato, and Aristotle. In view of the fact that these thinkers, particularly Socrates and Plato, did not believe that animals have souls, it becomes evident why for many centuries psychology's main attention has been given to human beings. The ancient philosophers asserted that the soul is the seat of consciousness. It is consciousness that makes mental life possible. This is why psychology is often thought of as the science of the mind.

Indeed, this meaning is the one given to it by William James, the dean of American psychologists. Working at Harvard a little more than one hundred years ago, James defined psychology as "the science of mental life." He believed that the purpose of psychology should be to investigate such mental processes as thinking, memory, and perception. (There is more about James later in this chapter.)

This is where we stand now. Although psychology no longer is thought of as the study of the soul, this original meaning colors our present-day approach, with its emphasis on human behavior and the importance of cognition.

(a) The Greek word *psyche* means _____.

(b) William James defined psychology as _____.

   Answers: (a) soul; (b) the science of mental life.

Contemporary, scientific psychology has four explicit goals: (1) describe, (2) explain, (3) predict, and (4) control behavior. These goals are the same common-sense goals that we all use in everyday life. Let's say that Jane tells her husband, Harry, that their son, seven-year-old Billy, was a brat today. Is this a good description of Billy's behavior? No, it's not. It's too general, too abstract. On the other hand, let's assume that Jane says that Billy refused to do his homework and told her, "Homework is stupid. I'm not going to do it anymore." This constitutes a much better description of behavior because is it is specific and concrete.

Similar specific descriptions may suggest to both parents that Billy misbehaves more than most children. Jane and Harry now wonder *why* Billy is beginning to misbehave more and more. Is he frustrated? Does he have an inferiority complex? Does he have low self-esteem? Does he have Attention Deficit Disorder (ADD)? Does he have an imbalance of certain key neurotransmitters in his brain? Does he have a childhood neurosis? As you can see, potential explanations are plentiful. They have to be evaluated.

This is where prediction and control come in. Let's say that Dr. Helen G., the family pediatrician, suggests that Billy *is* indeed suffering from Attention Deficit Disorder. Let's also assume that Dr. G. is convinced that Billy eats too many foods with refined sugar and that this causes, through a complex biochemical reaction, a depletion of certain neurotransmitters. She recommends a diet of natural foods with little refined sugar. The physician is *predicting* that the change in diet will take away the undesirable symptoms.

Let's say that the diet is tried. Billy sticks to it. If there is no change in Billy's misbehavior after several weeks, both Dr. G. and the parents will conclude that the explanation was incorrect. On the other hand, if the diet is therapeutic, and Billy's behavior becomes more manageable, then *control* has taken place. The explanation will appear to be adequate.

The four goals of scientific psychology are _____.

> *Answer:*   to describe, explain, predict, and control behavior.

The Classical Schools of Psychology: Five Great Thinkers and Their Ideas

It has been said that psychology has a long past and a short history. This statement should be taken to mean that although psychology has its roots in philosophy, as a scientific discipline psychology is only a little over 120 years old. As noted earlier, the roots of psychology can be easily traced back about 2,400 years to ancient Greek philosophers. However, the beginning of scientific psychology is usually associated with the date 1879, the year that a German scientist named Wilhelm Wundt founded the first psychological laboratory at the University of Leipzig in Germany.

Modern psychology arose in the context of what are known as **schools of psychology.** The concept of a school of psychology can be easily understood by thinking of a school of fish. In this case the word *school* is used similarly to the word *group.* A school, or group, of fish follows a leader fish. So it is with a school of psychology. There is a leader and a group of followers. The school has a viewpoint and a set of important assumptions.

(a) As a scientific discipline, psychology is only a little over how many years old?

_____

(b) The first psychological laboratory was founded in 1879 by _____.

> *Answers:*   (a) 120; (b) Wilhelm Wundt.

From a historical perspective, the first school of psychology to be established was **structuralism.** Its founding personality was Wilhelm Wundt (1832–1920). As already noted, he founded the world's first psychological laboratory. Wundt was trained in *physiology,* the study of the functions of the body. He became interested in studying not so much the physiology of the sense organs such as the eyes and ears, but in how simple sensations associated with the sense organs combined to form what we call human consciousness.

Imagine that you are looking at an oil painting of a landscape. You perceive trees, a river, a valley, and a sky. But what are the elemental sensations, the *basic building blocks,* that make the visual grasp of the picture possible? What, in a word, is the "structure" of your consciousness? Wundt trained assistants in the art of **introspection,** a skill characterized by paying attention not to the whole pattern of a stimulus, but to an elemental part of a stimulus. Consequently, a trained introspectionist was not supposed to say, "I see a tree." Instead, he or she was supposed to say, "I see here a patch of green," and "I see there a bit of brown," and so forth. These bits and pieces were the psychological "atoms" that made up the complex "molecule" of the tree or other visual object.

Wundt's studies of vision suggested that there are only three basic kinds of visual sensations. First, there is *hue,* or color. Second, there is *brightness.* For example, a light gray card is brighter than a dark gray card. Also, a page of print illuminated with an intense light is brighter than a page illuminated with a light of lower intensity. Third, there is *saturation.* This refers to the "richness" or "fullness" of a color.

No matter what visual stimulus Wundt's subjects looked at, there were no other kinds of sensations experienced than the three identified above. Consequently, Wundt concluded that all visual experiences are structured out of these same three types of elemental experiences. Similar statements can be made about the other senses such as hearing, taste, and touch. (See chapter 4.)

According to Wundt, the primary purpose of psychology is to study the structure of consciousness. By the structure of consciousness, Wundt meant the relationship of a group of sensations, a relationship that produces the complex experiences we think of as our conscious mental life. This approach to psychology has been called *mental chemistry.* As earlier indicated, the "atoms" of experience are the sensations. The "molecules" of experience are our complex perceptions.

Wundt is considered to be not only the first scientific psychologist, but also the founder of psychology as an academic discipline. (Many beginning psychology students think this honor belongs to Sigmund Freud. Although Freud *is* the most famous psychologist who ever lived, he occupies a different place in psychology's history than does Wundt.)

(a) Reporting a sensation alone without being confused by other sensations describes what process? _____

(b) According to Wundt, the primary purpose of psychology is to study _____.

Answers: (a) Introspection; (b) the structure of consciousness.

William James (1842–1910), teaching at Harvard in the 1870s, was following Wundt's research with interest. James had an interest not only in psychology, but also in physiology and eventually in philosophy. James founded a psychological laboratory at Harvard; he also authored *The Principles of Psychology,* the first psychology textbook published in the United States. The book was published in 1890, and this can also be taken as the date when the school of psychology known as **functionalism** was born. The principal personality associated with it is James, and he is said to be the dean of American psychologists.

According to James, psychology should be more interested in how the mind *functions,* or works, than how it is structured. Consequently, James stressed the importance of studying such processes as thinking, memory, and attention. You will recall that James defined psychology as "the science of mental life." This definition is certainly reflected in the processes just identified.

In brief, functionalism as a school of psychology asserts that that the primary purpose of psychology should be to study the functions of human consciousness, not its structures.

According to James, psychology should be interested primarily in how the mind
_____.

Answer: functions.

The German psychologist Max Wertheimer (1880–1943), like James, was also dissatisfied with Wundt's structuralism. Wertheimer believed that Wundt's emphasis on the importance of simple sensations as the building blocks of perceptions was misguided. According to Wertheimer, a melody, for example, is more than an aggregate of sensations. It is a pattern. And the perception of the melody depends much more on the pattern itself than on the individual notes. A melody played in the key of F can be transposed to the key of C, and *it is still the same melody.* However, all of the notes, the sensations, are *different.*

The general pattern that induces a complex perception is described with the German word **Gestalt.** Gestalt is usually translated as a "pattern," a "configuration," or an "organized whole."

In 1910 Wertheimer published an article setting forth the basic assumptions of Gestalt psychology, and this is usually taken to be the starting date of the school. The article reported a series of experiments using two of his friends, Kurt Koffka and Wolfgang Kohler, as subjects. These two men went on to also become well-known Gestalt psychologists. In the experiments, Wertheimer demonstrated that the perception of motion can take place if stationary stimuli are presented as a series of events separated by an optimal interval of time. This sounds complicated. However, in practice it's simple enough. If you flip at just the right speed through a special kind of cartoon book, you can perceive motion as the series of still pictures flicker by. Perceiving motion in a motion picture is the same thing. At the level of sensation, you are being presented with a series of still slides. At the level of perception, you are experiencing motion. The presence of motion can't be explained by the nature of the sensations. Consequently, it must be the pattern of presentation, or the Gestalt, that is inducing the perceived motion.

It became the goal of Gestalt psychology to study the effects that various Gestalten (the plural of *Gestalt*) have on thinking and perception. As you will discover in chapter 6, Kohler's research related Gestalt principles to insight learning.

In brief, Gestalt psychology asserts that patterns, or configurations, of stimuli have a powerful effect on how we think and perceive the world around us.

(a) Three of the meanings of the German word *Gestalt* are _____.

(b) The goal of Gestalt psychology was the study the effects that various Gestalten have on _____.

> *Answers:* (a) pattern, configuration, and organized whole; (b) thinking and perception.

Returning to the United States, **behaviorism** is a fourth classical school of psychology. Its founding personality is John B. Watson (1878–1958). A wave of enthusiasm for Watson's ideas swept him to the presidency of the American Psychological Association (APA) in 1915, and this can be taken as the starting date for behaviorism. Doing research first at the University of Chicago and then at Johns Hopkins University, Watson came to the conclusion that psychology was placing too much emphasis on consciousness. In fact, he asserted that psychology is not a mental science at all. The "mind" is a mushy, difficult-to-define concept. It can't be studied by science because it can't be observed. Only you can know what's going on in your mind. If I say I'm studying your mind, according to Watson, it's only guesswork.

Consequently, Watson asserted that the purpose of psychology should be to study *behavior itself,* not the mind or consciousness. Some critics of Watson say that he denied the very existence of consciousness. Others assert Watson was primarily saying that references to the consciousness, or mental life, of a subject don't provide solid explanations of behavior. In either event, Watson's view is today thought to be somewhat extreme and is referred to as *radical behaviorism,* a psychology that doesn't employ consciousness as an important concept.

Behaviorism has been very influential in American psychology. As you will find in chapter 6, it inspired a psychologist named B. F. Skinner to study the process of learning. Skinner in time became the most famous behaviorist of the twentieth century.

(a) Watson said that the mind can't be studied by science because it can't be _____.

(b) Behaviorism asserts that the purpose of psychology should be to _____.

> *Answers:* (a) observed; (b) study behavior itself, not the mind or consciousness.

In order to identify a fifth classical school of psychology, it is necessary to return to the European continent, specifically to Austria; the school is **psychoanalysis.** The father of psychoanalysis is Sigmund Freud (1856–1939). Freud was a medical doctor with a specialty in neurology. His findings and conclusions are based primarily on his work with patients. Early in his career he concluded that a large number of people with neurological symptoms such as paralysis, a numb feeling in a hand or foot, complete or partial blindness, chronic headaches, and similar complaints had no organic pathology. They were *not* biologically sick. Instead their symptoms were produced by intense emotional conflicts.

Freud's original work was done with a colleague named Josef Breuer (1842–1925). Breuer and Freud collaborated on the book *Studies on Hysteria*. Published in 1895, it is the first book written on psychoanalysis. This can also be taken to be the starting date for the school. After the publication of this first book, Freud went on alone without Breuer; it was a number of years before he worked again with colleagues.

The word **hysteria** is a diagnostic label. It used to be assigned to a patient if he or she was experiencing neurological symptoms that were thought to be imaginary in nature. The patient is not malingering. He or she believes that the symptoms are real. Today this is a well-recognized disorder, and is called a **somatoform disorder, conversion type.** This simply means that an emotional problem such as chronic anxiety has converted itself to a bodily expression. (The Greek word *soma* means "body.")

In order to explain chronic emotional suffering, Freud asserted that human beings have an unconscious mental life. This is the principal assumption of psychoanalysis. No other assumption or assertion that it makes is nearly as important. The unconscious mental level is created by a defense mechanism called **repression.** Its aim is to protect the ego against psychological threats, information that will disturb its integrity. (The ego is the "I" of the personality, the center of the self.) The kind of mental information repressed tends to fall into three primary categories: (1) painful childhood memories, (2) forbidden sexual wishes, and (3) forbidden aggressive wishes.

Psychoanalysis is not only a school of psychology, but also a method of therapy. You will find more about this in chapter 15. Freud believed that by helping a patient explore the contents of the unconscious mental level, he or she could obtain a measure of freedom from emotional suffering. It is important to note that of the five classical schools of psychology, psychoanalysis is the only one that made it an aim to improve the individual's mental health.

(a) Freud was a medical doctor with a specialty in _____.

(b) The principal assumption of psychoanalysis is that _____.

    Answers: (a) neurology; (b) human beings have an unconscious mental life.

Ways of Approaching the Study of Behavior: Searching for Explanations

As noted earlier, one of the goals of scientific psychology is to explain behavior. When someone does something, particularly something unexpected, often the first question that pops into our minds is why. If the answer can be resolved to our satisfaction, we have an explanation. There is often more than one way to explain the same behavior. Sometimes rational thinkers disagree. This has resulted in a set of *viewpoints,* major ways in which behavior can be explained. These viewpoints greatly influence how research is done, how psychologists approach the study of behavior.

Viewpoints in psychology are major ways _____.

> *Answer:*   in which behavior can be explained.

The first viewpoint to be identified is the **biological viewpoint.** The biological viewpoint asserts that behavior can be explained in terms of such factors as genes, the endocrine system, or the brain and nervous system. The biological viewpoint assumes that we are all organisms, made out of protoplasm, and the most solid explanations are those that recognize this.

Let us say that a child is suffering from mental retardation. Assume that the child receives a diagnosis of Down's syndrome, a set of signs and symptoms suggesting that the child has three chromosomes on what is normally the twenty-first pair of chromosomes. Mental retardation is very frequently associated with this condition. Consequently, the genetic condition provides an explanation of the mental retardation.

Assume that thirty-four-year-old Jane C. says, "I feel lazy." This may seem to be a psychological condition. If it is later discovered that she has a sluggish thyroid gland and a low basal metabolism, her laziness may be explained in terms of her low thyroid production.

Bill, a forty-five-year-old engineer, suffers from chronic depression. If it is discovered that he has low levels of the neurotransmitter *serotonin,* a chemical messenger in the brain, he may be prescribed a psychiatric drug that brings the serotonin to an optimal level. His depression has been explained in terms of the brain's neurotransmitters.

As you can see, the biological viewpoint is a powerful and useful one. It is the viewpoint that tends to be favored by psychiatry, a medical specialty, and physiological psychology (see "Fields of Psychology" on page 12).

The biological viewpoint asserts that behavior can be explained in terms of such factors as

_____.

> *Answer:*   genes, the endocrine system, or the brain and nervous system.

The second viewpoint to be identified is the **learning viewpoint.** The learning viewpoint assumes that much, perhaps most, behavior is learned. Behaviors are acquired by experience. The learning viewpoint owes much to the influence of the philosopher John Locke (1632–1704), who said that the mind at birth is a **tabula rasa** (i.e., a "blank slate"), meaning that there are no inborn ideas.

Let's say that Opal smokes two packages of cigarettes a day. She thinks of it as a "bad" habit, and the learning viewpoint agrees with this commonsense way of looking at Opal's smoking behavior. The behavior was acquired by processes such as observation and reinforcement. (There will be more about these processes in chapter 6.)

According to the learning viewpoint, both "good" and "bad" habits are acquired by experience. We acquire more than habits by learning. We learn to talk a specific language, we learn attitudes, we learn to like some people and dislike others, and so forth. Learning is a vast ongoing enterprise in every human life.

(a) Locke said that the mind at birth is a *tabula rasa* or _____.

(b) According to the learning viewpoint, both "good" and "bad" habits are _____.

   Answers: (a) blank slate; (b) acquired by experience.

The third viewpoint to be identified is the **psychodynamic viewpoint.** This viewpoint owes much to the influence of Freud and psychoanalysis. It asserts that a human personality contains a field of forces. Primitive sexual and aggressive impulses are often in conflict with one's moral and ethical values. An individual's emotional conflicts can induce or aggravate chronic anxiety, anger, or depression. The psychodynamic viewpoint is of particular value when one seeks to understand the behavior of a troubled person. (There is more about psychoanalysis and the psychodynamic viewpoint in chapter 13.)

The psychodynamic viewpoint asserts that a human personality contains _____.

   Answer: a field of forces.

The fourth viewpoint to be identified is the **cognitive viewpoint.** This viewpoint asserts that an immediate cause of a given action or an emotional state is what a person thinks. For example, before you actually go to the supermarket you usually think something such as, "I'll stop at the store to get some milk and cereal on the way home from work." For a second example, when a person experiences depression, he or she may first think something such as, "My life is pointless. Nobody loves me."

Interest in the thinking process can be easily traced back to the writings of William James. He is often said to be not only the dean of American psychologists but the first cognitive psychologist in the United States. The cognitive viewpoint has lead to a great interest in concept formation, rational thinking, and creative thinking. (There is more about thinking in chapter 9.)

The cognitive viewpoint asserts that an immediate cause of a given action or an emotional state is _____.

   Answer: what a person thinks.

The fifth viewpoint to be identified is the **humanistic viewpoint.** This viewpoint asserts that some of our behavior can only be understood in terms of psychological processes that are uniquely human. This viewpoint owes much to *existentialism,* a philosophical position originating in Europe that places an emphasis on the importance of free will and responsibility.

Two processes that tend to receive emphasis are the need for self-actualization and the will to meaning. **Self-actualization,** as defined by the psychologist Abraham Maslow, is the need to fulfill your talents and potentialities. The **will to meaning,** as defined by the psychiatrist Viktor Frankl, is a deep desire to make sense out of life and discover values to live by.

(a) Existentialism places on emphasis on the importance of _____.

(b) Two processes that tend to receive emphasis in the humanistic viewpoint are _____.

Answers: (a) free will and responsibility; (b) self-actualization and the will to meaning.

The sixth viewpoint to be identified is the **sociocultural viewpoint.** This viewpoint assumes that much of our behavior is determined by factors associated with society and culture. For example, when a country has a great long-lasting depression, there is often a rise in personal problems such as depression and alcohol abuse. Society and culture find their expression in the family and its values, in religious traditions, and in general codes of conduct. (The importance of the sociocultural viewpoint is reflected in chapter 16.)

The sociocultural viewpoint assumes that much of our behavior is determined by factors associated with _____.

Answer: society and culture.

Very few contemporary psychologists identify with a single school of psychology or subscribe to a single explanatory viewpoint. **Eclecticism** is the point of view that there is something of merit in most of the schools of psychology and in the various viewpoints described. The majority of today's psychologists describe themselves as eclectic. Eclecticism is by and large desirable. It is integrative and reflects an open-minded attitude. On the other hand, critics of eclecticism say that it is vapid and stands for nothing. Consequently, a competent psychologist must make an effort to steer a clear course between either a dogmatic adherence to a single viewpoint or an opposite extreme characterized by a lack of conviction and confidence.

Eclecticism is the point of view that there is _____ in most of the schools of psychology and the various viewpoints described.

Answer: something of merit.

Fields of Psychology: Of Laboratories and Clinics

Psychology as a profession expresses itself in different *fields,* or domains of interest. There are a number of fields of psychology, such as clinical, experimental, counseling, developmental, physiological, human factors, and industrial.

Clinical psychology is the field associated with psychotherapy and psychological testing. A clinic is a place where sick people go for help; consequently, clinical psychologists try to help persons with both well-defined mental disorders and serious personal problems. The word **psychotherapy,** in terms of its roots, means a "healing of the self." In practice, a clinical psychologist who employs psychotherapy attempts to work with a troubled person by using various methods and techniques that are designed to help the individual improve his or her mental health. This is done without drugs. An informal description of psychotherapy refers to it as "the talking cure." (There is more about methods of psychotherapy in chapter 15.)

Psychological testing is a process involving, in most cases, the administration of paper-and-pencil intelligence and personality tests. Test results can be helpful in both making an evaluation of the state of a person's mental health and suggesting a course of treatment. (There is more about psychological testing in chapter 13.)

A clinical psychologist should not be confused with a psychiatrist. A fully qualified *clinical psychologist* has earned a Ph.D. degree (doctor of philosophy with a specialization in psychology). **Psychiatry** is a medical specialty that gives its attention to mental disorders. A fully qualified *psychiatrist* has earned an M.D. degree (doctor of medicine). Although psychiatrists can and do practice psychotherapy, they can also prescribe drugs. Clinical psychologists, not being medical doctors, do not prescribe drugs.

Clinical psychology is the largest single field of psychology. About 40 percent of psychologists are clinical psychologists.

(a) Clinical psychology is the field associated with what two work activities? _____

(b) What kind of a specialty is psychiatry? _____

    Answers: (a) Psychotherapy and psychological testing; (b) It is a medical specialty.

Experimental psychology is the field associated with research. Experimental psychologists investigate basic behavioral processes such as learning, motivation, perception, memory, and thinking. Subjects may be either animals or human beings. Ivan Pavlov's experiments on conditioned reflexes, associated with the learning process, used dogs as subjects. (See chapter 6.)

The great majority of experimental psychologists are found at the nation's universities. Their duties combine research and teaching. In order to obtain a permanent position and achieve academic promotion, it is necessary for the psychologist to publish the results of experiments in recognized scientific journals.

Experimental psychology is not a large field of psychology in terms of numbers of psychologists. Only about 6 percent of psychologists are experimental psychologists. On the other hand, experimental psychology represents a cutting edge of psychology; it is where much progress is made. The overall concepts and findings in a book such as this one have been made possible primarily by experimental work.

Experimental psychology is the field associated with _____.

Answer: research.

The remaining fields of psychology will be briefly described in terms of what psychologists associated with them do.

A **counseling psychologist** provides advice and guidance, often in a school setting. Sometimes he or she will, like a clinical psychologist, attempt to help individuals with personal problems. However, if the problems involve a mental disorder, the individual will be referred to a clinical psychologist or a psychiatrist.

A **developmental psychologist** is concerned with maturational and learning processes in both children and adults. Although a developmental psychologist is usually thought of as a "child psychologist," it is important to realize that a given developmental psychologist might have a particular interest in changes associated with middle-aged or elderly people.

A **physiological psychologist,** like an experimental psychologist, does research. Subject areas include the structures and functions of the brain, the activity of neurotransmitters (i.e., chemical messengers), and the effect that hormones produced by the endocrine glands have on moods and behavior.

A **human factors psychologist** combines a knowledge of engineering with a knowledge of psychology. For example, he or she may be part of a team that is attempting to redesign an aircraft control panel in an attempt to make it more "user friendly" in order to reduce pilot error associated with misperceptions.

An **industrial psychologist** usually works for a corporation. The principal aim is to provide a work environment that will facilitate production, reduce accidents, and maintain employee morale. A theme that guides industrial psychology is "the human use of human beings."

(a) A counseling psychologist provides _____.

(b) A human factors psychologist combines a knowledge of what two subject areas? _____

Answers: (a) advice and guidance; (b) Engineering and psychology.

1. The primary subject matter of psychology is
   a. the philosophical concept of the psyche
   b. the behavior of organisms
   c. the conscious mind
   d. the unconscious mind

2. Which one of the following is *not* a goal of scientific psychology?
   a. To abstract behavior
   b. To explain behavior
   c. To predict behavior
   d. To control behavior

3. What characterizes a school of psychology?
   a. Its physiological research
   b. Its stand on Gestalt psychology
   c. Its orientation toward psychoanalysis
   d. Its viewpoint and assumptions

4. Functionalism, associated with William James, is particularly interested in
   a. introspection
   b. the structure of consciousness
   c. how the mind works
   d. developmental psychology

5. Which one of the following is correctly associated with the German word *Gestalt?*
   a. Neuron
   b. Organized whole
   c. Physiological psychology
   d. Repression

6. What school of psychology indicates that it is important to study behavior itself, not the mind or consciousness?
   a. Behaviorism
   b. Structuralism
   c. Psychoanalysis
   d. Functionalism

7. The principal assumption of psychoanalysis is that
   a. habits determine behavior
   b. human beings do not have an unconscious mental life
   c. human beings have an unconscious mental life
   d. all motives are inborn

8. The cognitive viewpoint stresses the importance of
   a. learning
   b. thinking
   c. motivation
   d. biological drives

9. What viewpoint stresses the importance of the activity of the brain and nervous system?
   a. The psychodynamic viewpoint
   b. The learning viewpoint
   c. The humanistic viewpoint
   d. The biological viewpoint

10. Psychotherapy is a work activity associated with what field of psychology?
    a. Experimental psychology
    b. Developmental psychology
    c. Clinical psychology
    d. Physiological psychology

ANSWERS TO THE SELF-TEST

1-b   2-a   3-d   4-c   5-b   6-a   7-c   8-b   9-d   10-c

ANSWERS TO THE TRUE-OR-FALSE PREVIEW QUIZ

1. False. Modern psychology is defined as the science that studies the behavior of organisms.
2. True.
3. True.
4. False. The biological viewpoint assumes that behavior can be explained in terms of such factors as genes, the endocrine system, or the brain and nervous system.
5. True.

KEY TERMS

actions

behavior

behaviorism

biological viewpoint

clinical psychology

cognitive processes

cognitive viewpoint

counseling psychologist

data

developmental psychologist

eclecticism

emotional states

experimental psychology

functionalism

Gestalt

human factors psychologist

humanistic viewpoint

hysteria

industrial psychologist

introspection

learning viewpoint

organism

physiological psychologist

psyche

psychiatry

psychoanalysis

psychodynamic viewpoint

psychological testing

psychology

psychotherapy

repression

schools of psychology

self-actualization

sociocultural viewpoint

somatoform disorder, conversion type

structuralism

tabula rasa

will to meaning

2 Research Methods in Psychology: Gathering Data

PREVIEW QUIZ

True or False

1. **T F** Forming a hypothesis is an important step in the scientific method.
2. **T F** Naturalistic observation is characterized by the use of a control group.
3. **T F** The clinical method is a research technique associated primarily with the treatment of individuals with mental or behavioral disorders.
4. **T F** The testing method explores human behavior by using psychological tests of attributes such as intelligence, personality, and creativity.
5. **T F** The experimental method is flawed as a method because it provides no way for a researcher to obtain control over variables.

(Answers can be found on page 28.)

In the opening chapter you learned that scientific psychology has four explicit goals—to describe, explain, predict, and control behavior. In order to accomplish these goals it is essential to employ effective research methods. In this chapter you will become familiar with the principal ways in which psychologists gather data and put the scientific method to work.

Objectives

After completing this chapter, you will be able to

- describe the three main steps in the scientific method;
- identify the principal research methods used by psychology;
- recognize some of the advantages and disadvantages of the various research methods;
- understand the difference between a positive and a negative correlation;
- specify key concepts associated with the experimental method.

The Scientific Method: Do the Facts Support Your Educated Guess?

In the days of psychology's long philosophical past, the method used to investigate the behavior of human beings was **rationalism.** This is the point of view that great discoveries can be made just by doing a lot of hard thinking. This is still a workable approach in some fields of philosophy, and it has certainly been a workable method in mathematics.

In psychology, however, rationalism alone can lead to contradictory conclusions. At an informal level, rationalism is sometimes called "armchair philosophizing." Using only writing and thinking, the British philosopher John Locke (1632–1704) decided that there are no inborn ideas. Using the same approach as Locke, the German philosopher Immanuel Kant (1724–1804) concluded that the human mind does have some **a priori information,** meaning that there are inborn ideas of a certain kind. So you can see that rationalism alone is an unsatisfactory method for psychology if it claims to be a science.

Contemporary psychology combines rationalism with empiricism. Naturally, thinking is used. However, facts are gathered. **Empiricism** is the point of view that knowledge is acquired by using the senses—by seeing, hearing, touching, and so forth. Empiricism represents what William James called a **tough-minded attitude.** The attitude can be expressed with the words "I'm stubborn. I can be convinced—but you've got to show me."

Today's researchers do their best to gather *data,* information relevant to questions they ask about human behavior. In order to gather data, various methods are used. And these methods are the principal subjects of this chapter.

(a) What is the point of view that great discoveries can be made just by doing a lot of hard thinking? _____

(b) What is the point of view that knowledge is acquired by using the senses? _____

   Answers: (a) Rationalism; (b) Empiricism.

Before we look at the various individual methods used to gather data, let's take a look at the general approach that inspires all of the methods. This general approach is called the **scientific method.** It is a systematic approach to thinking about an interesting possibility, gathering data, and reaching a conclusion.

There are three main steps in the scientific method. The first step is to form a **hypothesis,** a proposition about a state of affairs in the world. Informally, a hypothesis is an educated guess about the way things are. Let's say that Nora is a teacher. She observes at an informal level that students seem to do better on tests when the room is slightly cool than when it is too warm. She forms this hypothesis: Room temperature has an effect on test performance.

Let's say that she's interested enough to explore the merits of the hypothesis. Nora takes the second step in the scientific method. She *gathers data.* Probably she will compare student test performance under at least two different conditions. We'll return to this aspect of data gathering when the experimental method is presented later in this chapter.

The third step in the scientific method is to *accept or reject the hypothesis.* If the data support the hypothesis, Nora will accept it. If the data do not support the hypothesis, Nora will reject it.

Unfortunately, it is possible to make decision errors. Sometimes a hypothesis is accepted that should not be accepted. This is called a **Type I error.** Sometimes a hypothesis is rejected that should be accepted. This is called a **Type II error.** The history of science, unfortunately, provides many examples of both kinds of errors. The astronomer Percival Lowell (1855–1916), based on his observations, concluded that there were canals and probably an advanced civilization on Mars. Later research showed that there are neither canals nor an advanced civilization there. He made a Type I error.

For many years, before the research of the French biologist Louis Pasteur (1822–1895), medical doctors rejected various versions of the hypothesis that some diseases can be caused by germs. They were making a Type II error.

(a) The three main steps in the scientific methods are to _____.

(b) What kind of error is made when a hypothesis is accepted that should not be accepted?
_____

   Answers: (a) form a hypothesis, gather data, and accept or reject the hypothesis; (b) A Type I error.

Naturalistic Observation: Looking at Behavior without Interference

Naturalistic observation requires a researcher to study behavior as it is happening in its own setting. The researcher should have a "no interference" policy. When people or animals know they are being observed, they may not behave in the same way as when they're not being observed. Sometimes it is necessary for the researcher to allow for a period of adaptation to his or her presence.

Let's say that Clayton, an anthropologist, is interested in studying the behavioral patterns of a certain tribe. He lives among its people for a span of time, is accepted by them as a friend, and they grow to trust him. He takes field notes as objectively as possible. Eventually he publishes his findings for other scientists to read. This is the essence of naturalistic observation as a method. (**Anthropology,** like psychology, studies human behavior. Anthropology tends to focus on physical, social, and cultural development.) Naturalistic observation has also been used extensively to study the behavior of animals in their own habitats in the wilderness.

Although psychology occasionally employs naturalistic observation, in practice, research in psychology has tended to favor other methods.

Naturalistic observation requires a researcher to study behavior as it is _____.

Answer: happening in its own setting.

The Clinical Method: Studying Troubled People

The **clinical method** is a research technique associated primarily with the treatment of individuals with mental or behavioral disorders. It arose within the associated frameworks of psychiatry and clinical psychology. For example, a therapist may treat a troubled person for a span of time. Initially, research may not be the goal. However, at the conclusion of the case, the therapist may decide that the case has many interesting features that make a contribution to our understanding of either the therapy process, behavior, or both. Consequently, the therapist writes up the case, and it is published in a professional journal.

You will recall from chapter 1 that Freud once worked with a colleague named Josef Breuer. One of Breuer's patients was a young woman identified as Anna O. Anna suffered from various symptoms of hysteria (see chapter 1). "The Case of Anna O." is the first case in psychoanalysis, and it was published together with other case histories in Breuer and Freud's book *Studies on Hysteria* in 1895. Consequently, it can be said that psychoanalysis has its roots in the clinical method.

The clinical method arose within the associated frameworks of _____.

Answer: psychiatry and clinical psychology

The Case Study Method: One Subject at a Time

The **case study method** involves the study of one individual over a span of time. It is similar to the clinical method. The difference between the the two methods is that the subject in the case study method is not necessarily troubled.

Here is an example of the case study method. The Gestalt psychologist Max Wertheimer and the physicist Albert Einstein were personal friends. Based on a number of interviews with Einstein, Wertheimer studied the creative thought processes utilized by Einstein in his formulation of the Special Theory of Relativity. Wertheimer's observations and conclusions are the basis of one of the chapters in his book *Productive Thinking* (1959).

The difference between the clinical method and the case study method is that the subject in the case study method is not necessarily _____.

Answer: troubled.

The Survey Method: Large Samples from Larger Populations

A **survey** attempts to take a large, general look at an aspect of behavior. Examples of topics include sexual behavior, eating behavior, how people raise children, spending habits, and so forth. A researcher may be interested in studying a population. A **population** is a well-defined group. It need not be large. For example, a home aquarium with ten fish is correctly said to have a population of ten. However, in practice populations are often large (e.g., the population of the United States, the population of California, the population a particular city). Consequently, it is common to conduct the survey taken on a **sample** of the population. The sample should be taken at random from the population. A **random sample** allows the laws of chance to operate and provides an equal opportunity for any member of the population to be included in the sample. Members of the population fill out questionnaires, are interviewed, or are otherwise evaluated. This constitutes the survey.

Among the more famous surveys conducted during the twentieth century are the Kinsey surveys of sexual behavior published about fifty years ago. Conducted by the Indiana University researcher Alfred Kinsey, the surveys, first of males and then of females, provided valuable information concerning sexual behavior. These studies gave a great impetus to the survey method as a way of studying behavior.

(a) The survey attempts to take what kind of a look at an aspect of behavior? _____

(b) A population is _____ .

    Answers: (a) A large, general look; (b) a well-defined group.

A serious drawback of the survey method is the problem of bias in the sample. In 1936 Alfred ("Alf") Landon, the Republican governor of Kansas, ran for president against Franklin Delano Roosevelt, the incumbent. It was widely expected that Landon would win because a telephone poll conducted by a magazine called *The Liberty Digest* predicted Landon's victory. Although the survey method used by the poll took names at random from the phone book, it appears that during the Great Depression, with the nation plagued by 30 percent unemployment, more Republicans than Democrats had telephones. Consequently, the survey made an incorrect prediction.

The difficulty associated with biased sampling from a population of interest is a general problem, one that is not limited to surveys. Most research is conducted on samples, not populations. A researcher, no matter what research method he or she employs, needs to assess the quality of the sample obtained.

An important drawback of the survey method is the problem of _____ .

    Answer: bias in the sample.

The Testing Method: Mental Measurements

The **testing method** explores human behavior by using psychological tests of attributes such as intelligence, personality, and creativity. These tests are often of the paper-and-pencil variety, and the subject completes the test following a set of instructions. In some cases the test is given in interview form on a one-to-one basis by an examiner. Individual intelligence tests are often administered in this manner.

An example of the testing method is provided by the research of Lewis Terman (1877–1956) on gifted children. Using the Stanford-Binet Intelligence Scale as a research tool, Terman studied subjects with very high intelligence quotient (IQ) scores from childhood to late adulthood. (Associates continued the study after Terman's death.) The research supported the hypothesis that high intelligence is desirable. On the whole, gifted children had better health and lower divorce rates than most people. (There is more about intelligence and IQ in chapter 10.)

(a) Identify three kinds of human attributes associated with the testing method. _____

(b) Children with high intelligence quotient (IQ) scores are called _____.

> *Answers:*   (a) Intelligence, personality, and creativity; (b) gifted.

Two problems associated with psychological testing are **validity** and **reliability.** In order for a psychological test to be useful it needs to be both valid and reliable. A *valid* test measures what it is supposed to measure. If a test that is given to measure the intelligence of subjects instead actually measures the individual's motivation to take the test, the test is invalid.

A *reliable* test gives stable, repeatable results. If a subject is tested twice with the same instrument within a few days, the two scores obtained should be very close to each other. One of the functions of the next method to be identified, the **correlational method,** is to establish both the validity and reliability of psychological tests.

(a) A valid test measures what it is _____.

(b) A reliable test gives _____.

> *Answers:*   (a) supposed to measure; (b) stable, repeatable results.

The Correlational Method: When X Is Associated with Y

The word *correlation* refers to the relationship between two variables. These are usually designated as X and Y on a graph. If scores on one variable can be used to predict scores on the second variable, the variables are said to *covary.* Let's say that X stands for shoe size on the right foot. Y stands for shoe size on the left foot. If the both feet are measured on one hundred subjects, it is obvious that a measurement on the right foot will predict, with some variations, a measurement on the left foot (and vice versa). This example also illustrates that a correlation does not necessarily provide a basis to conclude that causation is present. The size of the right foot does not cause the size of left foot. The sizes covary because they both probably have the same genetic cause in common; they don't cause each other.

In the above example, a **positive correlation** is said to exist. This means that increases in variable X suggest increases in variable Y. On the other hand, if increases in variable X were to suggest decreases in variable Y, a **negative correlation** would be said to exist. Of course, in some cases there is no relationship. Then a **zero correlation** is said to exist.

(a) If scores on one variable can be used to predict scores on a second variable, the variables are said to _____.

(b) If increases in variable X suggest increases in variable Y, what kind of correlation is said to exist? _____

Answers: (a) covary; (b) A positive correlation.

The magnitude of a correlation is measured with the use of the **correlation coefficient,** a statistical tool developed by the mathematician Karl Pearson about one hundred years ago in association with the researcher Francis Galton. Galton used Pearson's tool to measure the correlation between the eminence of fathers and that of their sons. He found that eminent fathers tended to have eminent sons. For example, a father who was a judge might have a son who was an army general. Obscure fathers tended to have obscure sons. Galton used this evidence to accept the hypothesis that heredity determines a person's abilities. The research is flawed by the simple fact that eminent fathers are in positions to help their sons also attain eminence. In other words, the effects of environment may be as important as heredity in determining a person's vocational achievement. Although Galton's research on heredity is not taken seriously today, it did produce the very useful tool known as the correlation coefficient.

Correlation coefficients can range from −1.00 to +1.00. A perfect negative correlation is −1.00, and +1.00 stands for a perfect positive correlation. There can also be correlation coefficients between these two values. For example, −.85 indicates a high negative correlation, and +.62 indicates a moderate positive correlation.

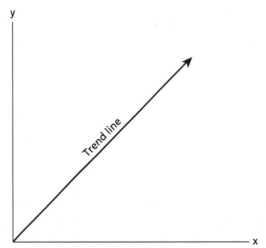

Graph for a positive correlation. The trend line shows that in general as X increases, Y also increases.

Earlier it was indicated that the correlational method can be used to establish both the validity and reliability of tests. If an intelligence test has a high positive correlation with student grades, this suggests that the test is valid. If Form A of a psychological test has a high positive correlation with Form B of the same test, the test is reliable.

(a) What does the correlation coefficient measure? _____

(b) Correlation coefficients can range from _____.

    Answers: (a) The magnitude of a correlation; (b) –1.00 to +1.00.

The Experimental Method: A Tool with Great Power

Of all of the methods presented, the experimental method is the one that gives a researcher the most confidence when making the decision to accept or reject a hypothesis. The **experimental method** is a research tool characterized by a control over variables, the identification of a cause (or causes), and a well-defined measure of behavior. These aspects of the experimental method give it great power.

Four key concepts will help you understand the experimental method: (1) the control group, (2) the experimental group, (3) the independent variable, and (4) the dependent variable. Definitions will be presented followed by an example incorporating all four concepts into an experiment. The **control group** receives no treatment; it is dealt with in a more or less conventional manner. It provides a standard of comparison, a set of observations that can be contrasted with the behavior of the experimental group.

The **experimental group** receives a novel treatment, a condition (or set of conditions) that is presumed to affect behavior. It is the target group, the one that will perhaps provide original or particularly interesting data.

(a) The experimental method is a research tool characterized by _____.

(b) Which group receives no treatment? _____

    Answers: (a) a control over variables; (b) The control group.

The **independent variable** is one that is assigned to the subjects by the experimenter. There will be at least two values, or measures, of this variable. It is the variable that is thought of as a *cause* of behavior.

The **dependent variable** is a measure of the behavior of the subjects. In most experiments, this variable can be expressed as a set of scores. The dependent variable is associated with the *effect* of a cause. Scores make it possible to compute statistical measures and make evaluations based on the data.

(a) The word *cause* is best associated with what variable? _____

(b) The dependent variable is a measure of _____.

    Answers: (a) The independent variable; (b) the behavior of the subjects, an effect.

You will recall that near the beginning of this chapter a teacher named Nora was said to have formed the hypothesis that room temperature has an effect on test performance. Let's say that Nora wants to do an experiment to evaluate this hypothesis.

Nora writes the names of sixty students on a set of cards. The cards are shuffled and then dealt into two groups, Group A and Group B. A coin is flipped. She says in advance that if heads comes up, Group A will be the control group. If tails comes up, Group B will be the control group. Heads comes up, and Group A becomes the control group. By default, Group B is designated the experimental group.

It is important to note that the process by which subjects are assigned to groups is a **random process,** meaning all subjects have an equal chance of being included in either group. The aim of this procedure is to cancel out the effects of individual differences in the subjects that may have an effect on the experiment. Such variables as age, sex, weight, intelligence, and income level are not, for the moment, under study. A practical way to minimize the effects of such variables is to assign subjects randomly to conditions.

The independent variable will be room temperature. Let's say that most of the time Nora's students take tests in a room that is 68 degrees Fahrenheit. The control group will be tested in a room at this temperature.

Up until now Nora has been thinking that a "cool" room will have a positive effect on test performance. The time has come to define "cool" more precisely. An **operational definition** is required, a definition of a variable such as "cool" in terms of its measurement operations. Nora decides that her operational definition of "cool" will be a temperature of 55 degrees Fahrenheit. The word *cool* is an imprecise, subjective term. On the other hand, 55 degrees Fahrenheit is precise and objective. The experimental group will be tested at this temperature.

Let's say that subjects in both groups are given the same twenty-question multiple-choice test. Scores range from a low of 5 to a high of 20 correct. The mean (i.e., average) score for subjects in the control group is 11. The mean score for subjects in the experimental group is 14. On the surface, it appears that Nora will make the decision to accept her experimental hypothesis. It appears that a cool room does in fact facilitate test performance.

Before a firm decision can be made to accept or reject a hypothesis, a statistical evaluation of the data must be made. A difference between means is sometimes due to chance.

An experiment can, of course, be much more interesting than the one described, and there can be two or more independent variables. However, Nora's experiment was presented because it reveals the essentials of the experimental method.

(a) Subjects should be assigned to groups by what kind of a process? _____

(b) An operational definition is a definition of a variable in terms of _____.

> *Answers:* (a) A random process; (b) its measurement operations.

SELF-TEST

1. The point of view that knowledge is acquired by using the senses is called
   a. rationalism
   b. voluntarism
   c. behaviorism
   d. empiricism

2. Which one of the following *is not* a step associated with the scientific method?
   a. Reject all operational definitions
   b. Form a hypothesis
   c. Gather data
   d. Accept or reject the hypothesis

3. Sometimes a hypothesis is rejected that should be accepted. This is called
   a. a Type I error
   b. an alpha error
   c. a Type II error
   d. an intrinsic error

4. Naturalistic observation requires a researcher to study behavior
   a. in animals only
   b. as it is happening in its own setting
   c. using two independent variables
   d. by making sure the subjects know they are being observed

5. The behavior of Anna O. was studied with the assistance of what method?
   a. The clinical method
   b. Naturalistic observation
   c. The experimental method
   d. The correlational method

6. A population is
   a. a very large sample
   b. defined by its bias
   c. a subset of a sample
   d. a well-defined group

7. The research of Lewis Terman on gifted children is an example of
   a. the experimental method
   b. the clinical method
   c. the testing method
   d. the validity method

8. The size of the right foot can usually be used to predict the size of the left foot. This is an example of a
   a. zero correlation
   b. negative correlation
   c. positive correlation
   d. lack of covariance

9. In an experiment, the control group
   a. receives no treatment
   b. receives a novel treatment
   c. is expected to provide particularly interesting data
   d. is the error variance group

10. The variable that is assigned to the subjects by the experimenter is called
    a. the dependent variable
    b. the independent variable
    c. the organismic variable
    d. the congruent variable

ANSWERS TO THE SELF-TEST

1-d   2-a   3-c   4-b   5-a   6-d   7-c   8-c   9-a   10-b

ANSWERS TO THE TRUE-OR-FALSE PREVIEW QUIZ

1. True.
2. False. Naturalistic observation does not use a control group.
3. True.
4. True.
5. False. One of the advantages of the experimental method is that it provides a researcher a way to obtain control over variables.

KEY TERMS

a priori information

anthropology

case study method

clinical method

control group

correlation coefficient

correlational method

dependent variable

empiricism

experimental group

experimental method

hypothesis

independent variable

naturalistic observation

negative correlation

operational definition

population

positive correlation

random process

random sample

rationalism

reliability

sample

scientific method

survey

testing method

tough-minded attitude

Type I error

Type II error

validity

zero correlation

3 The Biology of Behavior: Is the Brain the Organ of Mental Life?

True or False

1. **T F** A neurotransmitter is a chemical messenger.
2. **T F** The two divisions of the brain are the sympathetic division and the parasympathetic division.
3. **T F** The two pituitary glands are located on top of the kidneys.
4. **T F** The left hemisphere of the brain tends to mediate verbal and mathematical thinking.
5. **T F** The general adaptation syndrome is a reaction pattern associated with stress.

(Answers can be found on page 43.)

Chapter 2 made it evident that research is based on observations—events that can be seen and heard in the external world. A good starting point for such observations is the biology of the organism itself. A substantial amount of reliable data has been gathered concerning how the brain, the nervous system, and other structures actually function.

Objectives

After completing the chapter, you will be able to

- explain the way in which a neuron functions;

- describe the structure of the nervous system;

- specify some of the principal structures and functions of the brain;

- differentiate between the functions of the left and right hemispheres of the brain;

- identify the endocrine glands and their functions.

In the 1983 Steve Martin film *The Man with Two Brains,* a woman's personality is changed when her own brain is removed and then replaced with a different one. The plot is based on the assumption that the brain is the organ of mental life. This assumption, associated with the biological viewpoint (see chapter 1), sees the *activity* of the brain and nervous system as the basis of consciousness. The relationship between the brain and the mind in this way of looking at things is roughly the same as the relationship of a piano to the melody that one hears when the piano is played. The piano, like the brain, is a physical organ. The melody, like the mind, is somewhat less tangible.

This chapter explores behavior from the biological point of view. Of particular interest are (1) the brain and nervous system and (2) the endocrine system.

The biological viewpoint sees the _____ of the brain and nervous system as the basis of consciousness.

Answer: activity.

The Neuron: The Building Block of the Nervous System

The principal functional units of the brain and the nervous system are neurons. The **neuron** is a living cell with a cell wall and a nucleus. Unlike other cells of the body, neurons specialize in transmitting messages. Of particular importance are two structures called the **dendrite** and the **axon.** A neuron often has more than one dendrite; dendrites are reminiscent of a root system. They act like antennas, picking up information and sending it in the direction of the cell body. The axon extends from the cell body like a long filament. Although there can be more than one dendrite, there is always just one axon. The axon consistently sends information away from the cell body, often to an adjacent neuron.

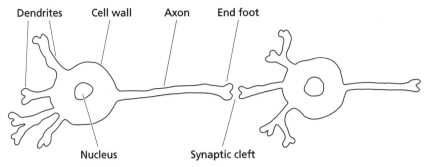

Two adjacent neurons with selected structures.

At the end of the axon there is an **end foot,** a slightly bulging structure that releases neurotransmitters. A **neurotransmitter** is a chemical messenger that allows a neuron to communicate with either other neurons or muscle fibers. The neurotransmitter travels across a physical gap called the **synaptic cleft.** The functional connection between, for example, two neurons is called the **synapse.** Note that there is a formal distinction between a synaptic cleft and a synapse. The first refers to a physical characteristic; the second refers to a functional characteristic. It is common to hear people refer to the gap itself as the synapse, and this is incorrect.

In order for a neurotransmitter to work, it must find a **receptor site** on an adjacent cell. The receptor site has a physical shape that matches that of the neuron. A useful analogy is a key and a lock. The neurotransmitter is like the key; the receptor site is like the lock.

(a) An axon consistently sends information _____.

(b) A neurotransmitter is also referred to as a _____.

(c) In order for a neurotransmitter to work, what must it find on an adjacent cell? _____

Answers: (a) away from the cell body; (b) chemical messenger; (c) A receptor site.

Neurotransmitters have received a lot of attention in recent years. Their activity often forms the basis of biological theories of mental disorders. For example, low levels of the neurotransmitter **serotonin** are associated with depression. Specific drugs called **selective serotonin reuptake inhibitors (SSRIs)** increase the amount of useable serotonin at the synapse. (Prozac is such a drug.)

For a second example, excessive activity of the neurotransmitter **dopamine** is associated with schizophrenia, a mental disorder characterized by delusions. There is evidence to suggest that chronic schizophrenic patients have too many receptor sites for dopamine, and this causes excessive dopamine activity. It is this activity that induces delusions. Some of the principal antipsychotic drugs block receptor sites for dopamine. (See the section on drug therapy in chapter 15.)

(a) Identify a neurotransmitter associated with depression. _____

(b) Identify a neurotransmitter associated with schizophrenia. _____

Answers: (a) Serotonin; (b) Dopamine.

Three basic kinds of neurons are (1) sensory, (2) association, and (3) motor. **Sensory neurons** make it possible for us to be in contact with the outside world. They are sensitive to light, sound, chemicals that induce taste sensations, and so forth. The rods and cones in the retina of your eye are sensory neurons.

Association neurons communicate with each other. Most of the neurons in your brain are association neurons. They allow you to think, remember, and perceive. It is the rich complexity of association neurons that makes self-consciousness possible.

Motor neurons communicate with muscle fibers, and these too are cells of the body. Complex contractions and relaxations of muscle fibers make it possible for us to talk, walk, and otherwise act.

(a) Sensory neurons make it possible for us to be in contact with _____.

(b) Association neurons communicate with _____.

(c) Motor neurons communicate with _____.

Answers: (a) the outside world; (b) each other; (c) muscle fibers.

The brain contains about 3 billion neurons. The rest of the nervous system contains approximately the same amount. The population of the planet Earth is rapidly approaching 6 billion people. It is impressive to think that the quantity of neurons you possess is roughly equivalent to the human population of our world.

When a neuron releases neurotransmitters it is like a gun; when it "fires," it sends forth a spray of neurotransmitters. The formal term for "fire" is **depolarize.** When a neuron depolarizes, it alternates from (1) a resting negative electrical potential to (2) a positive electrical potential, and (3) returns to a negative electrical potential again. This completes a cycle. In some cases a neuron can complete 2,000 to 3,000 cycles in a single second.

A **nerve** is a bundle of axons. Think of the axons as thin rope fibers and the nerve as the thick rope itself. Nerves are identified as afferent or efferent. **Afferent nerves** move toward an objective. **Efferent nerves** move away from a source. The optic nerve is an afferent nerve; it carries visual messages toward the brain.

On the other hand, when you pick up a pen you are using efferent nerves. Messages are being carried away from the brain.

(a) When a neuron releases neurotransmitters it is either said to "fire" or to _____.

(b) Nerves that move away from a source are called _____.

> *Answers:*   (a) depolarize; (b) efferent.

The Nervous System: The Body's Communication Network

Neurons are not, of course, scattered at random in the body. They are organized. This organization is called the **nervous system.** The nervous system is the body's communication network. Its function is often compared to the country's telephone system or the Internet. The nervous system allows any part of the body to be in contact with any other part of the body within a fraction of a second.

The nervous system has two main divisions. These are the **central nervous system** and the **peripheral nervous system.** The central nervous system consists of the brain and the spinal cord. The brain is the subject of the next section. Let's turn our attention to the peripheral nervous system.

This peripheral nervous system itself has two divisions. These are the **autonomic nervous system** and **somatic nervous system.** The word *autonomic* is similar to the word *automatic,* and it does in fact have a similar meaning. The autonomic nervous system is somewhat independent or self-moving. This means it doesn't always have to have instructions coming from the brain. Some of its activities are said to be involuntary.

(a) The two main divisions of the nervous system are the _____ and the _____.

(b) The two divisions of the peripheral nervous system are the _____ and the _____.

> *Answers:*   (a) central nervous system; peripheral nervous system; (b) autonomic nervous system; somatic nervous system.

The autonomic nervous system is involved in the regulation of such bodily processes as digestion, blood pressure, pulse, breathing, and internal temperature. This system has two additional divisions. These are the **sympathetic division** and the **parasympathetic division.**

The sympathetic division is active primarily when there is an *increase* in autonomic activity. Excitement provides an example. When you are excited, your blood pressure goes up, your pulse increases, and the rate of respiration rises. These are all due to the activity of the sympathetic division. The sympathetic division is sometimes compared to the gas pedal on a car; it makes the whole system go forward with increased speed. (There are exceptions to the generalization made in this paragraph.)

(a) The two divisions of the autonomic nervous system are the _____ and the _____.

(b) What division of the autonomic nervous system is active primarily when there is an increase in autonomic activity? _____

Answers: (a) sympathetic division; parasympathetic division; (b) The sympathetic division.

The parasympathetic division is active primarily when there is a *decrease* in autonomic activity. Relaxation provides an example. When you are relaxed, your blood pressure goes down, your pulse decreases, and your respiration rate falls. The parasympathetic division is sometimes compared to the brakes on a car; they can be used to make the whole system slow down. (Again, there are exceptions to the generalization made in this paragraph.)

As you will see in chapter 6, the chapter on learning, classical conditioning refers primarily to the activity of the autonomic nervous system.

Let's return to the somatic division of the peripheral nervous system. The Greek word **soma** means "body." Consequently, the somatic division controls the actions of the body. When you walk, talk, move your arms, or use your fingers, the somatic division regulates these actions. As you will see in chapter 6, operant conditioning refers primarily to the activity of the somatic nervous system.

(a) What division of the autonomic nervous system is active primarily when there is a decrease in autonomic activity? _____

(b) The Greek word *soma* means _____.

Answers: (a) The parasympathetic division; (b) "body."

The Brain: The CEO of the Organization

The brain is actually a part of the nervous system. As indicated earlier, the brain and the spinal cord constitute one of the two major divisions of the nervous system—the central nervous system. Our main concern in this section is with the brain, not the spinal cord. However, let us note that the **spinal cord,** protected by the bones of the spine, is a two-way communication highway. Sensory messages from the feet, the hands, and other parts of the body are sent to the brain. Motor messages from the brain are used to move the legs, the arms, and other parts of the body. If the spinal cord is damaged, this can greatly impair the individual's ability to both experience and move the body.

The brain resides at the top of the spinal cord and, as indicated, is the chief executive officer (CEO) of the nervous system. It is traditional in studying the brain to describe its structures and their functions. Each structure is given a name and a location in the brain. Then the purpose of the structure is identified.

Let's start toward the bottom of the brain and work our way up. Immediately above the spinal cord is the *brain stem*. It has the obvious function of connecting the brain to the spinal cord, and may even be thought of as an extension of the spinal cord. Located within the brain stem is a structure called the **reticular activating system (RAS).** It sends forth nerves to the higher levels of the brain. The RAS functions like both a light switch and a rheostat. When you wake up suddenly, the RAS has stimulated you to do so. When you fall asleep quickly, the RAS has also induced this behavior. On the other hand, when you are drowsy, the RAS is acting like a rheostat. It is reducing the flow of the kind of information that makes you attentive and alert. Also, you can be overly alert—what people call "hyper." In this case, the flow of information to the higher levels of the brain is excessive.

(a) The spinal cord acts as _____.

(b) What structure acts like both a light switch and a rheostat? _____

> *Answers:* (a) a two-way communication highway; (b) The reticular activating system.

The **medulla** is located toward the front of the brain stem. One of its principal functions is to regulate the respiration rate. The **pons,** associated with the medulla, is a bulging structure also located toward the front of the brain stem; it resides above the medulla. It too is involved in the regulation of breathing. In addition, it plays a role in the regulation of sleep and attention.

The **cerebellum** (i.e., "little brain") is located toward the back of the brain stem. Maintaining your sense of balance and coordinating your muscle movements are functions of the cerebellum.

The **hypothalamus** is located just under the thalamus and above the brain stem. (The prefix *hypo* means "under" or "beneath." A few paragraphs down you will find a reference to the thalamus.) The hypothalamus has a number of functions. Of particular interest is the regulation of biological drives. For example, both excitatory and inhibitory impulses for hunger arise from the hypothalamus. One starts eating and then stops eating depending, to some extent, on signals from the hypothalamus. Freud spoke of a psychological agent called the **id,** the constellation of our primal, pleasure-oriented impulses. The hypothalamus is *not* the id, because the id is a psychological concept and the hypothalamus is a physiological structure. Nonetheless, it is correct to say that to a large extent it is the activity of the hypothalamus that gives rise to the psychological processes Freud associated with the id.

(a) One of the principal functions of the medulla is to regulate _____.

(b) The regulation of biological drives is associated to a large extent with what structure? _____

    Answers: (a) respiration rate; (b) The hypothalamus.

The **pituitary gland**—one of the endocrine glands—is located toward the front of the hypothalamus. It is usually called the "master gland" of the body. This is because it plays a role in regulating the action of the other endocrine glands. This will be discussed in the section on the endocrine system, pages 39–41.

Located just above the hypothalamus is the **thalamus.** One of the principal functions of the thalamus is to act as a relay center for the sense organs. For example, the optic nerves transmit visual information to a center in the thalamus. The information is then relayed to a higher area in the cerebral cortex.

The **cerebral cortex** is the highest part of the brain. The word *cortex* means "bark" or "covering." The cortex, a large structure, does in fact sit on top of, or cover, the lower regions of the brain. The cortex has a number of functions. It has dedicated areas for vision, hearing, taste, touch, and smell. It has motor areas

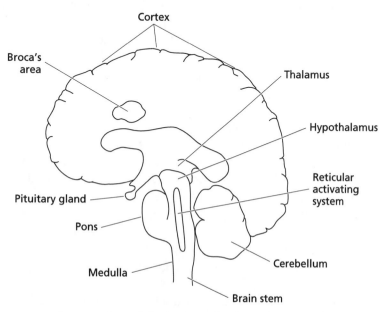

Cross section of the brain with selected structures.

allowing for voluntary movements. It has association areas allowing for learning, thinking, and memory. There are two speech areas allowing for language comprehension and language production. For example, **Broca's area** is involved primarily in language production. A group of structures in the cortex called the **limbic system** play important roles in our motivational and emotional lives. For example, damage to the limbic system can be associated with **anhedonia** (or **ahedonia**), an inability to experience pleasure.

(a) The "master gland" of the body is the _____.

(b) One of the principal functions of the thalamus is to act as _____.

(c) What large structure of the brain is associated with our ability to think? _____

Answers: (a) pituitary gland; (b) a relay center for the sense organs; (c) The cerebral cortex.

The Two Hemispheres of the Brain: Does the Right Side Know What the Left Side Is Doing?

The prior description of the brain was based on a cross-section of the brain associated with looking at a person's profile. On the other hand, looking at the brain from above, one discerns two cerebral hemispheres. These two hemispheres are connected by a structure called the **corpus callosum** ("thick body"). The function of the corpus callosum is to provide a way for the two hemispheres to communicate with each other. In the vast majority of people the corpus callosum is intact. Consequently, sharp differences between the way the two different hemispheres work are not usually evident.

However, in a very small number of people the corpus callosum has been cut as a treatment for intractable epilepsy. It is possible in such patients to study the different ways the two hemispheres work. It is evident from studies of subjects with a severed corpus callosum that the **right hemisphere** mediates nonverbal patterning—the kind of mental functioning required in drawing, making up a melody, dancing, and creating visual images. The right hemisphere is sometimes called the "romantic" hemisphere.

The **left hemisphere** mediates verbal and mathematical thinking—the kind of mental functioning required in writing, talking, scientific analysis, working an algebra problem, and so forth. The left hemisphere is sometimes called the "logical" hemisphere.

The right side of the brain *does* know what the left side is doing if the corpus callosum is intact—as it usually is.

(a) What structure connects the two hemispheres of the brain? _____

(b) What hemisphere of the brain is sometimes called the "romantic" hemisphere? _____

Answers: (a) The corpus callosum; (b) The right hemisphere.

The Endocrine System: Moods and Your Glands

You have a set of glands in your body that have a lot to do with your moods, your emotional states, and your behavior in general. Working together, these glands are called the **endocrine system.** The glands themselves are called **endocrine glands** because they secrete their substances directly into the bloodstream without ducts. (*Endo* means "within" or "inside." In contrast, **exocrine glands,** such as salivary or digestive glands, secrete their substances "outside" of the bloodstream.) The substances secreted by the endocrine glands are called **hormones.** These, like neurotransmitters, act as chemical messengers.

The **pineal gland** is a tiny gland located nearly in the center of the brain. It is called "pineal" because it is shaped something like a pine cone. Of historical interest is the fact that the philosopher René Descartes suggested, perhaps because it is small and centered, that the pineal gland is the place where the soul

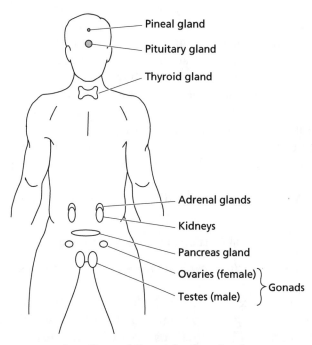

Locations of the endocrine glands.

interacts with the body. Today's research indicates that the pineal gland secretes a hormone called **melatonin.** This hormone plays a role in controlling the biological timetable for sexual maturation. Another of its functions is to regulate the sleep cycle.

(a) The endocrine glands secrete their substances (without ducts) directly into the _____.

(b) The pineal gland secretes a hormone called _____.

 Answers: (a) bloodstream; (b) melatonin.

The *pituitary gland,* about the size of a pea, is located in front of the hypothalamus. As already noted, it is called the "master gland" because it secretes a group of hormones that affect the action of the other glands. Among these hormones there are **adrenocorticotrophic hormone (ACTH),** a hormone that acts on the adrenal glands, **thyrotrophin,** a hormone that acts on the thyroid gland, and **follicle-stimulating hormone,** a hormone that acts on the gonads. One of the hormones secreted by the pituitary gland is **growth hormone (GH).** GH has an effect on growth and stature. People who are abnormally tall have a pathology of the pituitary gland and are said to suffer from the disease of **giantism.**

The **thyroid gland** is located toward the base and front of the neck. It is a relatively large gland and is shaped somewhat like a butterfly. In areas of the world where the soil is deficient in iodine, some individuals develop a disease of the thyroid gland called **goiter.** The gland can swell to the size of an orange or larger. One of the reasons that salt is often iodized is to prevent goiter.

The principal function of **thyroxin,** the hormone secreted by the thyroid gland, is to regulate **metabolism,** the rate at which you burn food. If not enough thyroxin is secreted, and your metabolic rate is abnormally low, you will tend to gain weight easily; at a behavioral level you may be sluggish and unenthusiastic. If too much thyroxin is secreted, and your metabolic rate is abnormally high, you will have difficulty gaining weight; at a behavioral level you may be impulsive and hyperactive.

(a) What hormone secreted by the pituitary gland is associated with a disease such as giantism? _____

(b) The principal function of the hormone thyroxin is to regulate _____.

 Answers: (a) Growth hormone (GH); (b) metabolism.

There are two **adrenal glands,** and these are located on top of the kidneys. The adrenal glands produce such hormones as the corticosteroid hormones and epinephrine. The **corticosteroid hormones** regulate the way the body utilizes such substances as glucose, salt, and water during times of stress. **Epinephrine** induces an increased sense of arousal and excitement. It plays an important role in the **fight-or-flight reaction,** an involuntary process in which the body prepares itself to cope with threatening situations. (The word **adrenalin** is synonymous with epinephrine. However, when the word *Adrenalin* appears in capitalized form, it refers to a specific drug with a trade name.)

Psychology has given increased attention to the role that the adrenal glands play in the body's adaptation to stress because of the work of the Canadian researcher Hans Selye (1907–1982). Using rats as subjects, Selye discovered that under conditions of chronic stress the body goes through a series of stages, including resistance and eventual exhaustion, that lead to an early death. The reaction pattern is called the **general adaptation syndrome.** Postmortem examinations revealed that the adrenal glands of the subjects were damaged and enlarged.

(a) Epinephrine induces an increased sense of _____.

(b) What reaction pattern is associated with chronic stress? _____

    Answers: (a) arousal and excitement; (b) The general adaptation syndrome.

The **pancreas gland** is a large gland located under the stomach. One of the hormones secreted by the pancreas is insulin. **Insulin** helps to regulate blood sugar. The disease diabetes is associated with an inadequate insulin production. The disorder **chronic hypoglycemia,** or low blood sugar, is, paradoxically, aggravated when one consumes either too much dietary sugar or too many refined carbohydrates. A person suffering from low blood sugar finds it difficult to concentrate, feel energetic, or otherwise function well.

The **gonads** are the sexual glands. In females the gonads are called the **ovaries.** In males the gonads are called the **testes. Estrogen** is one of the principal hormones produced by the ovaries. The secondary sexual characteristics in females, such as minimal facial hair and larger breasts, are determined by estrogen. **Testosterone** is one of the principal hormones produced by the testes. The secondary sexual characteristics in males, such as lack of breast development and the presence of facial hair, are determined by testosterone. There is also evidence to suggest that testosterone is associated, particularly in youth, with aggressive behavior. (It is important to note that both sexes produce estrogen and testosterone; however, the relative amounts differ.)

(a) Insulin helps to regulate _____.

(b) Identify a hormone associated principally with the ovaries. _____

(c) Identify a hormone associated principally with the testes. _____

    Answers: (a) blood sugar; (b) Estrogen; (c) Testosterone.

SELF-TEST

1. An axon
   a. can be found in the cell body of a neuron
   b. is a motor neuron
   c. sends information in the direction of the cell body
   d. sends information away from the cell body

2. Which one of the following is said to be a chemical messenger?
   a. A cell nucleus
   b. A neurotransmitter
   c. A metabolic cell
   d. A connector neuron

3. Informally, a neuron is said to "fire." The formal term for "fire" is
   a. signal recentering
   b. depolarize
   c. repolarize
   d. adaptation

4. The two main divisions of the nervous system are
   a. the brain and the spinal cord
   b. the somatic and the parasympathetic divisions
   c. the central nervous system and the peripheral nervous system
   d. the right hemisphere and the left hemisphere

5. What structure functions like both a light switch and a rheostat?
   a. The medulla
   b. The thalamus
   c. The reticular activating system
   d. The cerebellum

6. The hypothalamus is associated primarily with
   a. the regulation of biological drives
   b. abstract intelligence
   c. the curiosity drive
   d. motor coordination

7. The cerebral cortex is associated primarily with
   a. the inhibition of respiration
   b. the regulation of biological drives
   c. primal impulses
   d. thinking

8. The right hemisphere of the brain tends to mediate
    a. nonverbal patterning
    b. verbal thinking
    c. mathematical thinking
    d. symbolic logic

9. What hormone is associated with the pineal gland?
    a. Thyroxin
    b. Melatonin
    c. Growth hormone
    d. Insulin

10. The ovaries belong to what larger general category of endocrine glands?
    a. Stress glands
    b. Adrenal glands
    c. Gonads
    d. Pituitary glands

ANSWERS TO THE SELF-TEST

1-d   2-b   3-b   4-c   5-c   6-a   7-d   8-a   9-b   10-c

ANSWERS TO THE TRUE-OR-FALSE PREVIEW QUIZ

1. True.
2. False. The sympathetic division and the parasympathetic division refer to the two divisions of the autonomic nervous system. The two divisions of the brain are called the right hemisphere and the left hemisphere.
3. False. There is only one pituitary gland, and it is located in the brain. The two adrenal glands are located on top of the kidneys.
4. True.
5. True.

KEY TERMS

adrenal glands

adrenalin

adrenocorticotrophic hormone (ACTH)

afferent nerves

anhedonia (or ahedonia)

association neurons

autonomic nervous system

axon

Broca's area

central nervous system

cerebellum

cerebral cortex

chronic hypoglycemia

corpus callosum

corticosteroid hormones

dendrite

depolarize

dopamine

efferent nerves

end foot

endocrine glands

endocrine system

epinephrine

estrogen

exocrine glands

fight-or-flight reaction

follicle-stimulating hormone

general adaptation syndrome

giantism

goiter

gonads

growth hormone (GH)

hormones

hypothalamus

id

insulin

left hemisphere

limbic system

medulla

melatonin

metabolism

motor neurons

nerve

nervous system

neuron

neurotransmitter

ovaries

pancreas gland

parasympathetic division

peripheral nervous system

pineal gland

pituitary gland

pons

receptor site

reticular activating system (RAS)

right hemisphere

selective serotonin reuptake inhibitors (SSRIs)

sensory neurons

serotonin

soma

somatic nervous system

spinal cord

sympathetic division

synapse

synaptic cleft

testes

testosterone

thalamus

thyroid gland

thyrotrophin

thyroxin

4 Sensation: Studying the Gateways of Experience

True or False

1. T F The word *sensation* refers to the raw data of experience.
2. T F The trichromatic theory of color perception hypothesizes that we have three kinds of cones, differentially sensitive to three wavelengths of light, in the retina of the eye.
3. T F A sound wave has the remarkable property of being able to travel through a vacuum.
4. T F The units that make taste possible are clusters of neurons located on the tongue called *taste buds.*
5. T F You have no receptor neurons in the joints of your body.

(Answers can be found on page 55.)

The study of sensation—including such processes as seeing and hearing—grows logically from the study of the biology of behavior. Seeing, for example, is possible because we have biological structures such as the eye and the optic nerve. In this chapter we examine how basic sensory impressions relate to behavior.

Objectives

After completing this chapter, you will be able to

- differentiate among sensation, perception, and cognition;

- describe key aspects of the visual process;

- explain the trichromatic theory of color perception;

- describe key aspects of the hearing process;

- identify principal features of the processes associated with taste, the skin senses, smell, kinesthesis, and the vestibular sense.

A whole industry can sometimes be based on a single sense. The early motion picture industry appealed primarily to vision. Radio appeals primarily to hearing. Today's motion pictures and television make a combined appeal to vision and hearing. Other senses such as taste and smell play important roles in the food industry and the perfume industry.

It is difficult to overestimate the importance of the senses. They are our gateways to experience. Without our senses we would be creatures living in solitary confinement. We wouldn't know the world "out there," the world beyond the self. Learning would be impossible because, as you will see in chapter 6, the very definition of learning requires that we be capable of experience. Consequently, psychology considers it important to study the process of sensation, the basic process by which we obtain information about external reality.

Here is a useful way to think about the character of conscious experience. Imagine three ascending steps. The first step is associated with **sensation.** Sensation refers to the raw data of experience. Seeing a flash of light, hearing a single note sounded on a musical instrument, or feeling the touch of a fingertip, are all examples of simple sensations. Instead of yourself, imagine that an infant only a few days old is having these sensations. To the extent that they have little organization and little meaning, they are close to simple sensations.

The second step is associated with **perception.** Perception refers to organized experience. If a set of notes sounded on a musical instrument takes on a particular form, and you hear a melody, you have attained the level of perception. Perception is explored in chapter 5.

The third step is associated with **cognition.** Cognition refers to knowing. Thinking and concept formation are processes associated with cognition. If you perceive a melody and remember the name of the song, you have attained the level of cognition. You know what you're listening to. (Note that the familiar word *recognition* can be broken down into "re" and "cognition," suggesting that its root meaning is to "know again.") Cognition is explored in chapter 9.

(a) The three ascending steps of conscious experience are _____.

(b) Sensation refers to the _____.

   Answers: (a) sensation, perception, and cognition; (b) raw data of experience.

Vision: Seeing Is Believing

Most people think of vision as the primary sense. We need to see in order to drive, to read, to look at the people we love, and so forth. If asked what sense they consider the most important, most students in an introductory psychology class answer that it is vision.

In order to appreciate the visual process it is necessary first to give some attention to the stimulus that makes it possible. That stimulus is light. From the point of view of physics, there are two ways to look at light. It can be said that light consists of a set of electromagnetic waves. Or it can be said that light consists of a stream of particles, or quanta, called **photons.** In either case, light travels at the same speed—about 186,000 miles per second. For the purposes of psychology, we will limit our description of light to the electromagnetic wave theory.

An **electromagnetic wave,** consisting of a system of electrical and magnetic fields, is a unique kind of wave. It can even travel through a vacuum—without a medium to carry it. Otherwise, communication with voyagers to the Moon or with distant space probes would not be possible. Radio waves are one kind of electromagnetic wave.

(a) If light is looked upon as a stream of particles, or quanta, what are the particles called? _____

(b) A unique property of an electromagnetic wave is its ability to travel through _____.

   Answers: (a) Photons; (b) a vacuum.

The waves to which we give the name "light" are a narrow band of the **electromagnetic spectrum.** This spectrum ranges from relatively "long" radio waves at one end of the spectrum to relatively "short" gamma rays at the other end. In between the extremes we find the light waves. These range in length, measured crest to crest, from 750 nanometers to 400 nanometers. (A nanometer is one billionth of a meter.) The part of the electromagnetic spectrum we can see is called the *visible spectrum.* The principal colors of the visible spectrum, also known as the rainbow, starting at 750 nanometers, are red, orange, yellow, green, blue, indigo, and violet. The colors always appear in the same order either in a rainbow or when white light is broken up by a prism.

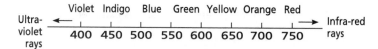

The visible portion of the electromagnetic spectrum.

Waves a little longer than 750 nanometers are called **infra–red rays.** Waves a little shorter than 400 nanometers are called **ultra–violet rays.** Both of these kinds of waves are invisible to the naked eye.

(a) The part of the electromagnetic spectrum we see is called the _____.

(b) Waves 750 nanometers in length are associated with what color? _____

    Answers: (a) visible spectrum; (b) Red.

Light is necessary for vision, but it is not sufficient. In order to see it is necessary to have a sense organ that can convert light waves into useful neurological information. This organ is, of course, the eye. In the front of the eye is the **cornea,** a kind of window that allows light to enter the eye. Because the cornea has a convex shape, it also is somewhat responsible for bending light waves and making them converge on the lens.

The **lens** is used to focus light waves, and it produces an inverted, or upside-down, image on the retina. The **retina** is a photosensitive neurological structure. Think of it as a target. The center of the target is called the **fovea,** and it plays a dominant role in visual acuity and color vision. The outer rim of the target, the **periphery,** plays an important part in signal detection and brightness vision. The neurons in the retina are called **photoreceptors** because they are light sensitive. The **optic nerve** conveys the retina's activity pattern to the brain.

The two kinds of photoreceptors are the cones and the rods. They have been given these names because of the shapes of their cell bodies. The **cones** are located primarily in the fovea. The **rods** are located primarily in the periphery. As already indicated, color vision is associated with the fovea, suggesting that the cones have a lot to do with this particular quality of sensation.

(a) The retina is a photosensitive _____.

(b) The two kinds of photoreceptors in the retina are the _____.

    Answers: (a) neurological structure; (b) rods and cones.

A leading theory of color vision is the **trichromatic theory.** This theory is also known as the Young-Helmholtz theory in honor of the scientists who first introduced it. The trichromatic theory hypothesizes that we have three kinds of cones. These are differentially sensitive to three wavelengths of light: (1) 750 nanometers, (2) 500 nanometers, and (3) 400 nanometers. The first wavelength, 750 nanometers, induces the sensation we call "red." The second, 500 nanometers, induces the sensation we call "green." And 400 nanometers induces the sensation we call "violet." The language in the preceding sentences has been carefully chosen in order to make it clear that the "color" is *not* in the stimulus itself (i.e., a light wave), but is produced by the firing of a certain kind of photoreceptor.

The trichromatic theory also accounts for the sensation of colors other than the three primary ones. The sensation of orange, for example, takes place because a wavelength of light such as 650 nanometers will cause the simultaneous firing of some neurons that usually fire at 750 nanometers and some that fire at 500 nanometers.

White light is sensed when all of the wavelengths arrive at the retina in a random or scrambled fashion. This causes the simultaneous firing of all three kinds of cones. It is often pointed out that the trichromatic theory works very well. It is the basis upon which color television sets are constructed.

(a) A leading theory of color vision is the _____.

(b) White light is sensed when all of the wavelengths arrive at the retina in a _____.

   Answers: (a) trichromatic theory; (b) random or scrambled fashion.

However, there are flaws in the trichromatic theory. For example, people who are red-green blind, lacking the two kinds of required photoreceptors, would not be predicted to sense yellow—yet they seem to have a normal capacity to sense yellow. As a consequence, other theories of color perception have been proposed. They have not received the level of acceptance of the trichromatic theory; but it is important to recognize that this major theory may explain some, but not all, of what is involved in the physiology of color vision.

There are three basic sensations associated with vision. First, the sensation of **hue** simply indicates, as already described, that we can see a range of colors. Second, the sensation of **brightness** indicates that we can see that objects are white or gray or black. We can also see that they are in low or high illumination. Third, the sensation of **saturation** indicates that we can see how richly or deeply a color seems to soak into an object.

The three basic sensations associated with vision are _____.

   Answer: hue, brightness, and saturation.

Hearing: The Sound of Music

If you enjoy hearing music, you appreciate the importance of the sense of hearing. Also, a moment's reflection helps us to realize that hearing is the primary way in which we overcome social isolation. It is by talking to each other, a behavior that requires hearing, that we visit with family and friends. If one cannot hear, it is important to learn skills such as lip reading and signing.

Like vision, the sense of hearing can be better understood by studying the stimulus that makes it possible. This stimulus is the *sound wave.* A sound wave requires a medium such as air or water. (The word *sonar* is associated with a sound wave in water.) Let's give our attention to a sound wave that uses air as its medium. First, there must be a vibrating source in order to get a sound wave going. An example of such a source is a guitar string. Another example is a human vocal cord. The vibrations emanating from the source set up a traveling wave of compressions, alternating with partial vacuums, in the air. The compressions strike the eardrum somewhat like a series of hammer blows. The frequency of a sound wave is measured with a unit called the **hertz (Hz).** One hertz is equal to one cycle per second. The greater the number of cycles per second, the higher the experienced pitch.

The intensity of a sound wave is measured with a unit called the **decibel (dB).** The greater the decibel level, the louder the sound.

(a) The unit of measurement called the hertz (Hz) measures _____.

(b) The unit of measurement called the decibel (dB) measures _____.

   Answers: (a) the frequency of a sound wave; (b) the intensity of a sound wave.

In order to experience the sensation of sound, it is necessary to have a functioning ear. These are the principal structures and functions of the ear. The eardrum, already mentioned, is also known as the **tympanic membrane.** Its vibrations induce a series of events. The motion of the tympanic membrane is conveyed to a structure called the **oval window.** The conveyance of the motion is made possible by the motion of three linked bones called the **malleus** ("hammer"), the **incus** ("anvil"), and the **stapes** ("stirrup").

Vibrations of the oval window in turn set up vibrations within a fluid contained in the **cochlea,** a bony structure reminiscent of a snail shell. A nervous system structure within the cochlea called the **basilar membrane** plays a role in hearing similar to the role that the retina plays in vision. The **auditory nerve** conveys the basilar membrane's activity pattern to the brain.

There are three basic sensations associated with hearing. First, **pitch** is the ability to hear sounds ranging from low to high. Second, **loudness** is associated with the magnitude of a sound. Third, **timbre** refers to the quality of a tone. In general, the quality of a note played on a piano has more timber, or "richness," than a note of the same pitch played on a flute.

(a) The eardrum is also known as the _____.

(b) What structure plays a similar role in hearing to the role that the retina plays in vision?

_____

(c) The three basic sensations associated with hearing are _____.

Answers: (a) tympanic membrane; (b) The basilar membrane; (3) pitch, loudness, and timbre.

Taste: "This Is Too Salty"

The stimuli that control much of the sense of taste are various chemical compounds such as those associated with salt, sugar, or lemon juice. The units that make taste possible are clusters of neurons located on the tongue called **taste buds.** The taste buds respond in such a way that they produce four basic taste sensations. These sensations are quite familiar. They are known as *sweet, salty, bitter,* and *sour.*

All tastes and taste names refer to combinations of these sensations in various patterns. How can there be many flavors if there are only four basic taste sensations? Think of the four sensations as a kind of alphabet. There are twenty-six letters in the standard English alphabet. Nonetheless, we have many thousands of words. Similarly, the four sensations are able to produce many flavors.

Taste buds are gathered in specific areas of the tongue. For example, the taste buds that produce the sensation of sweetness are located near the tip of the tongue. It is estimated that we have about 10,000 taste buds.

It should also be noted that the sense of taste interacts with other senses such as smell, vision, and touch. The aroma of a soup, the look of a steak, and differences in texture on the tongue all change our taste impressions.

(a) Taste buds, located on the tongue, are _____.

(b) The four basic taste sensations are _____.

Answers: (a) clusters of neurons; (b) sweet, salty, bitter, and sour.

Touch: Of Pain and Pressure

It is common to refer to touch as one of the basic senses. It is more accurate, however, to speak of the **skin senses,** basic experiences associated with different kinds of receptor neurons located in the skin. There are four skin senses: (1) light touch, (2) deep touch, (3) temperature, and (4) pain. The sensation of **light touch** can be induced by placing very little pressure on the surface of the skin or by slowly stroking the skin. You are aware that you are being touched even if your eyes are closed. Neurons located near the surface of the skin are the ones that give us the sensation of light touch.

Deep touch can be induced by placing substantial pressure on the surface of the skin. If someone shakes your hand too tightly or grips your arm with force, you will experience deep touch. Deep touch is also known as the sensation of *pressure*. Neurons located well below the surface of the skin are the ones that give us the sensation of deep touch.

(a) The four skin senses are _____.

(b) What skin sense can be induced by placing substantial pressure on the surface of the skin? _____

Answers: (a) light touch, deep touch, temperature, and pain; (b) Deep touch.

Temperature is induced by variations in the amount of heat being conducted to or away from the skin. When heat is being conducted toward the skin, we usually experience an increase in warmth. For example, the surrounding air temperature might be raised by turning on a furnace, and heat will be conducted toward the skin. When heat is being conducted away from the skin, we usually experience an increase in cold. For example, your bare feet will usually feel cold on a tile surface. This is because the skin of your feet makes such good contact with the hard surface that heat is carried away from your body. Two basic kinds of neurons for temperature are "hot" receptors and "cold" receptors.

Pain is a skin sense induced by tissue damage. A hard blow to the body or being cut by a knife will usually cause pain. Be clear that the kind of pain being described here is not the only type of pain. But the kind of pain associated with the skin is called *cutaneous pain*. Neurons in the skin that can detect tissue damage are the ones that give us this particular pain sensation.

(a) When heat is being conducted away from the skin we usually experience an increase in _____.

(b) What skin sense is induced by tissue damage? _____

Answers: (a) cold; (b) Pain.

Smell: The Nose Knows

You may think to yourself, "Someone in this room is wearing a perfume that I can't stand!" How do you know? You can't see the perfume. You can't hear the perfume. But you, with your sense of smell, *know.*

The sense of smell allows us to detect the presence of some, but not all, airborne chemical substances. The sense of smell is also known as **olfaction.** The receptor organ that makes the sense of smell possible is called the **olfactory epithelium,** and it is located high in the nose. It is to smell what the retina is to vision. Several kinds of neurons differentially sensitive to chemicals in gaseous forms induce the various smell sensations.

The exact number and kind of basic smell sensations, unlike the four basic taste sensations, are somewhat debatable. Nonetheless, it is possible to identify a number of elemental sensations. *Putrid* is one of them; it is the smell of something rotting or decomposing. Blossoms and blooms have a *floral* odor. A smell that is sharp or acrid, such as that produced by burning food, is said to be *pungent.* Cinnamon or cloves are said to have a smell that is *spicy.* The wood and bark of the camphor tree have a penetrating, fragrant odor. Camphor is also obtained by synthesis and is used in some medicines. The odor is described simply as *camphoric.*

(a) The sense of smell is also known as _____.

(b) The receptor organ that makes smell possible is called the _____.

Answers: (a) olfaction; (b) olfactory epithelium.

Kinesthesis: Can You Touch the Tip of Your Nose with Your Eyes Closed?

If you *can* touch the tip of your nose with your eyes closed, as most people can, you have an intact sense of kinesthesis. **Kinesthesis,** also known as **proprioception,** is the capacity to know the position in space of various parts of your body. (The term *proprioception* is related to the word "property." Your body belongs to you— it's your property.) Close your eyes and lift or lower a single finger. You know where it is at all times. When you walk you can sense the position of your legs even if you're not looking at them. Pianists and dancers rely heavily on kinesthesis.

The receptor neurons for kinesthesis are located in the connective tissue surrounding the body's joints as well as within the joints themselves.

(a) Kinesthesis is also known as _____.

(b) Kinesthesis is the capacity to know the position in space of _____.

Answers: (a) proprioception; (b) various parts of your body.

The Sense of Balance: Walking in an Upright Position

The sense of balance informs you that you are walking in an upright position. What you are sensing is the relationship of your body, and in particular your head, to the Earth's gravitational field. The sense of balance is made possible by receptor neurons located in the **semicircular canals.** Located in the inner ear, the canals are tubular bones filled with fluid. The movement of this fluid stimulates the firing of receptor neurons within the canals, and the information is transmitted to the brain.

The sense of balance is also known as the **vestibular sense.** A **vestibule** is a small antechamber or passageway. This is one way to describe the semicircular canals, important components of the apparatus involved in the sense of balance.

(a) The sense of balance is also known as the _____.

(b) The sense of balance is made possible by receptor organs located in the _____.

Answers: (a) vestibular sense; (b) semicircular canals.

SELF-TEST

1. Sensation refers to
    a. organized experience
    b. thinking and concept formation
    c. meaningful knowledge
    d. the raw data of experience

2. The waves to which we give the name "light" are a narrow band of
    a. the electromagnetic spectrum
    b. radio waves
    c. ultra-violet waves
    d. infra-red waves

3. The trichromatic theory proposes that we have
    a. three kinds of optic nerves
    b. a triad of lenses
    c. three kinds of cones
    d. three kinds of rods

4. A sound wave
    a. can travel through outer space
    b. cannot travel through water
    c. has frequency, but not amplitude
    d. requires a medium such as air or water

5. What structure in the ear is similar in function to the eye's retina?
    a. The basilar membrane
    b. The auditory nerve
    c. The tympanic membrane
    d. The oval window

6. The four basic taste sensations are
   a. sweet, salty, bitter, and hot
   b. sweet, bitter, burned, and salty
   c. sour, acid, sweet, and mint
   d. sweet, salty, bitter, and sour

7. One of the following is *not* a skin sense.
   a. Light touch
   b. Incongruent pleasure
   c. Deep touch
   d. Temperature

8. The receptor organ that makes smell possible is called the
   a. vestibular membrane
   b. olfactory epithelium
   c. odor membrane
   d. synaptic epithelium

9. What sense makes it possible for you to touch the tip of your nose with your eyes closed?
   a. The vestibular sense
   b. The cardiovascular sense
   c. Kinesthesis
   d. Synthesis

10. The vestibular sense lets you know when
    a. a signal is present
    b. a figure is perceived against a ground
    c. you are walking upright
    d. you have a subliminal perception

ANSWERS TO THE SELF-TEST

1-d 2-a 3-c 4-d 5-a 6-d 7-b 8-b 9-c 10-c

ANSWERS TO THE TRUE-OR-FALSE PREVIEW QUIZ

1. True.
2. True.
3. False. An electromagnetic wave, not a sound wave, has the remarkable property of being able to travel through a vacuum.
4. True.

5. False. Receptor organs in both the connective tissue surrounding the body's joints as well as within the joints themselves make possible the sense of kinesthesis, the capacity to know the position in space of various parts of your body.

KEY TERMS

auditory nerve
basilar membrane
brightness
cochlea
cognition
cones
cornea
decibel (dB)
deep touch
electromagnetic spectrum
electromagnetic wave
fovea
hertz (Hz)
hue
incus
infra-red rays
kinesthesis
lens
light touch
loudness
malleus
olfaction
olfactory epithelium
optic nerve

oval window
pain
perception
periphery
photons
photoreceptors
pitch
proprioception
retina
rods
saturation
semicircular canals
sensation
skin senses
stapes
taste buds
temperature
timbre
trichromatic theory
tympanic membrane
ultra-violet rays
vestibular sense
vestibule

5 Perception: Why Do Things Look the Way They Do?

PREVIEW QUIZ

True or False

1. T F   In the study of perception, a distinction can be made between the geographical world and the psychological world.
2. T F   Figure-ground perception is always stable and never reversible.
3. T F   Research suggests that there are innate, or inborn, organizing tendencies in perception.
4. T F   Learning appears to play no part in perception.
5. T F   Clairvoyance is another name for psychokinesis.

(Answers can be found on page 70.)

The link between sensation and perception is clear. Perception is possible because we have sensations. The raw data of experience—sensations— become organized wholes at the level of perception. We experience a world of objects—trees and songs—not flashes of light and random bits of sound. In this chapter you will learn how this organization arises.

Objectives

After completing this chapter, you will be able to

- state the Gestalt laws of perception;

- describe the role that learning plays in perception;

- explain what illusions teach us about perception;

- explain how both binocular vision and monocular cues play a role in depth perception;

- discuss some of issues associated with the topic of extrasensory perception.

Kurt Koffka (1886–1941), one of the founders of Gestalt psychology, said that the great question of perception is: "Why do things look the way they do?"

At first the question seems almost silly. We are tempted to answer, "Because things are they way they are." It would seem that tall things look tall because they *are* tall. And distant things look distant because they *are* distant. On the other hand, why does the Moon look larger just above the horizon than it does when it's overhead? It hasn't gotten any bigger, or any closer. And, if a series of disconnected dots are arranged in the pattern of, say, the letter F, it looks like the letter, not a bunch of disconnected dots—which, it could be argued, it actually is.

You learned in the last chapter that visual images on your retina are upside-down. Nonetheless, you perceive them as right side up. At the level of sensation, it's an inverted world. At the level of perception, the world doesn't look inverted at all.

Koffka's question does not have to be limited to the sense of vision. The same question could be adapted to the other senses. The principles set forth in this chapter, largely in connection with vision, can be readily applied to perception in general.

Sensation, as indicated in chapter 4, is the raw data of experience. **Perception,** on the other hand, is the organization and the meaning we give to primitive information. It can be said with some degree of confidence that we use sensory information to create a psychological world.

Returning to Koffka, he said that there is a distinction between the geographical world and the psychological world. The **geographical world** is the actual world "out there," the world as defined and described by physics. The **psychological world** is the world "in here," the world as experienced by the subject. Although common sense usually says it's the so-called "real world" or physical world that determines our behavior, it can be argued that common sense isn't sufficiently analytical. Reflection suggests that we behave in terms of what we perceive to be true, not necessarily in terms of what is actually true.

If ice is thin in the physical world, and it is solid in your psychological world, you are likely to skate on it. And, of course, you may make a serious mistake as a result.

In sum, it can be argued that we act to a large extent in terms of our perceptions. And it is for this reason that the study of perception is a basic one in psychology.

(a) Perception is the _____ and the meaning we give to primitive information.

(b) Koffka made a distinction between the geographical world and the _____ world.

   Answers: (a) organization; (b) psychological.

The Gestalt Laws: Is Our Perception of the World Due to Inborn Organizing Tendencies?

Imagine that you are looking up and you see a single bird flying in the sky. The bird is a **figure,** a well-defined perceptual object tending to stand out. The sky is **ground** (or **background**), the perceptual field that surrounds the figure. This is **figure-ground perception.** One of the features of this kind of perception is that the figure is usually smaller than the ground and tends to be seen as coming forward from the ground. Other examples include seeing a button on a blouse, a book on a table, or a car on the road.

It can be argued that this kind of perception, the ability to distinguish a figure from a field, is an inborn organizing tendency. We aren't taught to do it. We probably start doing it spontaneously early in infancy. An infant reaching for a milk bottle suggests to us that he or she perceives the bottle as a perceptual object, a figure in a field. Figure-ground perception is probably the most fundamental organizing tendency we possess.

Keep in mind once again that perception does not necessarily reflect the structure of the world itself. For example, a word printed in black ink on a white page is perceived as slightly in front of the white surface. We are tempted to think that this is because the word is "on" the page. But imagine that a black piece of paper is covered with a stencil. The entire page is inked white, with the exception of the word. Now, from a physical point of view, the white ink is on the black surface. Nonetheless, unless carefully studied, the word, emerging in black, will be perceived as slightly forward and on the page.

_____ perception is probably the most fundamental organizing tendency we possess.

   Answer: Figure-ground.

Various illusions demonstrate that figure-ground perception is reversible under some conditions. The example of the word on a page and the illusions all strongly suggest that figure-ground perception is a mental construction, not necessarily a fact about the physical world.

Max Wertheimer, as you will recall from chapter 1, is the father of Gestalt psychology. Adding to figure-ground perception, Wertheimer proposed a set of supplemental inborn organizing tendencies, or **Gestalt laws.** (The Gestalt laws are also traditionally called **innate tendencies,** which simply means "inborn." The words *innate* and *inborn* can be used interchangeably.)

First, **proximity** refers to the nearness of the elements that make up a perception. If four ink dots on a piece of paper are arranged in the form of a square, this Gestalt (i.e., organized whole) will, of course, be perceived to be a square. Let assume that two figures are drawn. Figure A has dots that are one inch apart. Figure B has dots that are three inches apart. Figure A will give a stronger impression of being a square than will Figure B.

When you look at stars in the sky and perceive constellations, it is because of the law of proximity. The "nearness" of some stars to each other creates clusters that we can easily imagine to be objects such as a dipper, a hunter, or a lion.

(a) Various illusions demonstrate that figure-ground perception is _____ under some conditions.

(b) What organizing tendency refers to the nearness of the elements that make up a perception? _____

Answers: (a) reversible; (b) Proximity.

Second, **similarity** refers to characteristics that elements have in common. Let's say that the word *airplane* is printed on a page in a single color of ink. Imagine that the same word is printed on a different page with its letters randomly appearing in black, red, and green. The second word is more difficult to perceive as a whole word, as a perceptual object, than is the first word. Similarity of the elements helps to make a perceptual object a coherent whole.

If a moth is dark gray and it lands on a tree with dark gray bark, it will be difficult to perceive the moth at all. This is because its similarity to the bark makes it, from a perceptual point of view, a part of the bark. However, if a light gray moth lands on the same tree, it will be easy to pick the moth out as a figure.

Third, **closure** is the tendency to fill in gaps in information and make a perceptual object into a complete whole. Imagine that an arc of 340 degrees is drawn on a piece of paper. Although at a sensory level this is an arc, you will tend to perceive it as a broken circle, as a coherent whole with a defect. (An unbroken circle has 360 degrees.) A newspaper photograph made up of nothing but disconnected dots is nonetheless perceived as a picture of people or things. Again, the principle of closure is at work.

Fourth, **common fate** exists when all of the elements of a perceptual object move or act together. (Their simultaneous activity is, in a sense, a "common fate.") When this happens, the perceptual object is quickly organized into a figure and is easily discriminated from a ground. For example, a polar bear with white fur surrounded by snow is more easily seen as a bear when it is moving than when it is stationary. Other organizing tendencies exist; however, the ones presented make clear the role that they appear to play in perception.

(a) What organizing tendency refers to characteristics that elements of perception have in common? _____

(b) The tendency to fill in gaps in information and make a perceptual object into a complete whole is called _____.

(c) Common fate exists when all of the elements of a perceptual object _____.

Answers: (a) Similarity; (b) closure; (c) move or act together.

Learned Aspects of Perception: Is the Infant's World a Buzzing, Blooming Confusion?

William James said that the infant's world is "a buzzing, blooming, confusion." There are flashes of light, noises, pressure on the skin, and so forth. But do they have any organization? Are patterns perceived? Or is there just a lot of random sensory activity? One gets the impression from James's comment that the infant, at least temporarily, inhabits a chaotic psychological world. We have seen from the exposition of the Gestalt laws that this is probably not completely correct. Innate organizing tendencies either immediately or very quickly help the infant to stabilize perceptions and introduce some sort of order into whatever is happening.

Nonetheless, it is important to appreciate that learning also plays a role in perception. The Gestalt laws may play a primary role, but learning certainly plays a secondary, and important, role.

Let's say that a simple melody is played on the piano in the presence of Tina, a two-week-old infant. Assume that Tina has had little or no experience with hearing music. Does she now actually perceive a melody in somewhat the same way that you perceive it? Or does she just hear a lot of disconnected tones? You can put yourself in Tina's position to some extent by imagining yourself listening to the music of another country, one that uses a tonal scale and patterns of harmony that are unfamiliar to you. When you first hear a song, it may seem to have little or no pattern. However, hearing it two or three times will help you to perceive the pattern. To the extent that you, or Tina, can hear any pattern at all on the first presentation, it is probably due to the Gestalt laws. The sharpening of perception on repeated presentations can be attributed to learning.

(a) William James's suggestion that the infant's world is a "buzzing, blooming, confusion" gives the impression that the infant, at least temporarily, inhabits a _____ psychological world.

(b) The sharpening of a perception on repeated presentations of a stimulus can be attributed to _____.

Answers: (a) chaotic; (b) learning.

One way to explain this sharpening of perception is to suggest that patterns of stimulation set off chain reactions in neurons located, let us say, in the association areas of the brain's cortex. Each time a given stimulus is presented, the same set of neurons fire. The research of the Canadian psychologist Donald O. Hebb suggests that repeated firings form a **cell assembly,** a stable group of neurons that are used over and over by the brain to create a representation of the external pattern. A pattern can, of course, be quite complex. If this is so, a given cell assembly may represent only a portion of a pattern. Hebb called a set of cell assemblies grouped together to form a larger pattern a **phase sequence.**

The existence of cell assemblies helps account for a memory of patterns and perceptual objects. When you hear a melody or recognize something you have seen before, it is quite possibly because an established cell assembly is firing.

Learning also plays a role in perception because we are conscious beings who attach labels to perceptual objects. This brings us to the **cognitive hypothesis** in perception, the hypothesis that we not only perceive, but know what we are perceiving. If you see a friend and think, "There's Erin," or hear a song and think, "That's 'God Bless America' by Irving Berlin," then you have increased the acuity of your perceptual world. **Cognitive learning,** learning in which consciousness plays an important role, is an important aspect of the perceptual process. There is more about learning in general and cognitive learning in particular in chapter 6.

(a) According to Hebb, a cell assembly is a stable group of _____.

(b) The hypothesis that we not only perceive, but know we perceive is called the _____.

Answers: (a) neurons; (b) cognitive hypothesis.

Illusions: What Do They Teach Us about Perception?

An **illusion** is a false perception, a perception that does not fit an objective description of a stimulus situation. An illusion is usually associated with a particular sense. Consequently, there are optical illusions, auditory illusions, and so forth. Illusions tend to be remarkably stable. They affect most normal observers in the same way. For example, for almost all of us the Moon is perceived to be larger when low and near the horizon than when it is high and overhead.

It is important to distinguish the concept of an illusion from a delusion and a hallucination. A **delusion** is a false belief. If Ray, a schizophrenic mental patient, believes that he has an eye with X-ray vision on the back of his head, this is a delusion. A **hallucination** is a perception created by the individual. It has no relationship to reality at all. If Ray sees and hears an invisible companion that nobody else can see or hear, this is a hallucination. Illusions are thought to be normal and experienced by most of us. Delusions and hallucinations are thought to be abnormal and experienced in an idiosyncratic fashion. (There is more about abnormal behavior in chapter 14.)

(a) An illusion is a _____.

(b) A delusion is a _____.

(c) A hallucination is a _____ created by the individual.

   Answers: (a) false perception; (b) false belief; (c) perception.

Illusions teach us that perceptions are, to some extent, created by the brain and nervous system, that we are not passive observers of our world. Let's return to figure-ground perception. We perceive the relationship between a figure and its associated ground as being a fact about the world itself. But is it? The **vase-faces illusion** can be perceived in two different ways. (See the illustration on page 64.) It can be seen as a vase. Or it can be seen as two profiles facing each other. When seen as a vase, this becomes figure and tends to stand forward a little in perception. The faces disappear and become absorbed into a receding ground. When seen as two faces, these become figure, and both tend to stand forward a little in perception. The vase disappears and becomes absorbed into a receding ground. These two different perceptual alternations will take place for most observers on a predictable basis. Also, it is impossible to simultaneously perceive both organizations. All of this suggests that figure and ground are organizing tendencies linked to perception, not facts about the external world.

How can the vase-faces illusion be explained? Here is one approach. The vase-faces drawing is said to be **ambiguous,** meaning that it can be perceived in more than one way. The process of **attention,** characterized by a tendency to focus on some stimuli and ignore others, determines that one organization will be temporarily favored over another. Let us say that the first organization favored is the vase. The region of the brain being stimulated by the vase organization becomes satiated ("overfilled") with the vase organization. It spontaneously rejects it for a second organization, one that is briefly refreshing. The **satiation hypothesis** suggests that the brain tends to reject excessive stimulation of one kind and tends to seek novel stimulation of another kind. Ambiguity, attention, and satiation are factors that all work together to produce the fluctuations in perception that take place when one experiences the vase-faces illusion.

The vase-faces illusion.

(a) Illusions teach us that we are not _____ of our world.

(b) A drawing that can be perceived in more than one way is said to be _____.

Answers: (a) passive observers; (b) ambiguous.

Returning to the Moon illusion, why does the Moon appear larger on the horizon than when it's overhead? The illusion is a variation of the **Ponzo illusion,** an illusion associated with linear perspective. Parallel lines, like those associated with railroad tracks or the sides of a roadway, appear to converge as they approach the horizon. At the horizon itself they meet, and this is called the **vanishing point.** If in a drawing two objects of the same size are simultaneously placed so that the first object is far from the horizon and the second one is near the horizon, the second object will be perceived as being larger than the first one. This is because, in a drawing, the retinal size of both objects is the same. However, the second object seems to be larger than it is in terms of comparisons we automatically make with other objects near the horizon.

Note that in everyday perception the Ponzo illusion does not occur. This is because the retinal size of an object near the horizon is smaller than that of an object closer to you. When the size of an image projected on the retina shrinks with distance, the apparent size of the object remains the same. This is a perceptual phenomenon called **size constancy.** For example, an approaching friend first seen when twenty feet away and then when closer to you appears to be the same size. However, in the case of the Moon illusion, the size of the Moon's image projected on your retina is about the same size when it is near the horizon and when it's "far" from it (when it's overhead). As the Moon orbits our planet, its actual distance from the Earth doesn't change significantly. Consequently, the conditions of the Ponzo illusion are met.

What we learn from illusions is that the world appears to us the way it does not only because it actually is the way it is. We also interpret sensory information, transforming it into a constructed perceptual, or psychological, world. And it is our perception of the world that determines much of our behavior.

(a) The Moon illusion is a variation of the _____.

(b) An object five feet away may look the same size as an object ten feet away. This is an example of _____.

Answers: (a) Ponzo illusion; (b) size constancy.

Depth Perception: Living in a Three-dimensional World

One of the fascinating questions of perception is this one: Why do we perceive a world of rounded shapes, of near and far things, of *depth* instead of a flat world with one surface? A second, related question is: How is this accomplished?

A given eye's retina is basically a surface, not a cube. (Although the eye itself is a three-dimensional "ball," the *surface* of the retina is not.) Think of the information on the surface of the retina as having some similarity to an oil painting made on a flat canvas. Note that it *is* possible to perceive depth in a landscape painting made on a flat canvas.

Depth perception is made possible by various *cues,* signals or stimuli that provide an observer with information. Depth perception is made possible by cues arising from binocular vision and monocular vision.

Binocular vision is vision with two eyes. The principal cue for depth perception associated with binocular vision is **retinal disparity.** The pupils of the eyes are about three inches apart. This gives the right eye a somewhat different view of a scene than the one obtained with the left eye. Notice that although you sense two images, you only perceive one. (This is another example of the difference between sensation and perception.) This is sometimes called the **zipper function** of the brain, the capacity of the visual portion of the cortex to integrate two images into a meaningful whole. The whole image, in part because of retinal disparity, appears to be three-dimensional.

(a) Binocular vision is vision with _____.

(b) The principal cue for depth perception arising from binocular vision is _____.

Answers: (a) two eyes; (b) retinal disparity.

Monocular vision is vision with one eye. If a person is deprived of binocular vision, then he or she can still perceive depth with the assistance of monocular cues. (Although the loss of the use of an eye *impairs* depth perception, it does not destroy it completely.) **Monocular cues** are available to one eye. These are the kinds of cues that give a landscape painting depth. Although you normally look at such a painting with both eyes open, in this case depth perception is not arising because of retinal disparity. Close one eye and look at the painting. The perception of depth will remain.

A first monocular cue is **linear perspective,** the tendency of parallel lines to seem to converge as they approach the horizon. Linear perspective was referred to earlier in connection with the Moon illusion. A second monocular cue is **interposition,** a cue created when one object blocks some portion of another object. If a person is standing in front of a tree, and the tree is partly blocked, it is easy to see that the tree is behind, not in front of, the person.

A third monocular cue is **shadows.** Shadows are differences in illumination gradients. These tend to help us see rounded surfaces as convex or concave. A fourth monocular cue is **texture gradient.** A texture gradient is perceived when we can see less detail in far away objects than those that are closer to us. Such a gradient appears spontaneously when we look at a field strewn with rocks.

A fifth monocular cue is **motion parallax,** the tendency when moving forward fairly rapidly to perceive differential speeds in objects that are passing by and in those that are being approached. For example, in a traveling car, nearby telephone poles approach rapidly and then flash by. Look down the road. The telephone poles seem to be approaching slowly. If you can see telephone poles very far away, they seem to be almost stationary.

All of these monocular cues work together to enhance depth perception.

(a) Monocular vision is vision with _____.

(b) The tendency of parallel lines to seem to converge as they approach the horizon is called _____.

(c) Differential speeds are associated with what monocular cue? _____

Answers: (a) one eye; (b) linear perspective; (c) Motion parallax.

Extrasensory Perception: Is It Real?

The novel *Slan* by A. E. van Vogt has become a science-fiction classic. First serialized in the magazine *Astounding Science Fiction* in 1940, the story relates the adventures of a boy with telepathic powers and his conflicts with nontelepathic adversaries. Telepathy has become a staple of science fiction and is taken for granted as a power of the mind in many novels and films. But is it real?

Before we address the fact or fiction of telepathy, let's explore the phenomenon as if it were real. This will permit us to understand more accurately what people mean when they use words such as *telepathy*.

Telepathy belongs to a larger category of phenomena called **extrasensory perception.** Extrasensory perception, or **ESP,** is the capacity to be aware of external events without the use of one of the conventional senses such as vision or hearing. ESP is referred to as the *sixth sense*, but as you learned in chapter 4, there are at least seven readily identified senses. ESP should more accurately be called the *eighth sense*.

There are three kinds of extrasensory perception: (1) precognition, (2) telepathy, and (3) clairvoyance. **Precognition** is the power to know what will happen in the future. Living almost five hundred years ago, the French physician and astrologer Nostradamus is one of the more famous individuals in history purported to have had precognitive powers.

(a) Identify the three kinds of extrasensory perception. _____

(b) Precognition is the power to know what will happen in the _____.

Answers: (a) Precognition, telepathy, and clairvoyance; (b) future.

Telepathy is the power to send and receive mental messages. The ability to read the minds of people who can't read yours is also considered to be a telepathic power. A spy with this ability would have a useful psychological tool. In the first half of the twentieth century Upton Sinclair, author of *The Jungle* and a defeated candidate for governor of California, conducted telepathic experiments with his wife and published a book called *Mental Radio*.

Clairvoyance is the power to have visions and "see" something out of the range of normal vision. (The word *clairvoyance* has French roots meaning "clear seeing.") Some clairvoyants are asserted to be able to give medical readings and visualize an illness in another person in the same way that an X-ray machine can. A person who can combine the two powers of precognition and clairvoyance is thought to be able to both predict and visualize future events. The term *seer* implies an ability to combine these powers.

(a) The power to send and receive mental messages is called _____.

(b) The word *vision* is associated with what kind of ESP? _____

Answers: (a) telepathy; (b) Clairvoyance.

Although not a form of ESP, there is another power often associated with it. This is **psychokinesis** or **PK.** Psychokinesis is the power to move objects using only energy transmitted by the mind. In the movie *The Empire Strikes Back,* the hero Luke Skywalker lifts a small spaceship out of the muck of a bog with PK. A gambler who believes in PK believes he can give the dice a mental nudge as they're rolling and influence the numbers that come up.

All four of the phenomena mentioned above are combined into a general class of mental abilities called **psi powers,** powers of the mind that are thought to transcend the conventional laws of physics and our ordinary understanding of natural science. Psi powers are sometimes also called "wild talents."

(a) The power to move objects using only the energy of the mind is called _____.

(b) What kind of powers are called "wild talents" such as ESP and PK? _____

Answers: (a) psychokinesis (PK); (b) Psi powers.

Do psi powers, ESP and PK, actually exist? If one were to make a decision on anecdotal evidence alone, then one would accept the reality of these powers. There are many stories and personal experiences that relate vivid and seemingly convincing events that tempt skeptical observers to become believers. However, anecdotes and personal experiences are hardly the stuff of science. They can't be verified. They are difficult or impossible to replicate. Often the only witness is one individual. When the number of subjects in a study is only one, the study has no reliability and can't be generalized. Consequently, wonderful stories aren't sufficient evidence in favor of the hypothesis that ESP and PK are real.

On the other hand, experimental science has explored psi powers. Joseph B. Rhine (1895–1980), working at Duke University, conducted many experiments on ESP and PK. He called the study of such phenomena **parapsychology.** Telepathy experiments were conducted with the aid of a set of twenty-five cards called **Zener cards.** There are five symbols and these are each repeated five times. PK experiments often involved the tossing of dice because probable outcomes could be accurately stated. Rhine's research favors accepting the hypothesis that psi powers are real. Others such as Charles T. Tart, using the experimental method, have obtained results that are similar to Rhine's.

On the other hand, many psychologists remain unconvinced. They point out that there are flaws in the methodology of the various parapsychological experiments. Also, it should be noted that such experiments do not consistently support the reality of psi powers. Skeptics assert that when parapsychological experiments are well designed and tightly controlled, many of the positive results fade away.

It is not possible at this time to make a simple statement saying that psychology either accepts psi abilities as real or rejects them as false. It *can* be asserted that many psychologists—perhaps most—are unwilling to accept the reality of these phenomena. They don't believe that the data are sufficiently convincing.

(a) Rhine called the study of such phenomena as ESP and PK _____.

(b) Many psychologists—perhaps most—are _____ to accept the reality of psi powers.

Answers: (a) parapsychology; (b) unwilling.

SELF-TEST

1. According to Koffka, the actual world "out there," the world as defined by physics is
   a. the phenomenal world
   b. the geographical world
   c. the psychological world
   d. the subjective world

2. The capacity to see a bird in the sky is an example of
   a. the Ponzo illusion
   b. a cell assembly working
   c. a monocular cue
   d. figure-ground perception

3. One of the following is *not* a Gestalt law.
   a. Proximity
   b. Similarity
   c. The cognitive hypothesis
   d. Closure

4. What hypothesis states that we not only perceive, but also know what we are perceiving?
   a. The cognitive hypothesis
   b. The sensory hypothesis
   c. The motor-neuron hypothesis
   d. The Wertheimer-Koffka hypothesis

5. An illusion is
   a. a false belief
   b. a kind of hallucination
   c. the same thing as a delusion
   d. a false perception

6. The vase-faces drawing is said to be ambiguous, meaning that
   a. its borders are fuzzy
   b. it can be perceived in more than one way

    c. it can be perceived in one way only

    d. it does not meet the criterion of subjectivity

7. The Moon illusion
   a. is caused by large changes in the Moon's distance from the Earth
   b. provides a good example of size constancy
   c. provides a case in which size constancy breaks down
   d. violates figure-ground perception

8. The principal depth perception cue associated with binocular vision is
   a. linear perspective
   b. texture gradient
   c. motion parallax
   d. retinal disparity

9. One of the following is *not* a kind of extrasensory perception.
   a. Psychokinesis
   b. Precognition
   c. Telepathy
   d. Clairvoyance

10. What is the status of psi powers in psychology as a science?
    a. Psi powers are proven facts
    b. No one has done experiments on psi powers
    c. The reality of psi powers is still open to question
    d. Telepathy is real, but clairvoyance is not

ANSWERS TO THE SELF-TEST

1-b   2-d   3-c   4-a   5-d   6-b   7-c   8-d   9-a   10-c

ANSWERS TO THE TRUE-OR-FALSE PREVIEW QUIZ

1. True.
2. False. Figure-ground perception is sometimes unstable and reversible (e.g., the vase-faces illusion).
3. True.
4. False. For example, learning often sharpens our perception.
5. False. Clairvoyance is the power to "see" something out of the normal range of vision. Psychokinesis is the power to move objects using only energy transmitted by the mind.

KEY TERMS

ambiguous

attention

binocular vision

cell assembly

clairvoyance

closure

cognitive hypothesis

cognitive learning

common fate

delusion

extrasensory perception (ESP)

figure

figure-ground perception

geographical world

Gestalt laws

ground (or background)

hallucination

illusion

innate tendencies

interposition

linear perspective

monocular cues

monocular vision

motion parallax

parapsychology

perception

phase sequence

Ponzo illusion

precognition

proximity

psi powers

psychokinesis (PK)

psychological world

retinal disparity

satiation hypothesis

shadows

similarity

size constancy

telepathy

texture gradient

vanishing point

vase-faces illusion

Zener cards

zipper function

6 Learning: Understanding Acquired Behavior

True or False

1. T F Learning is a more or less permanent change in behavior, or a behavioral tendency, as a result of experience.
2. T F A conditioned reflex is an inborn response pattern.
3. T F Operant behavior is characterized by actions that have no meaning for an organism, and, consequently, no consequences.
4. T F Observational learning takes place when an individual acquires behavior by watching the behavior of a second individual.
5. T F There is no such thing as short-term memory.

(Answers can be found on page 88.)

As indicated in the previous chapter, the perceptual world is a world of objects that form the basis of our organized experience. Consequently, this organization also provides the first stepping stone for the learning process. In order to learn it is essential to experience the world "out there" and respond to it. In this chapter you will find out how we acquire behavioral patterns through experience.

Objectives

After completing this chapter, you will be able to

- describe the principal aspects of the learning process;
- identify basic concepts in classical conditioning;
- explain the process of operant conditioning;
- give an example of the important role that consciousness plays in learning;
- specify the most important aspects of the memory process.

Think of ways to use the word *learned* in a sentence, using yourself as a subject of the sentence. Here are some examples collected from psychology students:

"I learned to drive a car."

"I learned quite a bit of Italian when I was stationed in Italy for two years."

"Little by little I have learned to hate my business partner."

"I learned a lot on the streets where I grew up."

"I learned to be a more loving, understanding person after I got married."

"I learned good table manners when I was a child."

"I learned to smoke by hanging out with friends who smoked."

The above examples of the ways students think about the learning process reveal that learning takes place under many conditions and in many situations. Although learning takes place in school, it is clear that much—perhaps most—learning goes on outside of the classroom. Indeed, the learning process affects almost everything we do.

Learning is a more or less permanent change in behavior, or a behavioral tendency, as a result of experience. There are several points to be made about this definition. First, learning is "more or less" permanent. This suggests that although learning tends to resist change once it is acquired, it sometimes does change. Learning can be forgotten. Learning is sometimes subject to a process known as *extinction* (to be explained later). Also, what has been learned can sometimes be shaped or modified. So learning is far from permanent.

Second, the term **behavioral tendency** indicates that learning is sometimes dormant, that it does not reflect itself in immediate action. This phenomenon is called *latent learning* and it too will be discussed later.

Third, note the focus on the word **experience** in the definition. In order to learn it is necessary to receive information. This is done through our sense organs. Imagine an infant born without vision or hearing. It would be terribly difficult for that infant to learn and develop normal intelligence. If the infant had no sense of touch or smell or balance, then learning would be next to impossible.

Learning is a more or less permanent change in behavior, or a behavioral tendency, as a result of _____.

Answer: experience.

Classical Conditioning: Responding to Signals

Imagine that you are reading a menu in a restaurant and your mouth begins to water. Is this an example of classical conditioning? Yes, it is. You were not born with a tendency to salivate when looking at a menu. This is behavior acquired through experience, and, consequently, a kind of learning. Salivating to words on paper is a conditioned reflex.

Classical conditioning was the first kind of learning to be studied experimentally. The pioneer researcher into classical conditioning was Ivan Pavlov (1849–1936), a Russian physiologist. **Classical conditioning** is characterized by the capacity of a previously neutral stimulus to elicit a reflex. If a dog is trained to salivate each time that it hears a tone of a specific frequency, then the tone is the previously neutral stimulus and the act of salivating is the reflex. Pavlov achieved his results primarily with a number of dogs that were trained to patiently cooperate with the researcher while being restrained in harnesses in the laboratory.

There are four basic terms, all closely related, that you need to learn as the foundation stones of your understanding of classical conditioning. These are (1) the unconditioned stimulus, (2) the conditioned stimulus, (3) the unconditioned reflex, and (4) the conditioned reflex.

The **unconditioned stimulus** is a stimulus that has an inborn power to elicit a reflex. Food in the mouth is such a stimulus. The physiology of the body is such that when salivary glands are stimulated by food, saliva will flow.

(a) Classical conditioning is characterized by the capacity of a _____ stimulus to elicit a reflex.

(b) The unconditioned stimulus is a stimulus that has an _____ power to elicit a reflex.

Answers: (a) previously neutral; (b) inborn.

The **conditioned stimulus** is created by the learning process. It acquires a power that is sometimes (not always) similar to that of the unconditioned stimulus. If a tone precedes food in the mouth a number of times, then the tone may acquire the power to elicit saliva. If a dog salivates when it hears a tone, then the tone is a conditioned stimulus. It can be argued that the dog has associated the tone with food and that the tone has become a signal conveying the meaning that food is coming soon. Indeed, this is one of the important meanings that Pavlov gave to classical conditioning. He thought of conditioned stimuli as signals.

The **unconditioned reflex** is an inborn response pattern. A dog has an inborn tendency to salivate when food is placed in its mouth. Salivating under these conditions is an unconditioned reflex. The word *response* is sometimes used in place of the word *reflex*. This usage, although common, is somewhat imprecise. A **response** to a stimulus is a behavior pattern that suggests a higher level of organization and complexity than that associated with a reflex. Salivating when reading a menu's description of a hamburger is a reflex. Ordering the item and asking that the meat be well done is a response.

A **conditioned reflex** is a learned response pattern. If a dog salivates to a tone, then the elicited flow of saliva is a conditioned reflex.

(a) What stimulus acquires a power that is sometimes (not always) similar to the unconditioned stimulus? _____

(b) The unconditioned reflex is an _____ response pattern.

(c) A response to stimulus is a behavior pattern that suggests a higher level of _____ and _____ than that associated with a reflex.

Answers: (a) The conditioned stimulus; (b) inborn; (c) organization; complexity.

Several important features of classical conditioning should be noted. First, the word **conditioning** implies a kind of learning that does not require reflection and reasoning. The learning takes place primarily through a process of association. Infants are capable of classical conditioning. If a baby's mouth begins to make sucking motions when a milk bottle is in view, then the sucking motions are conditioned reflexes.

Second, as indicated above, classical conditioning is not limited to dogs and animals. Although Pavlov used dogs as research subjects, the results of his research can be generalized to human beings.

Third, conditioned reflexes are **involuntary.** They are outside of the conscious control of the subject.

There are various behavioral patterns associated with classical conditioning. Three of these are extinction, stimulus generalization, and discrimination. **Extinction** takes place when the conditioned stimulus is presented a number of times without the unconditioned stimulus. If a conditioned dog is presented with a tone, it will salivate. However, if the tone is presented without food a sufficient number of times, the tone will cease to elicit the conditioned reflex. The dog has, in effect, *unlearned* the conditioned reflex. Extinction should not be confused with forgetting. Extinction is an active process that is designed to eliminate a conditioned reflex. The process of actively extinguishing a conditioned reflex is taken advantage of in desensitization therapy (see chapter 15).

(a) The word *conditioning* implies a kind of learning that does not require _____ and _____.

(b) Outside of the conscious control of the subject, conditioned reflexes are said to be _____.

(c) What phenomenon appears when the conditioned stimulus is presented a number of times without the unconditioned stimulus? _____

Answers: (a) reflection; reasoning; (b) involuntary; (c) Extinction.

Stimulus generalization occurs when a stimulus that is similar to an original conditioned stimulus elicits a conditioned reflex. For example, let's say that a dog is trained to salivate to a pitch that is the equivalent of middle C on the piano. If a pitch the equivalent of D, a note that is close to C, is sounded, the dog will also salivate. As the pitch goes higher, there may be some salivation. If the pitch gets high enough, salivation will stop. This is **discrimination,** the subject's ability to tell the difference between an original conditioned stimulus and other stimuli.

In a classical experiment, Rosalie Raynor, an assistant to John B. Watson, trained a child to be afraid of a white rat. In subsequent testing, the child, known in the research literature as Little Albert, showed fear reactions (conditioned reflexes) when he saw a different white rat, a Santa Claus mask (with white fur), or a rolled-up white terrycloth dishtowel. This research provides an example of stimulus generalization in a human being.

(a) What phenomenon occurs when a stimulus that is similar to an original conditioned stimulus elicits a conditioned reflex? _____

(b) A subject's ability to tell the difference between an original conditioned stimulus and other stimuli is called _____.

Answers: (a) Stimulus generalization; (b) discrimination.

Trial-and-Error Learning: Taking a Rocky Road

It is instructive to note that one of the most popular books on writing ever published is called *Trial and Error* by the novelist Jack Woodford. It sold many copies over a number of years, and communicated to would-be authors that the only way to learn to write was by taking the rocky road of learning by making one's own mistakes.

The first kind of learning to be studied experimentally in the United States was **trial-and-error learning.** Edward L. Thorndike (1874–1949) first studied maze learning in baby chickens (with the assistance and approval of William James). Later he studied the escape behavior of cats from puzzle boxes. The cats had to learn to pull a string that released a latch connected to a door. The cats learned to pull the string, but only very gradually. They showed no sudden burst of insight or comprehension. Thorndike concluded that the learning was a robotlike process controlled primarily by its outcomes. If a specific behavior helped a cat to escape, that behavior was retained by the cat. Thorndike called this process **stamping in,** meaning that an action that is useful is impressed upon the nervous system.

What stamps in a response, according to Thorndike, is satisfaction. The cat that escapes from a puzzle box is rewarded with food. Thorndike called the tendency to retain what is learned because satisfactory results are obtained the **law of effect.** Thorndike's law of effect is the forerunner of what today is usually known as the process of *reinforcement* (see the next section).

(a) If a specific behavior helps a cat to escape from a puzzle box, this behavior is retained by the cat. Thorndike called this process _____.

(b) Thorndike's law of effect is the forerunner of what today is usually known as the process of _____.

Answers: (a) stamping in; (b) reinforcement.

Operant Conditioning: How Behavior Is Shaped by Its Own Consequences

Operant behavior is characterized by actions that have consequences. Flick a light switch and the consequence is illumination. Saw on a piece of wood and the consequence is two shorter pieces of wood. Tell a joke and the consequence is (sometimes) the laughter of others. Work hard at a job all week and the consequence is a paycheck. In each of these cases the specified action "operates" on the environment, changes it in some way.

It was B. F. Skinner (1904–1990) who applied the term **operant** to the kind of behaviors described above. He saw that operant behavior is both acquired and shaped by experience. Consequently, he identified it as a kind of learning. In addition, he also categorized it as a form of conditioning because he believed that such concepts as consciousness and thinking are not necessary to explain much (perhaps most) operant behavior.

Skinner, long associated with Harvard, invented a device called the **operant conditioning apparatus;** its informal name is the **Skinner box.** Think of the apparatus as something like a candy machine for animals such as rats and pigeons. A rat, for example, learns that it can obtain a pellet of food when it presses a lever. If the pellet appears each time the lever is pressed, the rate of lever pressing will increase. Lever pressing is operant behavior (or simply an *operant.*) The pellet is a reinforcer. A **reinforcer** is a stimulus that has the effect of increasing the frequency of a given category of behavior (in this case, lever pressing).

(a) Operant behavior is characterized by actions that have _____.

(b) The formal term for a Skinner box is the _____.

   Answers: (a) consequences; (b) operant conditioning apparatus.

The concept of reinforcement plays a big part in Skinner's way of looking at behavior. Consequently, it is important to expand on the concept. Note in the above definition that a reinforcer is understood in terms of its *actual effects.* It is to be distinguished from a reward. A **reward** is perceived as valuable to the individual giving the reward, but it may not be valued by the receiving organism. In the case of a reinforcer, it is a reinforcer *only* if it has some sort of payoff value to the receiving organism. By definition, a reinforcer has an impact on operant behavior. Its function is always to *increase* the frequency of a class of operant behaviors.

One important way to categorize reinforcers is to refer to them as positive and negative. A **positive reinforcer** has value for the organism. Food when you are hungry, water when you are thirsty, and money when you're strapped for cash all provide examples of positive reinforcers.

(a) The function of a reinforcer is always to _____ the frequency of a class of operant behaviors.

(b) A _____ has value for the organism.

   Answers: (a) increase; (b) positive reinforcer.

A **negative reinforcer** has no value for the organism. It does injury or is noxious in some way. A hot room, an offensive person, and a dangerous situation all provide examples of negative reinforcers. The organism tends to either escape from or avoid such reinforcers. The operant behavior takes the subject *away* from the reinforcer. Turning on the air conditioner when a room is hot provides an example of operant behavior designed to escape from a negative reinforcer. Note that the effect of the negative reinforcer on behavior is still to *increase* the frequency of a class of operants. You are more likely to turn on an air conditioner tomorrow if you have obtained relief by doing so today.

It is also important to note that a negative reinforcer is *not* punishment. In the case of punishment, an operant is *followed* by an adverse stimulus. For example, a child sasses a parent and then gets slapped. Getting slapped comes *after* the child's behavior. In the case of a negative reinforcer, the adverse stimulus is *first* in time. Then the operant behavior of escape or avoidance follows.

(a) Operant behavior takes a subject _____ from a negative reinforcer.

(b) In the case of punishment, an operant is _____ by an adverse stimulus.

   Answers: (a) away; (b) followed.

Another important way to classify reinforcers is to designate them as having either a primary or a secondary quality. A **primary reinforcer** has intrinsic value for the organism. No learning is required for the worth of the reinforcer to exist. Food when you are hungry and water when you are thirsty are not only positive reinforcers, as indicated above, they are also primary reinforcers.

A **secondary reinforcer** has acquired value for the organism. Learning is required. Money when you're strapped for cash is a positive reinforcer, as indicated above, but it is a secondary one. You have to learn that cash has value. An infant does not value cash, but does value milk. A medal, a diploma, and a trophy all provide examples of secondary reinforcers.

(a) A _____ has intrinsic value for an organism.

(b) A _____ has acquired value for an organism.

   Answers: (a) primary reinforcer; (b) secondary reinforcer.

One of the important phenomena associated with operant conditioning is extinction. Earlier, we discussed how extinction takes place when the conditioned stimulus is presented a number of times without the unconditioned stimulus. Extinction also takes place when the frequency of a category of operant responses *declines*. If, using the operant conditioning apparatus, reinforcement is withheld from a rat, then lever pressing for food will decline and eventually diminish to nearly zero. The organism has learned to give up a given operant because it no longer brings the reinforcer.

Both animal and human research on extinction suggest that it is a better way to "break" bad habits than is punishment. If a way can be found to eliminate the reinforcer (or reinforcers) linked to a behavior pattern, the behavior is likely to be given up. Punishment tends to temporarily suppress the appearance of an operant, but extinction has not necessarily taken place. Consequently, the unwanted operant has "gone underground," and may in time surface as an unpleasant surprise. Also, punishment is frustrating to organisms and tends to make them more aggressive.

(a) Extinction takes place when the frequency of a category of operant responses _____.

(b) Punishment is frustrating to organisms and tends to make them more _____.

Answers: (a) declines; (b) aggressive.

Another important phenomenon associated with operant conditioning is the **partial reinforcement effect,** the tendency of operant behavior acquired under conditions of partial reinforcement to possess greater resistance to extinction than behavior acquired under conditions of continuous reinforcement. Let's say that rat 1 is reinforced every time it presses a lever; this rat is receiving continuous reinforcement. Rat 2 is reinforced every other time it presses a lever; this rat is receiving partial reinforcement. Both rats will eventually acquire the lever-pressing response. Now assume that reinforcement is withheld for both rats. The rat that will, in most cases, display greater resistance to extinction is rat 2. Skinner was surprised by this result. If reinforcement is a kind of strengthening of a habit, then rat 1, receiving more reinforcement, should have the more well-established habit. And it should demonstrate greater resistance to extinction than rat 2.

Nonetheless, the partial reinforcement effect is a reality, and Skinner became interested in it. He and his coworkers used many schedules of reinforcement to study the partial reinforcement effect. In general, it holds for both animals and human beings that there is indeed a partial reinforcement effect. **Random reinforcement** is determined by chance, and is, consequently, unpredictable. If behavior is acquired with random reinforcement, it exaggerates the partial reinforcement effect. Skinner was fond of pointing out that random payoffs are associated with gambling. This explains to some extent why a well-established gambling habit is hard to break.

(a) Operant behavior acquired under conditions of partial reinforcment tends to possess greater resistance to _____ than behavior acquired under conditions of continuous reinforcement.

(b) What kind of reinforcement is determined by chance? _____

Answers: (a) extinction; (b) Random reinforcement.

Assume that an instrumental conditioning apparatus contains a light bulb. When the light is on, pressing the lever pays off. When the light is off, pressing the lever fails to bring forth a reinforcer. Under these conditions, a trained experimental animal will tend to display a high rate of lever pressing when the light is on and ignore the lever when the light is off. The light is called a **discriminative stimulus,** meaning a stimulus that allows the organism to tell the difference between a situation that is potentially reinforcing and one that is not. Cues used to train animals, such as whistles and hand signals, are discriminative stimuli.

Skinner notes that discriminative stimuli control human behavior, too. A factory whistle communicating to workers that it's time for lunch, a bell's ring for a prizefighter, a school bell's ring for a child, and a traffic light for a driver are all discriminative stimuli. Stimuli can be more subtle than these examples. A lover's facial expression or tone of voice may communicate a readiness or lack of readiness to respond to amorous advances.

Skinner asserts that in real life both discriminative stimuli and reinforcers automatically control much of our behavior.

A stimulus that allows the organism to tell the difference between a situation that is potentially reinforcing and one that is not is called a _____.

Answer: discriminative stimulus.

Consciousness and Learning: What It Means to Have an Insight

Although classical and operant conditioning play a large part in both animal and human learning, it is generally recognized by behavioral scientists that these two related processes give an insufficient account of the learning process, particularly in human beings. Consequently, it is important to identify at least four additional aspects of learning. These are (1) observational learning, (2) latent learning, (3) insight learning, and (4) learning to learn.

Observational learning takes place when an individual acquires behavior by watching the behavior of a second individual. Albert Bandura, a principal researcher associated with observational learning, identified important features of this particular process. The second individual is a **model,** and either intentionally or unintentionally demonstrates behavior. If the observer identifies with the model and gains imaginary satisfaction from the model's behavior, then this is vicarious reinforcement. **Vicarious reinforcement** is characterized by imagined gratification. Psychologically, it acts as a substitute for the real thing. Let's say that Jonathan admires a particular tennis star. When the star wins an important tournament, Jonathan is ecstatic. This emotional state is a vicarious reinforcer.

It should be noted that the concept of watching a model is very general. Reading a mystery novel and identifying with the detective is a kind of observational behavior. The thrills associated with the hero's adventures are vicarious thrills.

(a) What kind of learning takes place when an individual acquires behavior by watching the behavior of a second individual? _____

(b) A _____ either intentionally or unintentionally demonstrates behavior.

(c) _____ is characterized by imagined gratification.

Answers: (a) Observational learning; (b) model; (c) Vicarious reinforcement.

Social learning theory, associated with Bandura's research, states that much of our behavior in reference to other people is acquired through observational learning. Let's say that Carol is a fifteen-year-old high school student. She is on the fringe of a group of adolescent females who admire a charismatic eighteen-year-old named Dominique. Dominique smokes, uses obscenities, and brags about her sexual exploits. Carol observes Dominique and obtains a lot of vicarious reinforcement from Dominique's behavior. If Carol begins to imitate Dominique's behavior, then social learning has taken place.

Both prosocial behavior and antisocial behavior can be acquired through observational learning. **Prosocial behavior** is behavior that contributes to the long-run goals of a traditional reference group such as the family or the population of the nation (see chapter 16). If an individual admires one or both parents, then the parents may be taken as role models. Many adolescents and young adults acquire attitudes and personal habits that resemble those of their parents. If one is patriotic and ready to defend one's nation during time of war, it is quite likely that the individual is taking important historical figures such as presidents and generals as role models.

Antisocial behavior is behavior that has an adverse impact on the long-run goals of a traditional reference group. From the point of view of Carol's parents, if Carol begins to act like Dominique, then Carol's behavior is antisocial.

(a) What theory states that much of our behavior in reference to other people is acquired through observational learning? _____

(b) _____ is behavior that contributes to the long-run goals of a traditional reference group.

(c) _____ is behavior that has an adverse impact on the long-run goals of a traditional reference group.

Answers: (a) Social learning theory; (b) Prosocial behavior; (c) Antisocial behavior.

Latent learning is a second kind of learning in which consciousness appears to play a large role. Pioneer research on latent learning is associated with experiments conducted by the University of California psychologist Edward C. Tolman and his associates. Let's say that a rat is allowed to explore a maze without reinforcement. It seems to wander through the maze without any particular pattern of behavior. It is probably responding to its own curiosity drive, but no particular learning appears to be taking place. Let's say that after ten such opportunities, reinforcement in the form of food in a goal box is introduced. The rat, if it is typical, will quickly learn to run the maze with very few errors. Its learning curve is highly accelerated compared to that of a rat that has not had an earlier opportunity to explore the maze. This is because the first rat was actually learning while it was exploring. The function of reinforcement in this case is to act as an **incentive,** a stimulus that elicits and brings forth whatever learning the organism has acquired.

Note that the learning was actually acquired when the rat was exploring. Therefore learning was taking place without reinforcement. Such learning is called *latent learning,* meaning learning that is dormant and waiting to be activated.

Let's say that Keith is an adolescent male. For years his mother has forced him, with no particular reinforcement, to make his bed and hang up his clothes neatly. But Keith has, from his mother's point of view, been a slow learner. He does both tasks poorly. He enlists in the army shortly after his eighteenth birthday. In basic training he makes his bed and hangs up his clothes neatly. He has been told that he will obtain his first weekend pass only if he performs various tasks properly. The fact that Keith shows a very rapid learning curve under these conditions provides an example of latent learning. He was learning under his mother's influence, but he wasn't motivated to bring the learning forth.

The process of latent learning calls attention to the **learning-performance distinction.** Learning is an underlying process. In the case of latent learning it is temporarily hidden. Performance is the way in which learning is displayed in action. Only performance can actually be observed and directly measured.

(a) _____ is learning that is dormant and waiting to be activated.

(b) _____ is the way in which learning is displayed in action.

    Answers: (a) Latent learning; (b) Performance.

Insight learning is a third kind of learning in which consciousness appears to play a major role. Groundbreaking research on insight learning was conducted by Wolfgang Köhler, one of the principal Gestalt psychologists. One of Köhler's principal subjects was an ape named Sultan. Sultan was presented with two short handles that could be assembled to make one long tool, a kind of rake. An orange was placed outside of Sultan's cage and it was beyond the reach of either handle. Sultan spent quite a bit of time using the handles in useless ways. He seemed to be making no progress on the problem.

Then one day Sultan seemed to have a burst of understanding. He clicked together the handles and raked in the orange. Köhler called this burst of understanding an **insight,** and defined it as a sudden reorganization of a perceptual field. Originally, Sultan's perceptual field contained two useless handles. With insight, Sultan's perceptual field contained a long rake. The conscious mental process that brings a subject to an insight is called **insight learning.**

A burst of understanding associated with the sudden reorganization of a perceptual field is called an _____.

Answer: insight.

Insight learning is also important for human beings. Let's say that a child in grammar school is told that pi is the ratio of the circumference of a circle to the diameter, and that a rounded value for pi is 3.14. The child memorizes the definition, but the definition has little meaning. If, on the other hand, the child is encouraged to measure the diameters and the circumferences of cans, pie tins, and wheels using a string and a ruler, the child may acquire the insight that round items are always about three times bigger around than they are across. Acquiring an insight is more satisfying than just memorizing material. Also, insights tend to resist the process of forgetting.

Harry Harlow, a former president of the American Psychological Association, using rhesus monkeys as subjects, discovered a phenomenon called *learning sets.* Assume that a monkey is given a discrimination problem. It is required to learn that a grape, used as a reinforcer, is always to be found under a small circular container instead of a square one. The learning curve is gradual, and a number of trials are required before learning is complete. A second similar problem is given. The discrimination required is between containers with two patterns, a crescent moon and a triangle. The learning curve for the second problem is more accelerated than the learning curve for the first problem. By the time a fourth or a fifth similar problem is given, the monkey is able to solve the problem in a very few trials. The monkey has acquired a **learning set,** an ability to quickly solve a given type of problem. The underlying process is called **learning to learn.**

Human beings also acquire learning sets. A person who often solves crossword puzzles tends to get better and better at working them. A mechanic who has worked in the automotive field for a number of years discovers that it is easier and easier to troubleshoot repair problems. A college student often finds that advanced courses seem to be easier than basic courses. All of these individuals have learned to learn.

An acquired ability to quickly solve a given type of problem is called a _____.

Answer: learning set.

Memory: Storing What Has Been Learned

What would life be like without memory? You would have no personal history. You would have no sense of the past—what you had done and what your childhood was like. Learning would be a meaningless concept, because learning implies retention. You will recall that the definition of learning includes the idea that learning is more or less permanent.

Memory is a process that involves the encoding, storage, and retrieval of cognitive information. Let's explore these three related processes one by one. **Encoding** is a process characterized by giving an informational input a more useful form. Let's say that you are presented with the letters TCA. They seem meaningless. You are told that the letters represent an animal that meows. You think, "The animal is a cat." You have just transformed the informational input TCA into CAT, and it has become more useful to you. The use of symbols, associations, and insights are all examples of human encoding.

The use of a **mnemonic device,** a cognitive structure that improves both retention and recall, is a special case of encoding. Let's say that in a physics class you are asked to memorize the colors of the rainbow in their correct order—red, orange, yellow, green, blue, indigo, and violet. You can use the name Roy G. Biv as a mnemonic device, using the first letter of each color.

(a) _____ is a process characterized by giving an informational input a more useful form.

(b) The use of the name Roy G. Biv to remember the colors of the rainbow is an example of a _____.

Answers: (a) Encoding; (b) mnemonic device.

Storage refers to the fact that memories are retained for a period of time. A distinction is made between short-term memory and long-term memory. **Short-term memory,** also known as **working memory,** is characterized by a temporary storage of information. If you look up a telephone number, hold it in at the conscious level of your mind for a few minutes, use it, and then promptly forget it, you are employing the short-term memory process. **Long-term memory** is characterized by a relatively stable, enduring storage of information. The capacity to recall much of your own personal history and what you learned in school provide examples of the long-term memory process.

If short-term memory is impaired, as it is in some organic mental disorders (see chapter 14), then this interferes with the capacity to form new long-term memories.

(a) _____ refers to the fact that memories are retained for a period of time.

(b) Short-term memory is also known as _____.

(c) _____ is characterized by a relatively stable, enduring storage of information.

Answers: (a) Storage; (b) working memory; (c) Long-term memory.

Retrieval of cognitive information takes place when a memory is removed from storage and replaced in consciousness. Three phenomena are of particular interest in connection with the retrieval process: recall, recognition, and repression. **Recall** takes place when a memory can be retrieved easily by an act of will. You see a friend and think, "There's Paula." You have recalled the name of your friend.

Recognition takes place when the retrieval of a memory is facilitated by the presence of a helpful stimulus. A multiple-choice test that provides four names, one of them being the correct answer, is an example of an instructional instrument that eases the path of memory. The item to be remembered is right there in front of you.

Repression takes place when the ego, as a form of defense against a psychological threat, forces a memory into the unconscious domain. This is a psychoanalytical concept, and it was proposed by Freud. He suggested that memories associated with emotionally painful childhood experiences are likely to be repressed (see chapter 13).

(a) _____ takes place when a memory can be retrieved easily by an act of will.

(b) _____ takes place when the retrieval of a memory is facilitated by the presence of a helpful stimulus.

(c) _____ takes place when the ego, as a form of defense against psychological threat, forces a memory into the unconscious domain.

Answers: (a) Recall; (b) Recognition; (c) Repression.

SELF-TEST

1. The unconditioned reflex is
   a. a kind of behavior acquired by experience
   b. always associated with voluntary behavior
   c. a learned response pattern
   d. an inborn response pattern

2. What takes place when the conditioned stimulus is presented a number of times without the unconditioned stimulus?
   a. Forgetting
   b. Extinction
   c. Discrimination
   d. Stimulus generalization

3. Thorndike said that when satisfactory results are obtained there is a tendency to retain what has been learned. He called this tendency the
   a. law of effect
   b. principle of reinforcement
   c. principle of reward
   d. law of positive feedback

4. Operant behavior is characterized by
   a. actions that have no meaning
   b. its inability to be affected by reinforcement
   c. its conscious nature
   d. actions that have consequences

5. What principle is associated with the phrase *greater resistance to extinction?*
   a. The law of effect
   b. The total reinforcement effect
   c. The partial reinforcement effect
   d. The pleasure-pain effect

6. Vicarious reinforcement is characterized by
   a. primary gratification
   b. imagined gratification
   c. extinction
   d. the discriminative stimulus

7. What did Köhler define as the sudden reorganization of a perceptual field?
   a. Operant conditioning
   b. Classical conditioning
   c. Insight
   d. Extinction

8. The concept of a learning set is associated with what underlying process?
   a. Spontaneous inhibition
   b. The law of effect
   c. Learned optimism
   d. Learning to learn

9. The use of a mnemonic device is a special case of
   a. encoding
   b. short-term memory
   c. antagonistic stimuli
   d. involuntary conditioning

10. Which one of the following is not associated with the memory process of retrieval?
    a. Recall
    b. Recognition

    c. Cognitive inhibition
    d. Repression

ANSWERS TO THE SELF-TEST

1-d   2-b   3-a   4-d   5-c   6-b   7-c   8-d   9-a   10-c

ANSWERS TO THE TRUE-OR-FALSE PREVIEW QUIZ

1. True.
2. False. A conditioned reflex is a learned response pattern.
3. False. Operant behavior is characterized by actions that have consequences for an organism.
4. True.
5. False. Short-term memory is an important aspect of the memory process.

KEY TERMS

antisocial behavior

behavioral tendency

classical conditioning

conditioned reflex

conditioned stimulus

conditioning

discrimination

discriminative stimulus

encoding

experience

extinction

incentive

insight

insight learning

involuntary

latent learning

law of effect

learning

learning set

learning to learn

learning-performance distinction

long-term memory

memory

mnemonic device

model

negative reinforcer

observational learning

operant

operant behavior

operant conditioning apparatus (Skinner box)

partial reinforcement effect

positive reinforcer

primary reinforcer

prosocial behavior

random reinforcement

recall

recognition

reinforcer

repression

response

retrieval

reward

secondary reinforcer

short-term memory

social learning theory

stamping in

stimulus generalization

storage

trial-and-error learning

unconditioned reflex

unconditioned stimulus

vicarious reinforcement

working memory

_7_ Motivation: Why Do We Do What We Do?

True or False

1. T F Biological drives are regulated by a principle known as hyperstatic integration.
2. T F General drives, unlike biological drives, are not inborn.
3. T F The need for autonomy is a motive to do what one wants to do.
4. T F According to Freud, all motives are conscious.
5. T F The need for self-actualization is the need to maximize one's talents and potentialities.

(Answers can be found on page 105.)

Chapter 6 emphasized the point of view that much of our behavior is determined by what we have learned. Another factor that determines much of our behavior is motivation. Motives can be thought of as the forces behind our actions. Learning and motivation have a close relationship. They interact. For example, a motive may impel an action, but learning directs the way it is expressed. In this chapter you will discover the significant role that motivation plays in behavior.

Objectives

After completing this chapter, you will be able to

- define the concept of motivation;
- list and describe the principal biological drives;
- specify the characteristics of the general drives;
- identify some of the principal acquired motives;
- explain the nature of unconscious motives;
- define the concept of self-actualization;
- explain the importance of the will to meaning.

Human beings spend most of their time during the day engaged in actions. They drive cars, raise children, have vocations, spend time with hobbies, go on vacations, gamble, take unnecessary risks, play, and so forth. Why do we do what we do? This is the great question associated with the subject of motivation.

The word **motivation** is related to words such as *motor, motion,* and *emotion.* (Emotion is discussed in chapter 8.) All of these words imply some form of activity, some kind of movement. And this is one of the principal features of life—a kind of restless movement that appears to arise from sources within the organism. These sources are called motives.

A **motive** is a state of physiological or psychological arousal that is assumed to play a causal role in behavior. Physiological arousal refers to such states as hunger and thirst. Psychological arousal refers to motives such as the need for achievement. The two factors, physiological and psychological, of course interact. For example, a biological drive such as sex tends to interact with a psychological motive such as the need to be loved.

It is important to note that from the point of view of psychology as a science, a motive is an intervening variable. An **intervening variable** is a variable used to explain behavior. It is assumed to reside within the organism and "intervene" between stimulus and response. An intervening variable can't be seen or otherwise directly observed. It is inferred from studying behavior. If we see someone buying a sandwich in a snack bar, we may infer that the individual is hungry. However, he or she may in fact be buying the sandwich for a friend. The important point is that when we act as investigators of the behavior of others, we do not experience their motives.

(a) The word *motivation* is related to words such as *motor, motion,* and *emotion.* All of these words imply some form of activity, some kind of _____.

(b) From the point of view of psychology as a science, a motive is an _____.

Answers: (a) movement; (b) intervening variable.

Biological Drives: The Need for Food and Water

We would not do anything at all if we were not alive. That is why in some sense it can be argued that the root cause of all behavior can be traced to a group of biological drives. **Biological drives** are inborn drives, and their principal feature is that they impel us to attend to our tissue needs, to maintain ourselves as organisms. The basic theme associated with biological drives is *survival*. We would die fairly quickly if we did not follow the dictates of our biological drives on a fairly regular basis.

The biological drives are familiar. The following are frequently specified: hunger, thirst, sleep, temperature, oxygen hunger, pain, and sex. Note that if the word *hunger* appears without an adjective in front of it, then the word refers to the hunger for food. Also note how any of the biological drives can act as a motive. For example, if your temperature level is such that you feel cold, you might be motivated to put a coat on.

Most of the drives direct us *toward* a stimulus. We seek food if we are hungry. We seek water if we are thirsty. Pain is unlike the other drives in this particular regard. Pain directs us *away* from a stimulus. It motivates us to escape from the source of the pain.

Sex also has a unique status among the biological drives. The general theme of the biological drives, as already noted, is survival. Usually we think of this as the survival of the individual. However, in the case of sex, survival is generalized beyond the individual. The long-run purpose of sex is to assure the survival of the species.

(a) Biological drives are _____ drives.

(b) The basic theme associated with biological drives is _____.

(c) Pain, unlike other drives, directs us _____ from a stimulus.

Answers: (a) inborn; (b) survival; (c) away.

An important physiological process associated with the biological drives is homeostasis. **Homeostasis** is a physiological process characterized by a tendency for biological drives to maintain themselves at optimal levels of arousal. The term *homeostasis* was introduced in the 1920s by the physiologist Walter B. Cannon, and it can be roughly translated as "an unchanging sameness."

The hunger drive provides an example of how homeostasis works. If your blood sugar is low, you will feel hungry. You will be motivated to seek food and eat. If you eat an appropriate amount of food, your blood sugar will gradually rise to an optimal level. On the other hand, if you happen to overeat, your blood sugar will rapidly rise to an overly high level. Under these circumstances, your pancreas will secrete extra insulin, returning your blood sugar from its overly high level to a lower one. The body's goal is to maintain blood sugar at an optimal level.

Hormones, secretions of the endocrine glands, also play a role in mediating the activity of the biological drives. We have already seen in chapter 3 how the hormone melatonin is involved in the regulation of sleep. It was also noted in the same chapter that the estrogen hormones and testosterone are associated with the sexual drive.

Biological drives play a significant role in the learning process. **Drive reduction theory** states that when an action pays off in such a way that it reduces the tension associated with a biological drive in a state of arousal, then that action is reinforced. It is reinforcing for a hungry rat in an operant conditioning apparatus to obtain food by pressing a lever. This principle can be readily generalized to some human behavior. A hunter's learned actions provide an example. These may include how to load a particular kind of gun or the skills involved in tracking a specific animal. If the ultimate goal of a series of actions is food, water, escape from pain, sexual gratification, or another biological drive, then the drive reduction principle may operate to shape learned behavior.

(a) Homeostasis is a physiological process characterized by a tendency for biological drives to maintain themselves at _____ levels of arousal.

(b) Drive reduction theory states than when an action pays off in such a way that it reduces the tension associated with a biological drive in a state of arousal, then that action is

_____.

Answers: (a) optimal; (b) reinforced.

General Drives: Looking for New Experiences

General drives, like biological drives, are inborn. Unlike biological drives, they do not appear to operate on the principle of homeostasis. Three general drives of particular interest are the curiosity drive, the activity drive, and the affectional drive.

The **curiosity drive** urges us to seek novel stimulation, to look for new experiences. The drive is active in infants. Present an infant with a familiar rattle. The infant may show a little interest, and then put the rattle aside. Present the infant with a second, unfamiliar rattle. Interest will be renewed. The renewed interest is explained by the curiosity drive. The different color or the different shape of the novel rattle elicits attention. The curiosity drive is activated by **change of stimulation.**

The need for stimulation is a profound one. Sensory deprivation research brings this point into bold relief. **Sensory deprivation** exists when vision, hearing, and the other senses are forced to operate with little or no information arising from the external world. Volunteer subjects deprived of light, sound, and other information to the senses often report sensory hallucinations. Some see flying fireballs. Others hear strange music. Some have out-of-body experiences. All of this suggests that it is necessary to have a flow of stimulation in order to maintain perceptual stability.

And change of stimulation, sought by the curiosity drive, has a greater value than constant stimulation. The same note played over and over and over again is experienced as boring. A series of notes played in different pitches and with time variations becomes an interesting melody.

(a) Like biological drives, general drives are also _____.

(b) The curiosity drive is activated by _____.

(c) What state exists when vision, hearing, and the other senses are forced to operate with little or no information arising from the external world? _____

Answers: (a) inborn; (b) change of stimulation; (c) Sensory deprivation.

The curiosity drive may also play a role in **risk-taking behavior,** behavior in which individuals unnecessarily place themselves in physical jeopardy. Examples of such behavior include sky diving, hang gliding, hot air ballooning, driving over the speed limit, and so forth. One interpretation of such behavior is to hypothesize that some individuals have self-destructive tendencies. And it is possible that such tendencies may play an important role in the behavior. A second interpretation of risk-taking behavior is to hypothesize that some individuals are somewhat bored with their day-to-day lives, lives that do not include enough change of stimulation. Risk-taking behavior is one way of increasing the level of stimulation, increasing central nervous system arousal, and experiencing excitement.

A second general drive to be identified is the **activity drive,** one that urges us to make motor movements even when our biological drives are satisfied. A rat that is not hungry, thirsty, nor otherwise in biological need can be placed in a wheeled cage. If it runs, the cage will spin. And the rat will run for no particular reason other than to run. Infants display a certain amount of restless motion. If an adult is forced to sit and wait for a long time in a physician's office, it is likely that the individual will cross and uncross his or her legs, get up and walk around, step outside for a few minutes, and so forth. The movement is an end in itself.

(a) _____ is behavior in which individuals unnecessarily place themselves in physical jeopardy.

(b) What drive urges us to make motor movements even when our biological drives are satisfied? _____

Answers: (a) Risk-taking behavior; (b) The activity drive.

A third general drive to be identified is the **affectional drive,** the need for the kind of emotional nurturance that helps to sustain a sense of well-being and an optimistic attitude toward life. The research psychologist Harry Harlow, a former president of the American Psychological Association, deprived a group of rhesus monkeys of their biological mothers. He raised the monkeys in social isolation. He discovered that, deprived of mother love, many of the monkeys displayed behavior somewhat similar to **infantile autism,** a pathological condition characterized by a lack of interest in others, self-destructiveness, and a preoccupation with rigid, self-oriented behavior.

The psychoanalyst Erik Erikson, an important personality theorist, theorized that the first stage of psychosocial development is **trust versus mistrust** (see chapter 13). If an infant develops a sense of trust during the first two years of life, this positive foundation will have a beneficial impact on future personality development. If an infant develops a sense of mistrust during the first two years of life, this negative foundation will have an adverse impact on future personality development. A major factor in the development of a sense of trust is the meeting of an infant's need for affection.

(a) What drive is characterized by the need for the kind of emotional nurturance that helps to sustain a sense of well being? _____

(b) What pathological condition is characterized by a lack of interest in others, self-destructiveness, and a preoccupation with rigid, self-oriented behavior? _____

(c) According to Erik Erikson, what is the first stage of psychosocial development? _____

Answers: (a) The affectional drive; (b) Infantile autism; (c) Trust versus mistrust.

Acquired Motives: Exploring the Need to Achieve

Acquired motives are motives in which learning plays a large role. This does not mean that acquired motives do not have underpinnings in biological and general drives. However, these drives have been modified by experience, and express themselves in ways that are unique to the individual. One way to look at acquired motives is to think of them as somewhat stable, persistent behavioral tendencies. Quite a bit is known about a person if one is familiar with the pattern of that person's acquired motives. These motives are also sometimes called **social motives,** meaning they affect the way we relate to other people.

First, the **need for achievement** is a motive to reach one's goals. All social motives can be thought of as ranging from high to low. A person with a high need for achievement is likely to be ambitious, strive to make a success of a business, or earn academic recognition. A person with a low need for achievement may lack ambition, be unconcerned about financial reward, and have very few dreams or aspirations.

(a) Acquired motives are motives in which _____ plays a large role.

(b) Because they impact on the way in which we relate to other people, acquired motives are sometimes called _____ motives.

(c) An ambitious person who manifests a strong desire to reach his or her goals probably has a high _____.

Answers: (a) learning; (b) social; (c) need for achievement.

Second, the **need for autonomy** is a motive to do what one wants to do without too much regard for what others expect. The need is reflected in phrases such as "do your own thing" or "I'm doing it my way." A person with a high need for autonomy is likely to pursue a pathway in life that is self-defined. A person with a low need for autonomy often feels that he or she is the victim of the demands of others.

Third, the **need for order** is a motive that urges the individual to impose organization on the immediate environment. A person with a high need for order is likely to keep good records, have important papers neatly filed, dislike clutter in the home, and so forth. A person with a low need for order doesn't seem to mind a certain amount of disorganization in the immediate environment. Neatness does not have a high priority.

Fourth, the **need for affiliation** is a motive to associate with others. A person with a high need for affiliation is likely to have a lot of friends, socialize frequently, and dislike being alone. A person with a low need for affiliation will have a few carefully selected friends, not be attracted to parties, and seek time alone.

(a) The need for _____ is a motive to do what one wants to do.

(b) The need for _____ is a motive that urges the individual to impose organization on the immediate environment.

(c) The need for _____ is a motive to associate with others.

Answers: (a) autonomy; (b) order; (c) affiliation.

Fifth, the **need for dominance** is a motive to control the behavior of others. A person with a high need for dominance will seek positions of authority in the workplace or to be the principal decision maker in a marriage. A person with a low need for dominance will tend to be somewhat submissive and often overly agreeable.

Sixth, the **need for exhibition** is a motive to be noticed by others. A person with a high need for exhibition is likely to talk loudly, dress in novel ways, or otherwise call attention to himself or herself. A person with a low need for exhibition is likely to be somewhat retiring and conforming when relating to others.

Seventh, the **need for aggression** is a motive to engage in conflict or to hurt others. A person with a high need for aggression may inflict physical harm on others by hitting, cutting, or shooting. However the need for aggression can also be expressed in psychological terms. A person with a high need for aggression is likely to be insulting and to make demeaning remarks. A person with a low need for aggression is likely to avoid conflict whenever possible and to avoid hurting the feelings of others.

There are other acquired motives. The list above is representative, not exhaustive.

Although the acquired motives were presented in terms of high and low needs, many people, perhaps most, do not manifest the extremes. It is possible to have a moderate need for achievement, a moderate need for autonomy, and so forth.

(a) The need for _____ is a motive to control the behavior of others.

(b) The need for _____ is a motive to be noticed by others.

(c) The need for _____ is a motive to engage in conflict or to hurt others.

Answers: (a) dominance; (b) exhibition; (c) aggression.

Unconscious Motives: Hidden Reasons for Our Behavior

Sigmund Freud, the father of psychoanalysis, believed that motives can be unconscious. **Unconscious motives** may operate outside of the control of the *ego,* the "I" of the personality. Freud asserted that there is a force in the mind called **repression.** Repression is an ego defense mechanism characterized by an involuntary tendency to shove mental information that threatens the integrity and stability of the ego down to an unconscious psychological domain (see chapter 13).

If Freud is correct, the reasons for human behavior are often obscure to the individual. People act on impulse, do things they regret, and often muddle through life. Some individuals appear to have only the murkiest of notions why they make certain choices and take certain turns in life. Freud's way of looking at human motivation is particularly useful when one is trying to explain why people do self-defeating things.

The two kinds of motives that tend to be repressed are forbidden sexual desires and forbidden aggressive urges. Note the importance of the word *forbidden*. A desire for sex with one's spouse would not qualify as a forbidden sexual desire. However, if Conrad, a married man, desires sex with his wife's sister, then this is likely to violate his moral code and to become repressed. Conrad finds himself, for example, becoming hostile to his wife's sister. He tells his wife that he doesn't like her sister and wishes she wouldn't visit so often. His wife can't understand why he has so much animosity toward her sister.

The explanation for the animosity lies in an ego defense mechanism called **reaction formation** (see chapter 13). A reaction formation reinforces the repression. By acting hostile toward a woman he is attracted to, the husband keeps her at a distance, alienates her, and protects himself against his repressed sexual desire. The behavior is, of course, self-defeating because he is undermining the quality of his relationship with his wife and a relative.

(a) According to Freud, what force in the mind creates unconscious motives? _____

(b) The two kinds of motives that tend to be unconscious are forbidden _____ desires and forbidden _____ urges.

Answers: (a) Repression; (b) sexual; aggressive.

One of the problems with unconscious motives is that they may lead to **acting out,** behavior in which the unconscious motives gain temporary ascendancy over the defense mechanism of repression. For example, Conrad has had one drink too many at a New Year's Eve party. He finds himself kissing or touching his wife's sister in an inappropriate way. She is furious, tells Conrad's wife, and Conrad's marriage is threatened. The next day, sober, he says he can't understand "what took possession of me."

Here is an example of how a forbidden aggressive urge can cause a problem in living. Linette, a mother of three children and a full-time homemaker, is married to Eric, an insurance broker. Eric is an authoritarian husband. He is demanding and controlling and has very little regard for Linette's feelings. She feels taken for granted. In terms of her religious tradition and her concept of how a good wife should behave, she does not allow herself the luxury of hostile feelings toward Eric at a conscious level. Her frustrations induce her to feel aggressive toward Eric, but her code of conduct is such that she needs to repress her wish to give him a piece of her mind or refuse to be the sweet person she usually tries to be. The repressed hostility takes its toll. She suffers from a moderate, chronic depression. When she is cooking, she burns food "by accident." She is an unenthusiastic sex partner.

According to Freud, forbidden sexual impulses and forbidden aggressive urges play a significant role in self-defeating behaviors. Actions that seem paradoxical and superficially unexplainable can be understood by examining the way in which repressed motives express themselves in devious ways.

(a) What term describes behavior in which the unconscious motives gain temporary ascendancy over the defense mechanism of repression? _____

(b) Linette burns her husband's food "by accident." This may be an example of _____.

Answers: (a) Acting out; (b) repressed hostility.

Self-Actualization: Becoming the Person You Were Meant to Be

Abraham Maslow, author of *Toward a Psychology of Being* and a principal advocate of the humanistic viewpoint in psychology, presented a large-canvas description of human motivation. This description is known as Maslow's **hierarchy of needs.**

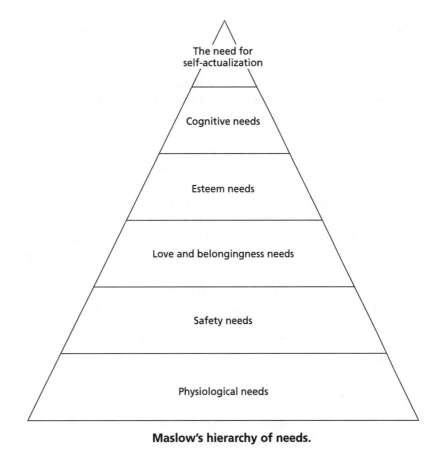

Maslow's hierarchy of needs.

According to Maslow, human needs can be ranked in terms of "lower needs" and "higher needs."

Imagine a pyramid in six layers. The needs ascend from the lower needs at the base of the pyramid to the higher needs at the apex. The first layer of the pyramid represents **physiological needs.** These are the need for food, water, and so forth. These are associated with the biological drives, already discussed toward the beginning of the chapter.

The second layer of the pyramid represents **safety needs.** These include the need for shelter, protection from injury, and so forth. Safety needs are reflected in such individual behaviors as wearing a seat belt and such social behaviors as organizing a police force.

(a) The first layer of a pyramid structured according to Maslow's hierarchy of needs represents _____ needs.

(b) The second layer of the pyramid represents _____ needs.

Answers: (a) physiological; (b) safety.

The third layer of the pyramid represents **love and belongingness needs.** These include the need for affection, the need to love, and the need to be loved. Love and belongingness needs are reflected in such behaviors as joining a club, forming friendships, getting married, and having children. The importance of love and belongingness needs is evident in many popular songs. They frequently focus on the elation one feels when a love relationship is going well or the despair one feels when such a relationship is going badly.

The fourth layer of the pyramid represents **esteem needs.** These include the need to be esteemed by others and self-esteem. The need to be esteemed by others is reflected in behaviors such as seeking a higher rank within an organization or working for a prestigious award or degree. **Self-esteem** is the sense of value that one feels about oneself. It is a kind of inner psychological ranking. Low self-esteem is associated with depression and a pessimistic outlook on life. High self-esteem is associated with a positive mood and an optimistic outlook on life.

The fifth layer of the pyramid represents **cognitive needs.** Cognitive needs include the need for mental stimulation, the need to use one's intelligence, and the need to exercise creative abilities. Cognitive needs are reflected in such behaviors as reading a book, writing a story, working a crossword puzzle, taking a class, solving a problem, and so forth.

(a) The third layer of the Maslow pyramid represents _____ and _____ needs.

(b) The fourth layer of the pyramid represents _____ needs.

(c) The fifth layer of the pyramid represents _____ needs.

Answers: (a) love; belongingness; (b) esteem; (c) cognitive.

The sixth and top layer of the pyramid represents the **need for self-actualization.** Of all the needs, this is the one that is primarily associated with the thinking and research of Maslow. Maslow hypothesized that this need is inborn. Also, it is **emergent,** meaning that it only becomes a pressing need when the other lower needs are relatively satisfied. The need for self-actualization is the need to maximize one's talents and potentialities. It is sometimes informally phrased as "the need to become the person you were meant to be."

The need for self-actualization is reflected in such behaviors as working toward success in a vocational field or seeking way of life that represents one's own idea of personal fulfillment. There is no field of work or style of life that can be specified, because the individual's choice and perception are of particular importance. For one person, self-actualization might mean the pursuit of an acting career. For another person, self-actualization might mean becoming a parent. The important thing, according to Maslow, is that the individual discovers what is right for himself or herself.

Maslow's research suggested that many, perhaps most, people are not self-actualizing. The price paid for a failure to be self-actualizing is a sense of disappointment in life and in oneself.

(a) The sixth layer of the Maslow pyramid represents the need for _____.

(b) The need for self-actualization is the need to maximize one's _____ and

_____.

Answers: (a) self-actualization; (b) talents; potentialities.

On the other hand, if one is in fact self-actualizing, there are important psychological rewards associated with the process. First, one will tend to experience both a general sense of psychological health and a pleasant day-to-day emotional tone. Second, the individual will from time to time have **peak experiences.** These are moments or joy or ecstasy when a hurdle is overcome, a task is completed, or a goal is reached.

Note that a person is not referred to as self-actualized, but as self-actualizing. Maslow is talking about the process of becoming, not an end state. Self-actualization as a process can be a rich source of psychological reward for most of one's life.

Maslow makes a distinction between deficiency motivation and being motivation. **Deficiency motivation** refers to those needs lowest on the hierarchy. We need to overcome deficiency states such as hunger, thirst, and danger in order to move upward toward the higher levels. **Being motivation** tends to be associated with the higher levels, particularly with the need for self-actualization. The theme of being motivation is growth.

(a) Peak experiences are moments of _____ or _____.

(b) What kind of motivation refers to needs lowest on Maslow's hierarchy? _____

(c) What kind of motivation refers to needs highest on Maslow's hierarchy? _____

   Answers: (a) joy; ecstasy; (b) Deficiency motivation; (c) Being motivation.

The Search for Meaning: Looking for the *Why* of Life

It would seem that self-actualization is the greatest height that can be reached by human motivation, and from reading Maslow's writings one would get that distinct impression. Nonetheless, it can be argued that there is one motivational level extending above self-actualization. The existential psychiatrist Viktor Frankl, author of *Man's Search for Meaning,* argues that the highest level for human beings is the **will to meaning,** the need for life to make sense and to have a purpose in the larger scheme of things.

Frankl asserts that the will to meaning is inborn, that it is a real psychological and emotional need. If a person lives a meaningful life, then that life will be full and rewarding. If a person lives a meaningless life, then that life will be empty and pointless. Frankl calls this adverse mental and emotional state the **existential vacuum.** One of its principal characteristics is demoralization, the conviction that nothing has any value and that nothing is worth doing.

Some of Frankl's assertions about the importance of our search for meaning arise from his own experiences in a Nazi concentration camp. Although he was a prisoner himself, he did not forget that he was a physician and a psychiatrist. He felt it was his responsibility to give comfort and aid to his fellow prisoners whenever possible. This became his reason for living, and he credits it with his ability to survive under extremely harsh conditions. He argues that when a human being has a reason for existence, he or she can often tolerate a high level of pain and frustration. It is instructive to note that the original title of *Man's Search for Meaning* was *From Death Camp to Existentialism.*

(a) Frankl argues that the highest level of motivation for human beings is the _____.

(b) The term used to identify an empty and pointless life is the _____.

   Answers: (a) will to meaning; (b) existential vacuum.

How is meaning fulfilled? Frankl argues that the will to meaning orients itself toward **values,** perceived aspects of the world that seem to have worth or importance to other individuals or to humanity in general. This may seem very exalted, but in practice it can be very basic. Being fair and decent in one's dealings with friends and relatives is an example of a value. Raising one's children in a loving way is another example. For most people, meaning can readily be found in living traditional social roles—being an effective teacher, parent, nurse, auto mechanic, loving partner, and so forth. Note that in all of these social roles there is some service or contribution to others. The will to meaning reaches beyond the self.

For some people, humanity in general is served by the will to meaning. When we think of great authors, scientists, or leaders, we see that their contributions to life extend beyond an immediate family to the larger human family. But the basic theme is the same—a concern with the welfare of others.

Frankl argues that values do not have to be invented. They need to be discovered. He says that a person suffering from an existential vacuum is like a person in a room with the lights out. The individual thinks that there is no furniture in the room because he or she can't see it. Then the lights are turned on and the furniture becomes visible. Values, like the pieces of furniture in the room, are real and present. But they have to be discovered by the light of human consciousness in order for the individual to have a meaningful life.

(a) Values are perceived aspects of the world that seem to have _____ or _____ to other individuals or to humanity in general.

(b) Frankl argues that values do not have to be invented. Instead, they need to be _____.

Answers: (a) worth; importance; (b) discovered.

SELF-TEST

1. From the point of view of psychology as a science a motive is
   a. a dependent variable
   b. an independent variable
   c. a radical variable
   d. an intervening variable

2. A physiological process characterized by a tendency for biological drives to maintain themselves at optimal levels of arousal is called
   a. homeostasis
   b. metamotivation
   c. hyperstatic integration
   d. heterostasis

3. Which of the following is clearly associated with the curiosity drive?
   a. The need to escape from pain
   b. The need for affiliation
   c. The search for meaning in life
   d. The tendency to seek novel stimulation

4. Which of the following is a motive to associate with others?
   a. The need for dominance
   b. The need for exhibition
   c. The need for aggression
   d. The need for affiliation

5. According to Freud, what force in the mind is responsible for the creation of unconscious motives?
   a. Repression
   b. Ego inhibition
   c. Superego excitation
   d. Homeostasis

6. Which one of the following is associated with cognitive needs?
   a. Seeking a higher rank within an organization
   b. Working a crossword puzzle
   c. Looking for love
   d. Searching for shelter

7. Self-actualization is most closely linked to which of the following?
   a. Feeling hungry
   b. Maximizing potentialities
   c. Seeking novel stimulation
   d. Wanting affection

8. What does Maslow call moments of joy or ecstasy experienced when a hurdle is overcome, a task is completed, or a goal is reached?
   a. Hedonic experiences
   b. Transcendental experiences
   c. Peak experiences
   d. Summit experiences

9. Frankl argues that the highest level of motivation for human beings is the
   a. will to meaning
   b. need for transcendental experience
   c. wish to become one with the All
   d. desire to exercise the will to power

10. If a person lives a meaningless life, then that life will be empty and pointless. Frankl calls this mental and emotional state
    a. major depressive episode
    b. bipolar disorder
    c. the existential vacuum
    d. biochemical depression

ANSWERS TO THE SELF-TEST

1-d   2-a   3-d   4-d   5-a   6-b   7-b   8-c   9-a   10-c

ANSWERS TO THE TRUE-OR-FALSE PREVIEW QUIZ

1. False. Biological drives are regulated by a principle known as *homeostasis.*
2. False. General drives, like biological drives, are inborn.
3. True.
4. False. According to Freud, some motives are unconscious.
5. True.

KEY TERMS

acquired motives	general drives
acting out	hierarchy of needs
activity drive	homeostasis
affectional drive	infantile autism
being motivation	intervening variable
biological drives	love and belongingness needs
change of stimulation	motivation
cognitive needs	motive
curiosity drive	need for achievement
deficiency motivation	need for affiliation
drive reduction theory	need for aggression
emergent	need for autonomy
esteem needs	need for dominance
existential vacuum	need for exhibition

need for order

need for self-actualization

peak experiences

physiological needs

reaction formation

repression

risk-taking behavior

safety needs

self-esteem

sensory deprivation

social motives

trust versus mistrust

unconscious motives

values

will to meaning

8 Emotions: Riding Life's Roller Coaster

PREVIEW QUIZ

True or False

1. T F The pleasant-unpleasant aspect of emotions is associated with the point of view, proposed by the philosopher Aristotle, known as hedonism.
2. T F The James-Lange theory proposes that feelings cause our actions.
3. T F Chronic stress appears to have no long-run effect on general health.
4. T F Type A behavior is associated with heart attacks and cardiovascular disease.
5. T F An approach-approach conflict exists when an individual perceives the same goal in both positive and negative terms.

(Answers can be found on page 118.)

The story of motivation does not begin and end with the motives discussed in chapter 7. Emotions are also part of the story of motivation. The very word emotion *contains "motion" in it. (Whenever we act we are, so to speak, in motion.) In this chapter you will find out how emotions can double as motives and also the way in which emotions add color and dimension to life.*

Objectives

After completing this chapter, you will be able to

- define the concept of emotions;
- identify the two basic psychological dimensions of emotions;
- describe the three aspects of all emotions;
- explain the three basic theories of emotions;
- specify how chronic stress affects general health;
- state the conditions of the four basic kinds of psychological conflict.

What would life be like without emotions?

In some ways life would be better. We would not experience the distress associated with anger, fear, and depression. We would never be in a bad mood. There would be no unhappiness.

On the other hand, without emotions there would be no joy, laughter, or excitement. We would never know the pleasure of a good mood. There would be no happiness.

Emotions give life much of its dimension and depth. Although emotions can sometimes diminish the quality of existence, they also often enrich life. The ups and downs associated with our emotional states give life something of the quality of a roller-coaster ride. Some people live a wild emotional life characterized by extreme highs and lows. Others lead a more rational emotional life—the highs and lows are not too extreme. But we all ride life's emotional roller coaster in one way or another. Consequently, emotions merit study and have an important place in psychology.

Emotions: What Are They?

The word *emotion* is a contraction of two words: *exit* and *motion*. The ancient Greeks believed that the smiles and the frowns associated with such states as happiness or sadness indicated that the soul was coming out of the body and revealing itself. It was making an "exit motion." This became "e-motion" or simply "emotion."

An **emotion** is, at the physiological level, a disruption in homeostatic baselines. There are changes in heart rate, respiration rate, and blood pressure. These are fluctuations in arousal. At the psychological level, these physiological changes are experienced as either greater excitement or increased calmness. Human beings also experience these changes as either pleasant or unpleasant.

(a) The word *emotion* is a contraction of what two words? _____ and _____

(b) An emotion is, at the physiological level, a disruption in _____ baselines.

Answers: (a) Exit; motion; (b) homeostatic.

It is evident from the above that there are two basic psychological dimensions to emotions: excitement-calm and pleasant-unpleasant. The pleasant-unpleasant dimension of emotions is identified as **hedonic tone.** The concept of **hedonism,** as presented by the philosopher Aristotle, was a motivational concept. Hedonism is the point of view that we approach stimulus situations that are pleasant and avoid situations that are unpleasant.

The two dimensions of emotions generate four categories of emotions: (1) excitement-pleasant, (2) excitement-unpleasant, (3) calm-pleasant, and (4) calm-unpleasant. All of the many words that we use to describe emotions can be readily placed in one of these categories. Words such as *happy, joy,* and *ecstasy* belong in category 1. Words such as *anger, fear,* and *rage* belong in category 2. Words such as *relaxed, blissful,* and *tranquil* belong in category 3. Words such as *sad, melancholy,* and *depressed* belong in category 4.

(a) What are the two basic psychological dimensions of emotions? _____ and _____

(b) Proposed by Aristotle, what is the philosophical viewpoint that we approach stimulus situations that are pleasant and avoid situations that are unpleasant? _____

(c) The two dimensions of emotions generate how many categories of emotions? _____

Answers: (a)Excitement-calm; pleasant-unpleasant; (b) Hedonism; (c) Four.

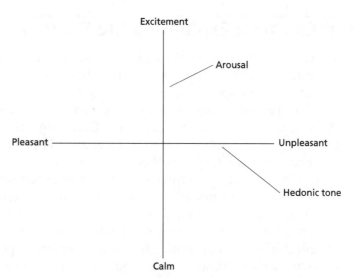

The two basic dimensions of emotions.

There are three aspects to all emotions: (1) cognitive, (2) physiological, and (3) behavioral. The **cognitive aspect of emotions** refers to what one is thinking when one feels an emotion. Thoughts such as "What a wonderful day," "I hate him," and "I think we're going to crash" are likely to either induce emotional states or be associated with them.

The **physiological aspect of emotions** refers to the disruption of homeostatic baselines. As already indicated, emotions are associated with either increased or decreased arousal. Fear is associated with increased arousal. Depression is associated with decreased arousal.

The **behavioral aspect of emotions** refers to what people *do* when they feel an emotion, what actions they take. Fear might induce a person to run away, if possible, from the stimulus source that is causing fear. If a person can't run, he or she might shake and tremble. If the fear is being caused by a threat from a menacing person, one might plead, turn over a purse or wallet, or beg for mercy. On the other hand, an emotion such as depression might induce a particular person to sit in a chair and mope. Another person in response to depression might go on an eating binge.

(a) What one is thinking when one feels an emotion is what aspect of emotions?

_____

(b) Disruption of homeostatic baselines refers to what aspect of emotions? _____

(c) The actions people take when they feel an emotion refer to what aspect of emotions?

_____

Answers: (a)Cognitive; (b) Physiological; (c) Behavioral.

Theories of Emotion: Explaining the Process

There are three principal theories of emotion that attempt to explain the general emotional process: (1) the James–Lange theory, (2) the Cannon–Bard theory, and (3) the cognitive appraisal theory.

The **James–Lange theory** was proposed independently by two men, William James in the United States and Carl Lange in Denmark. The theory states that an emotion can be induced by an action. The following example is based on observations made by James. Let's say that you see a bear in a forest. Common sense tells you that if you run away, the action of running is motivated by fear. On the other hand, according to James, common sense tells only half of the story. It is equally true that running *makes* you feel fear. At first presentation this does not seem reasonable. On the other hand, reflection suggests that the act of running has the effect of increasing arousal. If you were simply to get up now and run in place for two or three minutes, you would increase your pulse and heart rate; there would be increased arousal. Under the condition of running away from the bear, the act of running intensifies fear by increasing arousal.

If there is anything to the James-Lange theory, then one can influence one's feeling to some extent by willing one's actions. The familiar advice to walk, not run, when there is a fire in a public place conforms to the James-Lange theory. It is widely recognized that the act of running, by increasing arousal, will cause fear to escalate into panic.

In the musical play *The King and I,* Anna's young son confesses to her that he is afraid to enter Siam. Anna tells him that one of the tricks she uses to conquer fear is to whistle a happy tune. She says that by acting brave, he might become as brave as he's making believe he is. Again, the James-Lange theory is at work. An action is inducing a change in an emotional state. Fear is being turned into bravery.

(a) The James-Lange theory states that an emotion can be induced by an _____.

(b) The act of running has the effect of increasing one's state of _____.

    Answers: (a) action; (b) arousal.

The **Cannon-Bard theory,** also known as the **thalamic theory,** is based on the collaboration of the two researchers Walter B. Cannon and Philip Bard. The Cannon-Bard theory recognizes that the brain's thalamus is a relay station. When information comes in from the senses and arrives at the thalamus, the information is simultaneously sent up to the cortex and down to the spinal cord. This means that we become conscious of the cause of an emotion at the same time that our body is preparing to deal with it by making changes in physiological arousal.

Returning to the bear-in-the-forest example, the Cannon-Bard theory says that you are becoming aroused, and physiologically prepared to run, at the same time that you are able to think, "That's a bear!" This saves the individual precious time in an emergency.

(a) The Canon-Bard theory is also known as the _____.

(b) According to the Cannon-Bard theory, when information comes in from the senses and arrives at the thalamus, the information is _____ sent up to the cortex and down to the spinal cord.

    Answers: (a) thalamic theory; (b) simultaneously.

Proposed by the researcher Stanley Schachter, the **cognitive appraisal theory,** also known as the **labeling-of-arousal hypothesis,** states that a person's self-labeling of a state of arousal converts that state into a specific emotion. Let's say that Earl is driving, has taken a wrong turn, and is lost in an unfamiliar area of a big city. His pulse increases, his mouth feels dry, his muscles increase their tension. All of this is involuntary. He is experiencing increased arousal. He asks himself, "What's going on? Why is my pulse faster?" Let's say he thinks, "I'm afraid." By defining his state of arousal in this way, he clearly feels fear. On the other hand, let's say that he was to take a different cognitive approach. He's a person who often seeks adventure. He answers the questions posed above by thinking, "I'm getting a kick out of this. It's a kind of bang to be challenged." By defining his state of arousal in terms of a more positive outlook, he might be "having fun"—a positive emotional state—instead of experiencing fear. The hedonic tone, the sense that a state of arousal is pleasant or unpleasant, is often associated with the label that we assign to the state of arousal.

It is not necessary to make a distinct choice among the theories in order to determine which one is right and which one is wrong. All three theories have some degree of validity and help us to explain emotional states.

According to the cognitive appraisal theory, a person's _____ of a state of arousal converts that state into a specific emotion.

Answer: self-labeling.

Stress and Health: Wear and Tear Takes Its Toll

It is widely recognized that increases in arousal tend to be associated with stress. A formal distinction is made between a stressor and stress. A **stressor** refers to the source, or cause, of stress. The loss of a job, an argument with a spouse, a conflict situation, excessive cold or heat, and a physical threat are examples of stressors. **Stress** refers to wear and tear on the body. Chronic stress takes a toll. The body loses some of its resilience, its ability to bounce back.

Let's say that you take a small piece of metal and fold it back and forth. A crack appears in the metal after a number of foldings. Each act of folding is a stressor. The crack is the stress.

(a) What term is used to refer to the source, or cause, of stress? _____

(b) What term is used to refer to wear and tear on the body? _____

Answers: (a) Stressor; (b) Stress.

You will recall from chapter 3 that the Canadian researcher Hans Selye (1907–1982) did a substantial amount of research on stress. Rats were subjected to such stressors as excessive cold, excessive heat, and high-pitched whistles. Also, the stressors were chronic in nature. They became a constant part of the animal's environment. Under such conditions, the organism is forced to adapt, and Selye developed a set of observations about the organism's behavior under such conditions. This set of observations is called the **general adaptation syndrome (GAS),** a pattern that describes how an organism responds under conditions that induce chronic stress. There are three stages in the general adaptation syndrome: (1) The alarm reaction, (2) the stage of resistance, and (3) the stage of exhaustion.

The **alarm reaction** is characterized by an increase in arousal and general alertness. The pulse and respiration rates increase and the blood vessels of the striated muscles narrow. The organism prepares itself to deal with a threat. The alarm reaction is the individual's response to a novel stressor.

(a) What is the name of the pattern that describes how an organism responds under conditions that induce chronic stress? _____

(b) The _____ reaction is the individual's response to a novel stressor.

   Answers: (a) The general adaptation syndrome; (b) alarm.

The **stage of resistance** is characterized by reduced agitation and excitement. This stage represents an organism's response to a stressor that has become chronic. The individual learns to live with the stressor. During the stage of resistance, the organism seems to have adapted to adverse conditions. Learning and reproduction are possible.

The **stage of exhaustion** is associated with illness and death. The death is a premature one. Postmortem examinations of rats subjected to chronic stressors revealed that their adrenal glands were swollen. They had adapted at great physiological cost. During the stage of resistance, the adrenal glands had pumped out excessive amounts of their hormones and had overtaxed themselves.

(a) What stage of the general adaptation syndrome is characterized by reduced agitation and excitement? _____

(b) What stage of the general adaptation syndrome is characterized by illness and death?

   _____

   Answers: (a) The stage of resistance; (b) The stage of exhaustion.

The importance of the general adaptation syndrome has not been lost on physicians and psychologists. Research suggests that human beings, like Selye's rats, are also subject to the damaging effects of chronic stressors. Research on life change units and Type A behavior reveal the important role that stress plays in human illness.

Life change units (LCUs) refers to stressors arising from events in a person's life that require adaptation. The two researchers who pioneered the general approach are R. H. Rahe and T. H. Holmes. Studying a large group of subjects, they developed a measuring device called the **Social Readjustment Rating Scale (SRRS).** The scale, based on the perceptions of subjects, assigns weighted values to life changes. The maximum value is 100, and this is assigned to the death of a spouse. Getting married has a value of 50. Loss of a job has a value of 47. Being given a traffic ticket has a value of 11. There are a number of similar items on the scale. If a person collects 150 or more LCUs within a two–year period, there is a high likelihood that he or she will experience a distinct health problem.

(a) What is the name of the measuring device that employs life change units (LCUs)?

_____

(b) Too many LCUs accumulated within a relatively brief time span is associated with what kind of problem? _____

Answers: (a) The Social Readjustment Rating Scale; (b) A health problem.

The **Type A behavior pattern** is characterized by hostility and impatience. Research conducted by the cardiologists Meyer Friedman and Ray H. Rosenman strongly supports the hypothesis that individuals who display this pattern are more prone than people in general to heart attacks and cardiovascular disease.

The contrasting pattern is called the **Type B behavior pattern,** and it is characterized by an absence of general hostility and a willingness to allow events to take place at their own rate. As might be expected, individuals who manifest the Type B pattern are less prone to heart disease than individuals who manifest the Type A pattern.

The existence of the Type A pattern suggests that behavior can itself be a source of stress. Human beings are capable of **self-induced stress,** wear and tear on the body generated by their own thoughts, choices, attitudes, and actions. The Roman philosopher Cicero, writing about two thousand years ago, foreshadowed modern research on stress when he said, "To live long it is necessary to live slowly."

(a) What behavior pattern is characterized by hostility and impatience? _____

(b) Human beings are capable of _____ stress, wear and tear on the body generated by their own thoughts, attitudes, and actions.

Answers: (a) The Type A behavior pattern; (b) self-induced.

Conflict: Making Difficult Choices

Conflict is an important source of stress. **Psychological conflict** exists when we are forced to make difficult choices in life. According to the social psychologist Kurt Lewin, there are four basic ways to categorize conflict situations:

(1) the approach-approach conflict, (2) the avoidance-avoidance conflict, (3) the approach-avoidance conflict, and (4) the double approach-avoidance conflict.

The **approach-approach conflict** exists when an individual is presented with two desirable alternatives, but only one alternative can be obtained. Desirable alternatives are termed **positive goals.** A mild example of an approach-approach conflict is selecting a birthday card for a friend or relative. Let's say that Olympia is trying to pick a birthday card for her husband. She's narrowed her options down to two cards, but is having a hard time making a final selection. She's in an approach-approach conflict.

An approach-approach conflict might seem to induce relatively low stress. After all, the individual has at least two good choices. But such a conflict can in some cases induce quite a bit of stress. Eighteen-year-old Kirk has been accepted at two leading colleges. They are in different parts of the country. The selection he finally makes will have great long-run significance. He is in an intense approach-approach conflict.

(a) _____ exists when we are forced to make difficult choices in life.

(b) What kind of conflict exists when an individual is presented with two desirable alternatives, but only one alternative can be obtained? _____

(c) Desirable alternatives are termed _____ goals.

Answers: (a) Psychological conflict; (b) An approach-approach conflict; (c) positive.

An **avoidance-avoidance conflict** exists when the individual wants to either escape from or avoid two undesirable alternatives. Undesirable alternatives are termed **negative goals.** The central problem with this kind of conflict is that moving away from one negative goal takes one in the direction of the other negative goal. Nineteen-year-old Nancy is in her first year of college. She doesn't like academic work, is barely passing, and is thinking of dropping out. On the other hand, if she drops out, her parents have indicated they won't support her. She'll have to take a low-paying, unskilled job. If she stays in school, she'll be unhappy. If she takes a low-paying job, she'll be unhappy. She tells her best friend, "I'm between a rock and a hard place."

Associated with the research of the anthropologist Gregory Bateson, a term sometimes used to identify an avoidance-avoidance conflict is a **double bind.** A double bind is a no-win situation. Whatever the individual does, there is a sense of failure or loss.

(a) What kind of conflict exists when the individual wants to escape from or avoid two undesirable alternatives? _____

(b) Undesirable alternatives are termed _____ goals.

Answers: (a) An avoidance-avoidance conflict; (b) negative.

An **approach–avoidance conflict** exists when an individual perceives the same goal in both positive and negative terms. Glen is in love with Margaret and is thinking about marrying her. He sees her as beautiful, warm, and sexually desirable. On the other hand, Glen's parents are opposed to Margaret. They point out to him that she has a different religious affiliation than that of Glen and his parents. Margaret takes her religion seriously. So do Glen and his parents. The two religions are based on different assumptions. Glen's parents tell him that they don't see how he can ever have a happy marriage with Margaret. If Glen and Margaret have children, Margaret will want to raise them in her religious tradition. Glen will want to raise them in his.

When Glen is away from Margaret, he thinks about her constantly. He misses her, and often decides that he'll propose marriage no matter what the consequences. When he's actually with her, the words associated with the marriage proposal won't leave his mouth. He gets cold feet at the last minute. One of the characteristics of approach–avoidance conflicts is that the approach tendency tends to gain strength when the positive aspect of the goal seems momentarily out of reach. Conversely, the avoidance tendency tends to gain strength when in the presence of the goal; under these conditions the negative factors tend to loom large.

An individual caught in an approach–avoidance conflict often experiences a sustained period of emotional conflict before a final decision is made.

(a) What kind of conflict exists when an individual perceives the same goal in both positive and negative terms? _____

(b) An approach tendency tends to _____ when the positive aspect of a goal seems momentarily out of reach.

Answers: (a) An approach–avoidance conflict; (b) gain strength.

A **double approach–avoidance conflict** exists when an individual simultaneously perceives two goals in both positive and negative terms. This conflict is a more complex version of the singular approach–avoidance conflict. Let's say that Pamela is on a diet. She's having lunch in a restaurant. She is thinking about ordering either a burger with fries or a salad with broiled chicken. Goal 1, the burger and fries, is the more appealing choice to Pamela from the point of view of taste and general appeal. On the other hand, the negative aspect is that the combination will have too many calories and she'll be cheating on her diet. Goal 2, the salad with broiled chicken, is the more appealing choice to Pamela from the point of view of caloric content. On the other hand, the negative aspect is that she is weary of salad and wants to have a treat.

Pamela's dilemma presents a fairly mild version of the double approach–avoidance conflict. However, such conflicts can be quite intense. Imagine that Glen's parents introduce him to Naomi. She and her parents are recent arrivals in the neighborhood, and they practice the same religion as Glen and his parents. Naomi is young, pretty, and interested in Glen. He takes her out on a couple of dates. He finds himself attracted to her, but not nearly as attracted as he is to Margaret. By introducing Glen to Naomi, Glen's parents have thrust him into a double approach–avoidance conflict.

What kind of a conflict exists when an individual simultaneously perceives two goals in both positive and negative terms? _____

Answer: A double approach-avoidance conflict.

SELF-TEST

1. The word *emotion* is a contraction of the two words
   a. *evaluation* and *motor*
   b. *exit* and *motion*
   c. *emission* and *movement*
   d. *escape* and *mobile*

2. The two basic psychological dimensions of emotion are
   a. excitement-calm and low arousal–high arousal
   b. extraversion-introversion and pleasant-unpleasant
   c. homeostasis-alpha and homeostasis-beta
   d. excitement-calm and pleasant-unpleasant

3. Which one of the following is *not* a basic aspect of emotions?
   a. The cognitive aspect
   b. The formal-logical aspect
   c. The physiological aspect
   d. The behavioral aspect

4. The James-Lange theory of emotion states that
   a. emotions are illusions
   b. all emotions stem from unconscious motives
   c. an emotion can be induced by an action
   d. emotions are the motives for almost all actions

5. The cognitive appraisal theory of emotion states that
   a. the brain's thalamus is a relay station
   b. we become conscious of the cause of an emotion at the same time that our body is preparing to deal with it
   c. emotions are metaphysical concepts
   d. a person's self-labeling of a state of arousal converts that state into a specific emotion

6. Which one of the following is *not* a stage of the general adaptation syndrome (GAS)?
   a. The alarm reaction
   b. The stage of resistance
   c. The stage of frustration
   d. The stage of exhaustion

7. The concept of life change units (LCU's) is associated with which of the following?
   a. The Social Readjustment Scale
   b. The Wechsler Psychosocial Stressor Inventory
   c. The Lewin Cognitive Test
   d. The Selye Stress Test

8. The Type A behavior pattern is characterized by
   a. hostility and impatience
   b. a hedonistic attitude toward life
   c. learned optimism
   d. an absence of hostility and a willingness to allow events to take place at their own pace

9. In the analysis of psychological conflict, undesirable alternatives are termed
   a. positive goals
   b. negative goals
   c. neutral attributes
   d. orienting functions

10. What kind of a conflict exists when the individual wants to either escape from or avoid two undesirable alternatives?
    a. An approach-approach conflict
    b. An approach-avoidance conflict
    c. A double approach-avoidance conflict
    d. An avoidance-avoidance conflict

ANSWERS TO THE SELF-TEST

1-b   2-d   3-b   4-c   5-d   6-c   7-a   8-a   9-b   10-d

ANSWERS TO THE TRUE-OR-FALSE PREVIEW QUIZ

1. True.
2. False. The James-Lange theory of emotions proposes that an emotion can be induced by an action.

3. False. According to the general adaptation syndrome, chronic stress can have an adverse effect on general health.

4. True.

5. False. An approach-approach conflict exists when an individual is presented with two desirable alternatives.

KEY TERMS

alarm reaction	labeling-of-arousal hypothesis
approach-approach conflict	life change units (LCUs)
approach-avoidance conflict	negative goals
avoidance-avoidance conflict	physiological aspect of emotions
behavioral aspect of emotions	positive goals
Cannon-Bard theory	psychological conflict
cognitive appraisal theory	self-induced stress
cognitive aspect of emotions	Social Readjustment Rating Scale (SRRS)
double approach-avoidance conflict	stage of exhaustion
double bind	stage of resistance
emotion	stress
general Adaptation Syndrome (GAS)	stressor
hedonic tone	thalamic theory
hedonism	Type A behavior pattern
James-Lange theory	Type B behavior pattern

9 Thinking: Exploring Mental Life

PREVIEW QUIZ

True or False

1. T F   The philosopher Aristotle said that the human being is the thinking animal.
2. T F   Concepts put the world of experience into mental boxes.
3. T F   A heuristic approach to solving a problem is the same thing as using a formula to solve the problem.
4. T F   Functional fixedness is a kind of mental set that helps you to solve problems.
5. T F   The core of the creative process is rational, logical thought.

(Answers can be found on page 135.)

The last chapter made note of the fact that every emotion has a cognitive aspect. We not only feel, but we also think when we experience an emotion. In fact, thinking plays a role in almost all of our actions. This chapter is designed to further your understanding of the thinking process.

Objectives

After completing this chapter, you will be able to

- define thinking;

- specify three basic kinds of mental concepts;

- describe various strategies for solving problems;

- explain how mental sets can present obstacles to solving problems;

- distinguish between logical thinking and logical errors;

- state the core feature of the creative process.

When you think about a bird, you tend to concentrate on its ability to fly. The bird could be said to be the "flying animal." When you think about a fish, you tend to concentrate on its ability to swim. The fish could be said to be the "swimming animal." Similarly, when you think about human beings, one thing in particular seems to stand out—our ability to think. The philosopher Aristotle said that the human being is the thinking animal.

The philosopher René Descartes tried to find a bedrock for his own philosophical viewpoint. He mistrusted much learning and doubted the truth of much so-called knowledge. He asked himself what he could be certain of. His answer was that he was certain he existed. And how was he certain that he existed? Because he was thinking. He reasoned, "I think, therefore I am." And this became the starting point for his philosophical reflections.

More recently, William James, the founding personality of a school of psychology called functionalism, defined psychology as the science of mental life. And this is close to the commonsense view of psychology. Most people think of it in this way. It is the science of the mind; and the concept of the mind includes both our conscious awareness and our ability to think.

(a) The philosopher Aristotle said that the human being is the _____.

(b) The philosopher Descartes said that the fact that he was a thinking being made him confident that he _____.

(c) James defined psychology as the _____.

Answers: (a) thinking animal; (b) existed; (c) science of mental life.

Note in the paragraphs above that not only thinking was implied, but *thinking about thinking*. That's what we will be doing in this chapter. The process of thinking about thinking is called **metathought.** Although we take for granted that we can do it, a moment's reflection suggests how unusual an ability it is. Even if it is granted, as seems to some degree reasonable, that certain animals such as dolphins and chimpanzees can think, it is doubtful that they engage in metathought. They probably don't think, as we do, about the nature of thought itself.

As indicated above, the study of thinking has a long and respectable tradition in both philosophy and psychology.

Before we proceed with its study, let's define thinking. **Thinking** is a mental process characterized by the use of symbols and concepts to represent both inner and outer reality. A **symbol** is a word, mark, sign, drawing, or object that stands for something else. Consequently, the word *dog* is a symbol that stands for an actual dog. Concepts are defined below.

(a) Thinking about thinking is called _____.

(b) Thinking is a mental process characterized by the use of _____ and _____ to represent both inner and outer reality.

(c) Something such as a word, mark, sign, drawing, or object that stands for something else is called _____.

Answers: (a) metathought; (b) symbols; concepts; (c) a symbol.

Forming Concepts: Putting the World into Mental Boxes

A **concept** is a mental category. A basic tool of thought, it is a way in which we organize and simplify information. Concepts put the world of experience into mental boxes. Let's say you see a bowl of fruit containing an assortment of lemons and oranges. You see only two kinds of fruit. You don't feel overwhelmed by information. However, it is clear that no one lemon is exactly like any other lemon. And no one orange is exactly like any other orange. The concepts of lemons and of oranges simplify things for us. The concept of lemons includes these attributes: a yellow skin, elongated shape, and somewhat sour taste. The concept of oranges includes these attributes: orange-colored, round, and sweet. Differences between individual lemons and oranges are obscured when we employ the two concepts. And this is the functional value of the concepts. There are three basic kinds of concepts: (1) conjunctive, (2) disjunctive, and (3) relational.

A **conjunctive concept** strings together perceived attributes. A *conjunction* in grammar has the function of joining words and phrases. Similarly, a conjunctive concept joins attributes to make a perceptual whole. The concept of a lemon is conjunctive because to most of us a lemon is an object that has a yellow skin *and* an elongated shape *and* a somewhat sour taste.

To a child, forming the concept of a dog, a dog "is" an animal with some or all of these attributes: it barks *and* bites *and* has fur *and* a tail *and* four legs.

(a) A concept is a mental _____.

(b) Concepts help us to organize and simplify _____.

(c) A conjunctive concept _____ attributes to make a perceptual _____.

> *Answers:*   (a) category; (b) information; (c) joins; whole.

Note that when a child is acquiring the concept of a dog, there may be a period of confusion. Let's say that three-year-old Tammy is visiting an aquarium with her parents. An entertaining show is put on with seals. Tammy calls them "doggies" because they bark. The parents explain that seals are *not* dogs. If asked why, they might answer, "Because they don't have legs the way dogs do."

As is evident from the above, concepts are formed by both positive and negative exemplars. A **positive exemplar** is an object or an idea that fits the concept, that can be contained within it. A **negative exemplar** is an object or an idea that does not fit the concept, that cannot be contained within it. For Tammy, her pet dog at home is a positive exemplar of the concept "dog." The seal at the aquarium is a negative exemplar of the concept "dog." However, it is a positive exemplar of the concept "seal" or "aquatic animal." (Without an adjective before it, the word *exemplar* means "a typical example.")

(a) An object or idea that fits a given concept, that can be contained within it, is called called

_____.

(b) An object or idea that does not fit a given concept, that can not be contained within it, is called _____.

> *Answers:*   (a) a positive exemplar; (b) a negative exemplar.

A **disjunctive concept** treats perceived attributes in either-or terms. The classic example of a disjunctive concept is a strike in baseball. A strike is *either* a ball that goes through the strike zone and is not swung at *or* a ball that is swung at and missed, even if it's outside of the strike zone. Let's say that forty-year-old Carl says, "I will drink any kind of wine except muscatel or port." If he refuses a glass of wine at a friend's house, it is possible to reflect that the host must have offered Carl either muscatel or port. "Wines that Carl won't drink" is, in this case, a disjunctive concept.

A **relational concept** treats perceived attributes in terms of some connection between objects or ideas such as "more than," "less than," "bigger than," "more beautiful than," and so forth. A concept such as "cheapskate" is a relational concept. Nolan is a regular customer for breakfast in a family restaurant in a small town. He always leaves a twenty-five-cent tip even though 15 percent of his breakfast check comes to about one dollar. Ogden is also a regular customer for breakfast. He always leaves a three-dollar tip. Both Nolan and Ogden are successful businessmen. The servers in the restaurant refer to Nolan as a "cheapskate" and to Ogden as a "big spender." The two concepts are relational because they arise from the fact that Ogden's tip is more than Nolan's.

(a) A disjunctive concept treats perceived attributes in _____ terms.

(b) What kind of a concept treats perceived attributes in terms of some connection between object or ideas such as "more than," or "less than"? _____

Answers: (a) either-or; (b) Relational.

Solving Problems: What Is the Square Root of 12?

It is a fair question to ask: Why do we think at all? A good answer to the question is: One of the reasons we think is in order to solve problems.

Human beings lead complex lives. We have all kinds of problems to solve. Every day is filled with challenges. And it is necessary to think clearly and effectively if one is to be successful in meeting the problems and challenges of life.

Two basic ways to solve problems are to employ either (1) algorithms or (2) heuristic approaches. An **algorithm** is a formula. If followed carefully, it will always solve the problem. Formulas in math books are algorithms. So are recipes in cookbooks and step-by-step instructions for operating a microwave oven.

Let's say that you are given this problem: What is the square root of 12? You will probably turn to a calculator. You enter 12, push the square-root button, and the answer appears on the screen. In a sense, you haven't solved the problem. The calculator has solved the problem for you. It has the formula built into it. And even if you have forgotten the formula, it is possible for you to obtain the right answer. If you don't have a calculator, you can look up the square root in a table in the appendix of a mathematics book. Again, you are relying on an algorithm that you may or may not know.

(a) One of the reasons we think is in order to _____.

(b) A recipe in a cookbook is an example of an _____.

Answers: (a) solve problems; (b) algorithm.

Let's say that you decide to figure out the square root of 12 without a calculator or a book. What would you do? Some might remember the formula they were taught in school. They might apply it and obtain the square root. Others might say, "I forgot the formula. I can't get the answer." This response betrays an excessive reliance on algorithms to solve math problems. Even if the formula is forgotten, the problem can be solved.

Solving a problem without a formula involves the use of **heuristic approaches.** Heuristic approaches employ principles, rules-of-thumb, and insights to solve problems. A heuristic approach is based on the attitude "I can solve this problem even if I can't solve it in an elegant way." Returning to the search for the square root of 12, it is necessary to ask oneself this question: "What *is* a square root?" As most adults know, it is the number that when multiplied by itself will generate the squared number. For example, $3 \times 3 = 9$; the square root of 9 is 3. Once this is clearly seen, it should be possible to discover the square root of 12 without an algorithm. One can do it by trial and error. Try multiplying 4×4. The product is 16. Obviously the square root of 12 must be between 3 and 4. It has to be a decimal fraction. Try multiplying 3.5×3.5. The product is 12.25. The answer isn't 12, but it's close. One can close in on the answer by multiplying numbers somewhat smaller than 3.5. As already noted, a heuristic approach is not an elegant, efficient way to solve a problem. But it *will* get the job done, and should not be scorned. On the contrary, it is often essential to use heuristic approaches to solve problems when formulas are either not available or forgotten.

(a) Solving a problem without a formula involves the use of _____ approaches.

(b) Heuristic approaches employ principles, _____, and insights to solve problems.

    Answers: (a) heuristic; (b) rules-of-thumb.

A particular kind of heuristic approach is a means–end analysis. A **means–end analysis** is characterized by identifying a goal and then finding a way in which the goal can be obtained. Questions such as: "Where is this going?" and "How will I get there?" are associated with a means–end analysis.

For example, let's say that you are buying a home and are told by a broker that the payments are only $1,200 a month. This sounds good, and you might sign on the dotted line. Or, you might make a means-end analysis. You ask the broker, "How long will it take to pay off the house if I stick to the payment schedule?" You are told it will take thirty years. You reply that you have a goal. You want to pay off the house in twenty years. The broker explains that if you will pay $1,400 a month, following a different payment schedule, you can accomplish your goal. You have now been provided with the means—the way—to obtain your goal. It is up to you to decide if you can afford the larger payments.

What kind of heuristic approach is characterized by identifying a goal and then finding a way in which the goal can be obtained? _____

Answer: A means-end analysis.

If possible, it is desirable to be systematic when there is a problem to be solved. This is particularly true if the problem involves a project that will require a span of time involving days or even weeks. When an orderly approach to solving a problem is taken, psychologists have identified five important steps. These are (1) definition of the problem, (2) preparation, (3) incubation, (4) illumination, (5) and verification. This general approach can be applied to many problems. Usually a problem can be stated in question form. Examples include: "How do I get a weed-free lawn?" "How do you raise a child to have high self-esteem?" "How do you study effectively for examinations?" and "How do you lose weight?"

Assume that Laura, a thirty-three-year-old engineer, wife, and mother of two children, wants to lose some weight. It's a problem because she's been trying to lose weight off and on for a couple of years without much success. She decides to use her training as an engineer to solve her problem. So she takes a systematic approach. First, she **defines the problem** in a precise way. She decides that she will stop vaguely saying, "I want to lose some weight." Instead she asks the question, "How can I lose ten pounds in the next five weeks?"

What is the first step in systematic problem solving? _____

Answer: Defining the problem.

Second, she **prepares** to lose weight by gathering information. She obtains two books on nutrition, a third book on the psychology of weight control, and a fourth book on breaking habits. She takes notes on key points in the books.

Third, she lets the information **incubate** before she takes action. She reflects on what she has learned. She feels a little bit overwhelmed and confused by contradictory information in the books she has read. She thinks, "I'll just sleep on all of this stuff for a while and let my subconscious mind bring things together."

Fourth, **illumination** arrives in about a week. She feels she has new insights about weight control. She sees that she needs to stay away from fad diets. She decides that she has been eating too many refined carbohydrates and excessive amounts of saturated fat. She writes an eating plan for herself, one that she believes she can follow.

Fifth, Laura begins to eat in accordance with her plan. She **verifies** that the plan is working—or not working—by weighing herself in the morning every other day.

(a) What step in systematic problem solving involves reflection on what one has learned?
_____

(b) What step in systematic problem solving is associated with insight? _____

Answers: (a) Incubation; (b) Illumination.

Obstacles to Solving Problems: Mental Sets Can Cause Difficulties

The path of problem solving is often a rocky road. There are obstacles that can interfere with obtaining a solution. Two of the principal obstacles are mental sets and functional fixedness.

A **mental set** is a subconscious determining tendency. It is *there,* a part of our cognitive processes, but sometimes its content doesn't enter consciousness. In principle a mental set can either help you solve a problem or interfere with the discovery of a solution. Of principal interest is the way in which a mental set can interfere. However, before we proceed, let's first look at the way in which a mental set can help you solve a problem.

Let's say that you are given ten simple arithmetic problems. You are told to add and obtain sums. With the first problem or two you are consciously instructing yourself to add. Perhaps by the third problem you are adding without telling yourself "I need to add these numbers." The action of obtaining sums is now determined by a mental set to add. As you can see, this is somewhat helpful. It gives you less to think about and juggle at a conscious level.

(a) A mental set is a subconscious _____

(b) In principle a mental set can either help you solve a problem or _____ with the discovery of a solution.

Answers: (a) determining tendency; (b) interfere.

Here are two problems in which mental sets are likely to interfere with obtaining a solution. Problem 1: You are an elevator operator in the Empire State Building. Seven people get on the elevator in the lobby. Four get off at the fifth floor. Two get on at the twenty-first floor. Three get off at the twenty-seventh floor. What is the elevator operator's name?

Problem 2: When an airliner crashes on the border between the United States and Canada where do they bury the survivors?

The answer to Problem 1 is *your own name.* The problem starts, "*You* are an elevator operator . . ." The answer to Problem 2 is that survivors—who are alive—are *not* buried. If you had any difficulty with either problem it is because of mental sets. In Problem 1 the mental set is that this is an arithmetic problem. In Problem 2 the mental set is that this is a problem associated with international law.

In both cases a mental set was created by implication, not by an explicit statement. Consequently, a mental set that interferes with obtaining a solution contains a **false assumption,** a belief that is not correct.

A mental set can be given by nature. Consider the Wright brothers attempting to invent the airplane. They had to break the mental set that wings must flap. Birds do not have stationary wings like airplanes.

(a) A mental set that interferes with obtaining a solution contains a _____.

(b) The idea that wings have to flap is an example of a mental set given by _____.

   Answers: (a) false assumption; (b) nature.

Functional fixedness exists when there is a need to use a tool or familiar object in a novel way and one can't perceive the novel way. Let's say that a carpenter needs a plumb line in order to erect a perpendicular two-by-four piece of wood. He or she can't find the line in the tool box. Carpenter A might leave the job and drive somewhere to obtain a plumb line. Carpenter B might improvise a plumb line by tying a pair of pliers to the end of a string. Carpenter A, who has both string and a pair of pliers, is displaying functional fixedness because he or she can only think of using the pliers for gripping, not as a weight.

Functional fixedness is really a special case of mental set. There is often a mental set that a tool is designed for one and only one purpose. And this fixes the user's attention on that and only that particular function of the tool.

_____ exists when there is a need to use a tool in a novel way and one can't perceive the novel way.

   Answer: Functional fixedness.

Logical Thinking: How We Reason

In order to think effectively, it is necessary to think in a logical manner. **Logical thinking** is thinking that employs valid reasoning to reach a correct conclusion. Logical thinking is the foundation of **rational thought,** thought that fits the real world and allows us to function well in it. There are two basic kinds of reasoning involved in logical thinking: inductive reasoning and deductive reasoning.

Inductive reasoning is characterized by making observations and gathering information until a general conclusion is reached. It is the basic method of science. About 500 years ago the astronomer Nicholas Copernicus made observations that led him to formulate the heliocentric theory of the solar system. About 150 years ago the botanist Gregor Mendel raised sweet peas, studied the characteristics of their flowers, and formulated his theory of heredity.

When a detective gathers clues and reaches the conclusion that the butler murdered the millionaire, the sleuth is using inductive logic. (When Dr. Watson asks Sherlock Holmes how he reached a conclusion, Holmes answers, "Deduction, my dear Watson. Merely deduction." Strictly speaking, he was using induction, not deduction.)

Inductive reasoning also appears frequently in everyday life. Harold makes a series of observations about his car. It's using too much gas, it's pulling to the left, it's overheating, it's squeaking too much, and the brakes are mushy. He concludes that it's overdue for servicing. Or perhaps he concludes that he needs a new car. Rowena makes a series of observations about her fifteen-year-old daughter, Georgia. Her grades are falling, she is spending more time than usual talking secretively on the phone with one of her friends, she is dressing very carefully for school, she is reading romance novels, and she seems unusually dreamy-eyed. Perhaps Rowena, using inductive reasoning, reaches the conclusion that Georgia is developing an interest in adolescent males.

(a) Logical thinking is thinking that employs _____ to reach a correct conclusion.

(b) What kind of reasoning is characterized by making observations and gathering information until a general conclusion is reached? _____

Answers: (a) valid reasoning; (b) Inductive reasoning.

Deductive reasoning is reasoning in which a conclusion follows from a premise. The underlying structure of deductive reasoning is *if-then.* Such reasoning allows for predictions, and it is often the next step taken after inductive reasoning is employed. Sherlock Holmes tells Dr. Watson, "If the butler is really the murderer, then if we hide in the closet we should see him sneak into Jillian's bedroom when the clock strikes midnight." Rowena thinks, "If Georgia is getting interested in boys, then it won't be long before she will be asking me if she can go on a date."

According to Freud, there is a kind of thinking employed at the unconscious level of the mind that is overly primitive. It is neither inductive nor deductive. Freud called this kind of thinking **predicate thinking.** It is also called **paleological thought,** meaning "old" thought. It is presumably the kind of thinking used by primitive, prescientific people and by preschool children. According to Freud, when two sentences have identical predicates (i.e., "first parts") the objects or people in the sentences become associated in an illogical manner. Here is an example:

1. Automobile make X is driven by beautiful people.
2. Automobile make X is the kind of car I drive.
3. Therefore I am a beautiful person.

(a) What kind of reasoning is characterized by a conclusion that follows from a premise?

_____

(b) According to Freud, what kind of thinking is neither inductive nor deductive?

_____

Answers: (a) Deductive reasoning; (b) Predicate thinking (or paleological thought).

Predicate thinking is not the only way in which thinking can be led astray. Logical errors are common. Such errors include (1) overgeneralization, (2) false analogy, (3) appeal to authority, (4) arguing in circles, and (5) attack on character.

Overgeneralization, also known as **hasty generalization,** takes place when we reach a conclusion that goes substantially beyond the facts that inspire it. Nelson owns stock in ten different companies. The prices on two of his stocks decline by 40 percent. He begins telling friends, "I think there's going to be another Great Depression." Melinda's husband, Clark, forgets their wedding anniversary. The next day Melinda is on the phone telling her best friend, "I don't think Clark loves me anymore."

An **analogy** consists of the observation that two basically dissimilar things have some resemblance to each other. A **false analogy** exists when the comparison between two things is inappropriate. Books on anatomy and physiology often point out that the eye is like a camera. The eye has a lens like a camera. The film in the camera is like the retina; they are both light sensitive. The lens of a camera produces an inverted image on the film; the lens of the eye produces an inverted image on the retina. The eye-camera analogy is a useful one. On the other hand, let's say that Colby, who grew up on a ranch, compares his car to a horse. "The darn thing gets balky like a horse. Feeding it gas is like feeding a horse hay. It's getting old the way horses do." However, if one day we hear that Colby in a fit of anger shot the car because the darn thing refused to run, then we would recognize that Colby was employing a false analogy.

(a) What kind of logical error takes place when we reach a conclusion that goes substantially beyond the facts that inspire it? _____

(b) What kind of a logical error takes place when the comparison between two things is inappropriate? _____

Answers: (a) Overgeneralization (or hasty generalization); (b) False analogy.

Appeal to authority is characterized making by a reference to a respected person, believed to be well informed, when one's own logic or reasoning is weak. Nadine tells her friend Kitty, who eats no green vegetables, that she should eat more broccoli, peas, and spinach. Kitty asks, "Why?" Nadine says, "Because Dr. Genius says so in his book *Green Food for a Green Mind.*" Although Dr. Genius may know what he's talking about, in some cases an authority may be a pseudo-authority or give bad advice. It would have been far better if Nadine could have answered Kitty by saying, "Green foods contain folic acid, an important component of good nutrition. Also, vegetables have a lot of fiber, and this promotes regularity."

Arguing in circles takes place when one's premise contains the conclusion that one wants to reach. Edgar tells his girlfriend Janet, "I love you." Janet asks, "Why do you love me?" Edgar says, "I don't know. Just because I do." Janet presses. "But *why* do you?" Edgar, sweating and a little confused, says, "Because you're so lovable!" It would have been a better answer if Edgar could have said, "Because I like your personality and your sense of humor." Or, "Because you're more fun to be with than anyone I've ever met." His actual answer, based on a circular argument, was empty of any real meaning.

Attack on character picks out a negative attribute of another person and uses this attribute to discredit other aspects of the person's behavior. Kathleen is thinking about taking her car for repairs to Jake, a local auto mechanic. Mabel, a friend, tells Kathleen that she shouldn't take her car to Jake. "Why?" asks Kathleen. "Because I hear he cheats on his wife," says Mabel. Obviously, Jake's marital behavior has nothing to do with his ability to repair cars.

(a) Making a reference to a respected person, believed to be well informed, when one's own logic or reasoning is weak is called _____.

(b) What logical error takes place when one's premise contains the conclusion that one wants to reach? _____

(c) What logical error picks out a negative attribute of another person? _____

 Answers: (a) appeal to authority; (b) Arguing in circles; (c) Attack on character.

Creative Thinking: The Importance of Originality

Creative thinking is an important factor in writing poems, books, and songs. It is also plays an important role in advancing human understanding in fields of study such as physics, biology, and psychology. Inventions from the airplane to the automobile have required creative thinking. However, creative thinking should not be associated only with such exalted areas of activity such as literature, invention, and science. It is possible to speak of creative cooking, creative gardening, creative child rearing, creative decorating, and so forth. It is clear that creative thinking often has a place in everyday life.

The core feature of the creative process is **divergent thinking,** thinking that follows new pathways and explores alternative possibilities. Thomas Alva Edison (1847–1931) provides an example of a person who manifested quite a bit of divergent thought. When he was a child, one of his teachers thought that he was mentally retarded because his answers to questions were so odd, deviant, and unexpected. He is well known for improving the electric light bulb. However, he also invented wax paper and the phonograph. When he died he had patented 1,150 inventions, a record for American inventors that still stands.

Divergent thinking often involves breaking mental sets. The example of the Wright brothers realizing that wings don't have to flap has already been given. Divergent thinking also involves combining familiar elements in new combinations. Dumbo the flying elephant combines the familiar image of an elephant and its large ears with the also familiar image of a bird flying and flapping its wings. The cartoon character that results doesn't exist in the real world, but has entertained both adults and children for years.

(a) The core feature of the creative process is _____.

(b) Divergent thinking often involves breaking _____.

(c) Dumbo the flying elephant combines familiar elements in _____.

   Answers: (a) divergent thinking; (b) mental sets; (c) new combinations.

Convergent thinking, in contrast to divergent thinking, follows conventional thought pathways. It is the core feature in rational thought, thought that employs both inductive and deductive logic. Intelligence (see chapter 10) requires convergent thinking. When a student is asked to answer a multiple-choice test, he or she employs convergent thinking. There is thought to be one and only one best answer to a given question.

The Gestalt psychologist Max Wertheimer asserted that **productive thinking,** high-quality creative thinking, combines both divergent and convergent thinking in a functional way. Wertheimer and Albert Einstein were personal friends. In his book *Productive Thinking,* Wertheimer explores how Einstein arrived at the Special Theory of Relativity. It is clear that divergent thinking was required, because in the theory it is possible for space to warp and time to slow down. Both of these concepts were radical departures from standard concepts of physics held in the early part of the twentieth century. On the other hand, convergent thinking was also required, because Einstein employed a large base of theory and knowledge that made his own theory both reasonable and acceptable to scientists in general.

(a) What kind of thinking follows conventional thought pathways? _____

(b) Wertheimer said that what kind of thinking combines both divergent and convergent thinking in a functional way? _____

   Answers: (a) Convergent thinking; (b) Productive thinking.

It is possible to evaluate the quality of creative thinking by three criteria:

(1) **productivity,** (2) **originality,** and (3) **flexibility.** Leo Tolstoy (1828–1910), author of *War and Peace* and *Anna Karenina,* is generally thought to be one of the world's greatest authors. Why? Let's employ the three criteria. First, Tolstoy was extremely productive. He wrote many books, short stories, and essays. He left behind a large body of work.

Second, he was highly original. *War and Peace* broke the ground for a now-familiar kind of book, the war novel. *Anna Karenina* was one of the first great romantic tragedies presented in the form of a novel. It pioneered today's tearjerkers and soap operas. Although the patterns are familiar today, they were highly original when Tolstoy first presented them. In general, his stories and essays often presented characters and ideas from unusual perspectives.

Third, Tolstoy was unusually flexible. As already indicated, he expressed his ideas in several forms. Also, he changed his philosophy of life from an egocentric one to a selfless one, and wrote extensively about the shift in his viewpoint. As you can see, Tolstoy receives high marks on all three criteria.

(a) Tolstoy wrote many books, short stories, and essays. This example is associated with what criterion used to evaluate creative thinking? _____

(b) Tolstoy's works often presented characters and ideas from unusual perspectives. This example is associated with what criterion used to evaluate creative thinking? _____

Answers: (a) Productivity; (b) Originality.

SELF-TEST

1. The process of thinking about thinking is called
   a. cognitive existentialism
   b. symbolic production
   c. functional reflection
   d. metathought

2. What kind of a concept strings together perceived attributes?
   a. A relational concept
   b. A disjunctive concept
   c. An iconic concept
   d. A conjunctive concept

3. Which of the following identifies an object or an idea that fits a concept, that can be contained within it?
   a. Positive exemplar
   b. Negative exemplar
   c. Bipolar exemplar
   d. Transformational exemplar

4. Step-by-step instructions for operating a microwave oven provide an example of
   a. a heuristic approach
   b. a means-end analysis
   c. an algorithm
   d. an insight analysis

5. Let's say you figure out the square root of 12 without a formula. Instead, you rely on your understanding of the concept of a square root. What kind of a problem-solving approach are you using?
   a. An algorithm
   b. A heuristic approach
   c. A means-end analysis
   d. An operant reflection

6. Which of the following correctly defines a mental set?
   a. A conscious conditioned reflex
   b. An unconscious wish
   c. A subconscious determining tendency
   d. A false negative

7. What exists when there is a need to use a tool or familiar object in a novel way and one can't perceive the novel way?
   a. Cognitive slippage
   b. Mental facilitation
   c. Functional fixedness
   d. Transformational perception

8. What kind of reasoning is characterized by making observations and gathering information until a general conclusion is reached?
   a. Inductive reasoning
   b. Deductive reasoning
   c. If-then reasoning
   d. Relational reasoning

9. Deductive reasoning is reasoning in which
   a. a premise follows from a conclusion
   b. a premise follows from a hyperpremise
   c. a conclusion follows from a metaconclusion
   d. a conclusion follows from a premise

10. What is the core feature of the creative process?
    a. Convergent thinking
    b. Divergent thinking
    c. Congruent thinking
    d. Reliable facts

ANSWERS TO THE SELF-TEST

1-d   2-d   3-a   4-c   5-b   6-c   7-c   8-a   9-d   10-b

ANSWERS TO THE TRUE-OR-FALSE PREVIEW QUIZ

1. True.
2. True.
3. False. Heuristic approaches employ principles, rules-of-thumb, and insights to solve problems.
4. False. It *is* correct that functional fixedness is a type of mental set. However, functional fixedness exists when there is a need to use a tool or familiar object in a novel way and one can't perceive the novel way. Consequently, such fixedness interferes with solving a problem.
5. False. The core feature of the creative process is divergent thinking.

KEY TERMS

algorithm	inductive reasoning
analogy	logical thinking
appeal to authority	means-end analysis
arguing in circles	mental set
attack on character	metathought
concept	negative exemplar
conjunctive concept	originality
convergent thinking	overgeneralization
deductive reasoning	paleological thought
definition of the problem	positive exemplar
disjunctive concept	predicate thinking
divergent thinking	preparation
false analogy	productive thinking
false assumption	productivity
flexibility	rational thought
functional fixedness	relational concept
hasty generalization	symbol
heuristic approaches	thinking
illumination	verification
incubation	

10 Intelligence: In Pursuit of Rational Thought and Effective Action

True or False

1. T F The concept of intelligence is associated with the ability to think clearly and to function effectively in the environment.
2. T F The Stanford–Binet Intelligence Scale is based on the performance method of measuring intelligence.
3. T F Information, or general knowledge, is not associated with intelligence.
4. T F An intelligence quotient (IQ) score of 100 is evidence of superior intelligence.
5. T F A valid test is one that measures what it is supposed to measure.

(Answers can be found on page 152.)

Thinking, the subject matter of the previous chapter, plays a significant role in intelligence. Indeed, as the subtitle of this chapter suggests, rational thought is at the core of intelligence. We will now examine the concept of intelligence and the ways in which it can be measured.

Objectives

After completing this chapter, you will be able to

- define intelligence;
- describe the approach of the Stanford–Binet Intelligence Scale;
- specify key features of the Wechsler Intelligence Scales;
- explain the concept of an intelligence quotient (IQ);
- compare and contrast the concepts of validity and reliability in psychological testing.

Consider how you might use the word *intelligent* in a short sentence. Here are some answers that were obtained from members of an introductory psychology class:

"I want to marry an intelligent person."

"Is there intelligent life on Earth?"

"I want to raise intelligent children."

"To be intelligent is both a curse and a blessing."

"It's difficult to make intelligent decisions."

"I always have the feeling that that my friends are more intelligent than I am."

"I'm intelligent when it comes to math, but not in my way of relating to other people."

As you can see from these statements, the concept of intelligence is a pervasive one entering into most aspects of behavior and life.

Although the concept of intelligence is as familiar, in a way, as an old shoe, it has a quality of mystery about it. Familiarity should not breed contempt in this case. We shouldn't be confident that we really understand intelligence until we explore its more important features.

Intelligence: What Is It?

Intelligence is the global ability of the individual to think clearly and to function effectively in the environment. This definition of intelligence is based on the thinking and writing of the clinical psychologist David Wechsler (1896–1981), author of the widely used Wechsler Intelligence Scales. (There will be more about the Wechsler Scales later.)

If we examine the definition clearly, several important points emerge. First, intelligence is, to some extent, *global*. This means that it has a general quality that has an impact on many facets of life. When we think of someone as "smart," we expect him or her to be a smart businessperson, a smart parent, a smart student, and so forth. (Subsequently we will reexamine the global, or general, nature of intelligence and compare it with specific mental abilities.)

Second, intelligence is associated with the ability to *think clearly*. This means the ability to use both inductive and deductive logic in an appropriate manner. The core feature of intelligence, unlike creativity, is the ability to employ **convergent thinking,** defined in chapter 9 as the ability to think along conventional pathways. When a question is asked on an intelligence test, there is only one best answer. Consequently, intelligence tests measure convergent thinking. When one learns the basic information associated with a trade or profession, one is required to learn well-established facts and principles.

(a) Intelligence is the global ability of the individual to think _____ and to function _____ in the environment.

(b) The core feature of intelligence, unlike creativity, is the ability to employ what kind of thinking? _____

Answers: (a) clearly; effectively; (b) Convergent thinking.

Third, intelligence implies the ability to *function effectively in the environment*. A person with normal intelligence has survival skills. He or she can get things done correctly—everything from pumping gas to cooking a meal. The word **environment** includes almost any aspect of an individual's surrounding world. Therefore, it includes the **social environment,** the world of other people. A person with normal intelligence is able to get along reasonably well with others.

Note that the definition of intelligence says nothing about heredity and environment. The concept of intelligence, in and of itself, is a functional one. It refers to what a person can *do*. The question of how heredity and environment contribute to intelligence is, of course, an important one, and is treated in a later section in this chapter.

Returning to the global aspect of intelligence, in the first decade of the twentieth century the British researcher Charles Spearman concluded that there is a **general factor** running through all aspects of intelligence. He called this general factor *g*. Spearman also recognized that there were **specific mental abilities,** and he called this factor *s*.

(a) The word _____ includes almost any aspect of an individual's surrounding world.

(b) The concept of intelligence is a _____ one. It refers to what a person can do.

(c) Spearman concluded that there is a _____ factor running through all aspects of intelligence. He called this factor _____.

Answers: (a) environment; (b) functional; (c) general; *g.*

Interested in the nature of specific mental abilities, the American researcher Louis Thurstone made a factor analysis of intelligence tests in the 1930s. **Factor analysis** is a mathematical tool that allows a researcher to pull meaningful clusters out of a set of data. Based on his analysis, Thurstone concluded that there are at least nine primary mental abilities. These include (1) inductive reasoning, (2) deductive reasoning, (3) word fluency, (4) speed of perception, (5) verbal comprehension, (6) verbal fluency, (7) memory, (8) spatial visualization, and (9) mathematics.

More recently, the research psychologist Howard Gardner has suggested that we speak of **multiple intelligences** in preference to global intelligence. Taking this approach, one kind of intelligence may be more or less independent of another kind of intelligence. An example of what Gardner means is **kinesthetic intelligence,** the ability to comprehend the position of one's body in space. Such intelligence is important in athletic performance and dancing.

(a) What kind of analysis did Thurstone make of intelligence tests? _____

(b) Gardner has suggested that we speak of _____ in preference to global intelligence.

Answers: (a) A factor analysis; (b) multiple intelligences.

It is possible to bring together the concept of a general ability with the concept of specific abilities. The general factor, or *g,* is like the palm of a hand. It can be small or large. The specific abilities are like the fingers of a hand, and they can vary in length. This allows for many possibilities. Kurt has an unusually high level of general intelligence, but finds it difficult to comprehend mathematical concepts. Rita has an average level of general intelligence; however, she makes her living as a sculptor, and she displays an unusually high level of ability in the area of spatial visualization.

As you can see, it is difficult to pin intelligence down and say with any kind of finality what it *is.* This in part is due to the fact that intelligence has the status of a **hypothetical construct.** In science, a hypothetical construct is "constructed" by the mind of the scientist in order to explain a set of facts. In physics, the concept of an electromagnetic field is sometimes said to be such a construct. Science freely employs hypothetical constructs. Intelligence as experienced by *you* is not, of course, hypothetical. However, intelligence as measured by a psychologist with an intelligence test is hypothetical. The intelligence has to be *inferred* from scores, and there is room for error whenever one makes an inference. (See the section on validity and reliability on pages 145–147.)

(a) It is possible to bring together the concept of a general ability with the concept of _____ abilities.

(b) In scientific terms, intelligence has the status of a _____ construct.

(c) Intelligence has to be _____ from scores.

   Answers: (a) specific; (b) hypothetical; (c) inferred.

The Stanford-Binet Intelligence Scale: Intelligent Is as Intelligent Does

One of the first people to attempt to measure intelligence in an objective manner was the English scientist Sir Francis Galton (1822–1911). Working somewhat over one hundred years ago, he used the **biometric method,** meaning he tried to measure intelligence directly by evaluating such physiological measures as strength of grip and perceptual-motor speed. He found that there was little correlation between these measures and intelligence. Discouraged, he discontinued his research in this particular area of human behavior.

Only a few years after Galton abandoned the effort to measure intelligence, Alfred Binet, director of the psychological laboratory at the Sorbonne in Paris, was asked by France's Minister of Public Instruction to devise a way to detect subnormal intelligence. The aim was to give extra instruction and assistance to children with cognitive problems.

Binet, working in collaboration with the scientist Theodore Simon, published the Binet-Simon Scale in 1905. This was the first modern intelligence test, and today's tests still use its basic method—the **performance method.** In brief, the subject is asked to demonstrate the existence of intelligence by giving answers to questions. Correct answers reflect the existence of intelligence. Informally, the **Binet-Simon Scale** was based on the premise that intelligence *is* as the intelligent individual *does.*

(a) What method did Galton use in his unsuccessful attempt to measure intelligence? _____

(b) What method did Binet and Simon use in their successful attempt to measure intelligence? _____

   Answers: (a) The biometric method; (b) The performance method.

The Binet-Simon Scale established a measure called **mental age,** or **MA.** Mental age is determined by comparing one subject's score on the Binet-Simon Scale with the scores of a group of subjects of the same age. Let's say that a group of nine-year-old subjects is able, on average, to answer fifteen questions correctly on the Scale. If seven-year-old Alice is able to answer fifteen questions correctly, her mental age is nine even though her chronological age is seven. Binet and Simon expected mental age to rise over time, and it does. In view of the fact that mental age is a changeable number, this created a problem. (The way in which this problem was solved with the concept of an intelligence quotient, or IQ, will be discussed later.)

The Binet-Simon Scale was translated into English by the Stanford psychologist Lewis Terman. In 1916, only eleven years after Binet and Simon published their test, the **Stanford–Binet Intelligence Scale (SBIS)** was published in the United States. The SBIS became a popular way in which to measure intelligence, and it is still used today in revised form.

One of the questions that interested Terman was: Do highly intelligent children do, overall, better in life than children of normal intelligence? In order to answer the question, Terman started a **longitudinal study,** a research project that measures behavior over a span of time. In this case, the Stanford project, carried on after Terman's death, continued for more than seventy years. The results are clear. On the whole, highly intelligent children grew into highly intelligent adults. They fared better in general in all aspects of life. They had better health, fewer divorces, and better mental and emotional adjustment than subjects with average intelligence. This result should not be surprising. If intelligence is to mean anything at all as a concept, it must mean that it has value to the individual and society. As already indicated in the definition of intelligence, the ability to think clearly and to function effectively is part and parcel of what it means to *be* intelligent.

(a) What measure, abbreviated MA, is associated with the Binet-Simon Scale? _____

(b) Terman translated the Binet-Simon Scale into English and called it _____.

(c) A research project that measures behavior over a span of time is called what kind of a study? _____

Answers: (a) Mental age; (b) the Stanford-Binet Intelligence Scale (SBIS); (c) A longitudinal study.

The Wechsler Scales: Comparing Verbal Intelligence and Performance Intelligence

Working for a number of years as the chief psychologist for the Bellevue Psychiatric Hospital in New York City, David Wechsler conducted a substantial amount of research on intelligence. His work culminated in a set of highly regarded intelligence tests called collectively the **Wechsler Scales.** There are three individual tests, and in revised editions they are still used today. The three tests are: (1) the **Wechsler Preschool and Primary Scale of Intelligence (WPPSI),** (2) the **Wechsler Intelligence Scale for Children (WISC),** and (3) the **Wechsler Adult Intelligence Scale (WAIS).**

The Wechsler Scales have a clear-cut advantage over the Stanford–Binet Scale. The Stanford–Binet measures general intelligence without regard to specific mental abilities. The Wechsler Scales recognize that there are different kinds of intelligence. Two in particular are emphasized: verbal intelligence and performance intelligence. **Verbal intelligence** includes such abilities as word fluency, abstract reasoning, and mathematical ability. **Performance intelligence** includes such abilities as visualization, the perception of the relationship of parts to a whole, and the capacity to relate well to other people. As a consequence, it is possible to obtain two separate IQ scores, a verbal IQ and a performance IQ. The two IQ scores can be combined for an overall IQ score.

(a) What does the abbreviation WAIS stand for? _____

(b) What two kinds of intelligence are clearly identified in the Wechsler Scales? _____

Answers: (a) Wechsler Adult Intelligence Scale; (b) Verbal intelligence and performance intelligence.

The following description is based on the Wechsler Adult Intelligence Scale. Not only is the Scale divided into two large areas, it is also subdivided into a set of eleven subtests, six under the Verbal Scale and five under the Performance Scale. Keep in mind that the word *scale* is used because sets of questions proceed from easy to difficult. Evaluation is based on how high the subject can climb on the ladder of psychological difficulty. Here is the breakdown:

The Verbal Scale: Each of the following tests consists of a group of questions designed to assess a different area.

Information: level of general knowledge.

Comprehension: ability to understand questions and grasp concepts.

Arithmetic: capacity to grasp and employ mathematical concepts.

Similarities: ability to employ abstract thought.

Digit Span: tasks designed to measure attention span.

Vocabulary: grasp of the meaning of words.

The Performance Scale: Each of the following tests is a set of tasks designed to assess a different area.

Digit Symbol: mental flexibility and ability to employ arbitrary symbols.

Picture Completion: ability to detect the missing parts of an organized whole (i.e., a Gestalt).

Block Design: ability to relate a printed pattern to a physical construction.

Picture Arrangement: ability to comprehend the "before and after" aspect of time. Also useful in evaluating the subject's level of social intelligence.

Object Assembly: ability to place parts in a correct relationship to a whole.

Under optimal conditions, a trained psychologist administers the Wechsler Adult Intelligence Scale to a given to a subject on an individual basis. The results of the test, when properly scored and evaluated, provide a clear picture of the individual's level of cognitive functioning at both a general level and at the level of specific mental abilities.

(a) The Wechsler Adult Intelligence Scale consists of a set of how many subtests? _____

(b) What subtest in the Verbal Scale is designed to assess the subject's ability to understand questions and grasp concepts? _____

(c) What subtest in the Verbal Scale is designed to assess the subject's grasp of the meaning of words? _____

(d) What subtest in the Performance Scale is designed to assess the subject's mental flexibility and ability to employ arbitrary symbols? _____

(e) What subtest in the Performance Scale is designed to assess the subject's ability to relate a printed pattern to a physical construction? _____

Answers: (a) Eleven; (b) Comprehension; (c) Vocabulary; (d) Digit Symbol; (e) Block Design.

The Concept of an Intelligence Quotient: Following the Bell-Shaped Curve

As already noted, the concept of mental age (MA) is of limited value because it is unstable. As one's **chronological age (CA)** increases, so does one's mental age. Consequently, a German psychologist named William Stern suggested that a ratio based on the comparison of mental age with chronological age would tend to be relatively stable. Stern proposed the following formula:

$$IQ = \frac{MA}{CA} \times 100$$

IQ stands for **intelligence quotient.** The IQ is a quotient because it is the result of a division process.

MA stands for mental age.

CA stands for chronological age

CA is divided into MA and multiplied by 100. Stern suggested the multiplication step be employed with the aim of getting rid of decimals in the final quotient. For example, instead of an IQ being reported as 1.15, it is reported as 115.

Let's say that Irwin has a CA of 9 and an MA of 9; 9 ÷ 9 = 1. Multiply 1 by 100 and the product is 100. Consequently Irwin's IQ score is 100. This is a normal, or average, IQ. This makes sense in view of the fact that the average child of 9 years old will also have a mental age of 9. Let's say Irwin is tested again when he is 11 years old. His MA is now 11. A CA of 11 divided into an MA of 11 is 1. So Irwin's IQ is still 100.

Let's say that Lana has a CA of 8 and an MA of 10; 10 ÷ 8 = 1.25. Multiply by 100 and Lana's IQ score is 125, above normal.

Let's say that Jeffrey has a CA of 9 and an MA of 8; 8 ÷ 9 = .89. Multiply by 100 and Jeffrey's IQ score is 89, below normal.

(a) Stern suggested that a _____ based on the comparison of mental age with chronological age would tend to be relatively _____.

(b) What is the formula for IQ? _____

Answers: (a) ratio; stable; (b) $IQ = \dfrac{MA}{CA} \times 100$.

Research has demonstrated that the IQ score is a random variable, meaning a variable distributed according to the laws of chance. This means that in a large sample of scores the scores will tend to take on a bell-shaped distribution. This distribution, well studied by statisticians, goes by three names: (1) the **bell-shaped curve,** (2) the **normal curve,** and (3) the **Gaussian curve.** The third name is in honor of the nineteenth-century German mathematician Karl Friedrich Gauss, who first studied the curve's properties. Applying the curve to IQ scores, seven categories emerge. These are summarized in the accompanying table.

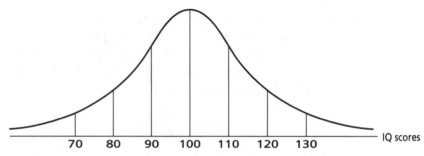

A large sample of IQ scores tends to display a bell-shaped distribution.

IQ Categories

IQ	Classification	Percent
130 and above	Very Superior	2.2
120–129	Superior	6.7
110–119	Bright Normal	16.1
90–109	Normal (or Average)	50.0
80–89	Dull Normal	16.1
70–79	Borderline	6.7
69 and below	Cognitively Deficient	2.2

(a) Research has demonstrated that the IQ score is a _____ variable.

(b) What are the two other names of the bell-shaped curve? _____

(c) What percent of subjects fall within an IQ range of 90 to 109, the Normal, or Average, classification? _____

(d) What percent of subjects fall within an IQ score of 130 or above, the Very Superior classification? _____

Answers: (a) random; (b) The normal curve and the Gaussian curve; (c) 50 percent; (d) 2.2 percent.

Validity and Reliability: Two Big Problems in Any Kind of Testing

Let's say that a confused auto mechanic gets certain important wires crossed on the display panel in your car. You are driving merrily along and your gas gauge reads "Full." However, soon you are forced to pull over to the side of the road. Your car has overheated and it's also out of gas. What has gone wrong? The gas gauge, unfortunately, was giving information on temperature, not fuel in the tank. Under these conditions, the gas gauge had lost its validity as a measuring instrument. Interestingly, it was functioning in a reliable manner. It was reliably giving you the wrong information! As you can see, validity and reliability, although related, are not the same thing.

Validity and reliability are important aspects of any kind of measurement and testing. Intelligence tests are—like gauges, clocks, and rulers—measuring instruments. Consequently, before they can be used to measure intelligence with any degree of confidence, their validity and reliability must be assessed.

A **valid test** is one that measures what it is supposed to measure. If an intelligence test really does in fact measure intelligence, then it is valid. But how can one ascertain that the test is valid? Just because the questions in a test *seem* valid does not mean they actually are. This kind of validity is called **face validity,** meaning that the questions have a surface appearance of validity.

(a) Like gauges, clocks, and rulers, intelligence tests are what kind of instruments? _____

(b) A _____ test is one that measures what it is supposed to measure.

Answers: (a) Measuring instruments; (b) valid.

In order to evaluate the validity of an intelligence test, it is necessary to compare test scores with an outside criterion. An **outside criterion** is a measurement instrument that is independent of the intelligence test being evaluated. A useful outside criterion is grade point average. If intelligence means anything at all, then students with high IQ scores should have high grade point averages. In research, this relationship is evaluated with a statistical tool called the **correlation coefficient,** a measure of the magnitude of the relationship between two variables (see chapter 2). If the correlation between IQ scores and grade point average is high, then it seems reasonable to conclude that the intelligence test in question has validity. The higher the correlation coefficient, the more valid the test is considered to be.

Other outside criteria that can be used are teacher ratings and evaluations made by parents.

(a) An _____ criterion is a measurement instrument that is independent of the intelligence test being evaluated.

(b) What statistical tool is used to evaluate the magnitude of the relationship between two variables? _____

Answers: (a) outside; (b) The correlation coefficient.

A **reliable test** is one that gives stable, repeatable results. Let's say that you use a certain thermometer to take the temperature of family members when an illness is suspected. In most cases, the thermometer will be reliable. You can depend on it.

An intelligence test has to be carefully assessed for reliability. This is also accomplished with the use of the correlation coefficient. Let's say that a 100-question test is split into two versions, Form A and Form B. The original 100 questions are randomly assigned to two forms. Form A has 50 questions. Form B has 50 questions. The two tests are administered, for example, one week apart to the same group of children. If Sheila obtains an IQ score of 119 on Form A, she should obtain a score close to 119 on Form B. However, if she obtains 119 on Form A and 87 on Form B, the reliability of the test is in question. Comparing paired scores for each child in the group, a high score on Form A should predict a high score on Form B. And a low score on Form A should predict a low score on Form B. If these predictions aren't obtained, then the test is not reliable.

A _____ test is one that gives stable, repeatable results.

Answer: reliable.

The two related factors of validity and reliability generate four possibilities for any kind of measuring instrument. The instrument may be (1) neither valid nor reliable, (2) valid, but not reliable, (3) reliable, but not valid, (4) both valid and reliable. This fourth happy circumstance is the one we usually associate with rulers, clocks, and thermometers. These are the primary measuring instruments of physics. They are some of the reasons why it has such a high status as a science.

In psychology, both personality tests and intelligence tests are forced to deal with the mutual problems of validity and reliability. Fortunately, with the use of the correlation coefficient applied to large sets of scores, a reasonable level of validity and reliability can be obtained. The Stanford-Binet Intelligence Scale and the Wechsler Scales have been subjected to a substantial amount of scrutiny and evaluation. On the whole, they are considered to be both valid and reliable measuring instruments.

The two related factors of validity and reliability generated how many possibilities for any kind of measuring instrument? _____

Answer: Four.

The Interaction of Heredity and Environment: How They Exert Joint Effects

What is the primary determinant of intelligence? Is it heredity? Is it environment? Or, is it possible that the best answer can't be given in either-or terms?

The topic under discussion in this section is sometimes called the **nature-nurture controversy,** and it has a long history in philosophy, biology, and psychology. **Nature** refers to heredity; the primary characteristic of nature, or heredity, is the **potential** to reach a given level of intelligence. **Nurture,** on the other hand, refers to environment; the primary characteristic of nurture, or environment, is its capacity to bring forth, in the case of intelligence, the maximum cognitive potential that an individual has. Or, conversely, environment has the capacity to inhibit and restrict that potential.

(a) The word _____ refers to heredity.

(b) The primary characteristic of heredity is the _____ to reach a given level of intelligence.

(c) The word _____ refers to the environment.

Answers: (a) *nature;* (b) potential; (c) *nurture.*

Let's say that a mother and a father insist that their two sons have had the "same" environment. Both were loved, ate the same kind of food, and received the same kind of cognitive stimulation. Now thirty-year-old Kendrick has a Ph.D. in physics. His brother, twenty-seven-year-old Mark, is an insurance broker. The parents say that since early childhood Kendrick has had a brilliant, unusual mind. Mark has always appeared to have normal intelligence. The parents are convinced that the difference in the cognitive functioning of their two sons is intrinsic, something that is built in to the two individuals. This general line of reasoning tends to support the importance of heredity. It can be argued that the individual differences in the two brothers have a genetic basis. Although siblings do have many genes in common, there is still plenty of room for unique genetic patterns.

A strong advocate of the importance of environment in shaping intelligence is likely to point out that, strictly speaking, the two brothers didn't have the same environment. That is why the word *same* appeared with quotes around it in the above paragraph. It is possible to suggest, as the pioneer psychotherapist Alfred Adler did, that a first child and a second child have, by definition, different environments. The first child lives for a time as an only child. The second child always lives in a world with a sibling. It is possible to hypothesize that a first child often receives, for a time, more attention and affection than a second child is likely to receive.

In spite of the Adlerian birth–order argument, when individuals are raised in the same home and with the same parents, variations in intelligence tend to support the genetic hypothesis.

(a) Individual differences in intelligence in siblings who have had highly similar environments are likely to have what kind of a basis? _____

(b) According to Adler, a first child and a second child have, by definition, _____ environments.

Answers: (a) A genetic basis; (b) different.

The fictional tale *Tarzan of the Apes* is a reflection of the genetic hypothesis. Tarzan, after all, develops the intelligence of a human being even though he's raised in an environment of ape intelligence. However, as indicated, Tarzan is a fictional character. Children raised by animals or in deprived circumstances are called **feral children.** When such children are discovered, they seldom display adequate cognitive functioning. A famous case is that of the wild boy of the forest of Aveyron in France. Discovered at the age of seven and studied by the nineteenth-century physician Jean–Marc-Gaspard Itard, the boy, given the name Victor, never did attain normal intelligence. Similar studies of feral children support Itard's research findings. So, in spite of the story of Tarzan, it appears that early experiences have to be within the context of a human social environment in order to bring out the individual's genetic potentiality.

A substantial body of research suggests that a **stimulus–rich environment** will make a large difference in measurable intelligence. A stimulus-rich environment, for human beings, is one that provides a great deal of affection along with mental stimulation of a verbal and symbolical nature. A child who is played with spontaneously, exposed to the printed word, provided with challenging toys, and encouraged to express himself or herself is likely to automatically maximize his or her genetic potentiality.

(a) The fictional tale of *Tarzan of the Apes* reflects what hypothesis as an explanation of intelligence? _____

(b) Children raised by animals or in deprived circumstances are called _____ children.

(c) A _____ environment, for human beings, is one that provides a great deal of affection along with mental stimulation of a verbal and symbolical nature.

Answers: (a) The genetic hypothesis; (b) feral; (c) stimulus-rich.

We can see that in a best–case scenario the function of the environmental factor is to elicit, or bring forth, the genetic potential of the child. It can't put that potential there, but it can help make it reach its highest and best level.

The concept of an interaction, a formal mathematical concept, is useful at this point. An **interaction** occurs when two (or more) variables affect each other in a complex way. In contrast, the relationship between two variables is said to be additive when they don't affect each other's value. For example, $3 \times 3 = 9$. The relationship between the numbers is interactive because the whole (the product) is more than the sum of its parts. On the other hand, $3 + 3 = 6$. In this case the relationship between the numbers is additive because the whole (the sum) *is* the sum of its parts.

Loosely speaking, a kind of "magic" occurs when there is an interaction. Something is produced that is not "in" the original variables. So it is with intelligence. It is very difficult to say, when there is an interaction, that one factor is of greater importance than another factor. It is the *joint effects* of the two factors working together that produce a result. In the case of intelligence, the nature-nurture controversy is something of a false issue. The correct formula for under-standing intelligence is this one:

Heredity × Environment = Intelligence

(The multiplication sign is used to symbolize an interaction.)

The answer to the heredity-environment debate should not be given in either-or terms. The answer should be given in *both-and* terms. Both heredity *and* environment, interacting, play important roles in determining intelligence.

(a) An _____ occurs when two (or more) variables affect each other in a complex way.

(b) What is the correct formula for understanding intelligence? _____

Answers: (a) interaction; (b) Heredity × Environment = Intelligence.

SELF-TEST

1. One of the following *is not* a primary characteristic of intelligence:
   a. The ability to think clearly
   b. Eccentric thinking
   c. Convergent thinking
   d. Functioning effectively in the environment

2. In behavioral science, intelligence has the status of
   a. a hypothetical construct
   b. a psychological atom
   c. a transcendental force
   d. an interim operant

3. What method was employed by Binet and Simon to measure intelligence?
   a. The biometric method
   b. The perceptual-motor method
   c. The performance method
   d. The physiological method

4. A research project that measures behavior over a span of time is called a
   a. discontinuity study
   b. gradient study
   c. longitudinal study
   d. continuity study

5. Which of the following is the correct formula for the intelligence quotient (IQ)?
   a. $IQ = MA \times CA + 100$
   b. $IQ = CA + MA \times 3.14$
   c. $IQ = MA + MA/100$
   d. $IQ = MA/CA \times 100$

6. An IQ score in the range 110 to 119 is associated with what classification?
   a. Very Superior
   b. Superior
   c. Bright Normal
   d. Normal (or Average)

7. A test that measures what it is supposed to measure is said to be
   a. consistent
   b. reliable
   c. valid
   d. congruent

8. A test that gives stable, repeatable results is said to be
   a. authentic
   b. reliable
   c. valid
   d. systematic

9. The inborn potential to reach a given level of intelligence is associated primarily with which of the following?
   a. Nature
   b. Nurture
   c. Environment
   d. Reinforcement

10. The correct formula for understanding intelligence is which of the following?
    a. Heredity $\times$ Environment = Intelligence
    b. Heredity + Environment = Intelligence
    c. Nature $\times$ Heredity = Intelligence
    d. Nurture $\times$ Environment = Intelligence

ANSWERS TO THE SELF-TEST

1-b   2-a   3-c   4-c   5-d   6-c   7-c   8-b   9-a   10-a

ANSWERS TO THE TRUE-OR-FALSE PREVIEW QUIZ

1. True.
2. True.
3. False. There is an information subtest in the Wechsler Intelligence Scales.
4. False. An intelligence quotient (IQ) score of 100 is associated with normal, or average, intelligence.
5. True.

KEY TERMS

bell-shaped curve (normal curve, or Gaussian curve)

Binet-Simon Scale

biometric method

chronological age (or CA)

convergent thinking

correlation coefficient

environment

face validity

factor analysis

feral children

general factor (or g)

hypothetical construct

intelligence

intelligence quotient (or IQ)

interaction

kinesthetic intelligence

longitudinal study

mental age (or MA)

multiple intelligences

nature

nature-nurture controversy

nurture

outside criterion

performance intelligence

performance method

potential

reliable test

social environment

specific mental abilities (or s)

Stanford-Binet Intelligence Scale (SBIS)

stimulus-rich environment

valid test

verbal intelligence

Wechsler Adult Intelligence Scale (WAIS)

Wechsler Intelligence Scale for Children (WISC)

Wechsler Preschool and Primary Scale of Intelligence (WPPSI)

Wechsler Scales

11 Developmental Psychology: How Children Become Adults

True or False

1. T F If a fertilized egg contains an **XX** chromosome pattern, the resulting infant will be a female.
2. T F According to Freud, the five stages of psychosexual development are: (1) oral, (2) anal, (3) phallic, (4) latency, and (5) genital.
3. T F In psychosocial development, the stage of identity versus role confusion is associated with old age.
4. T F Cognitive development focuses primarily on the emotional adjustment of the child.
5. T F An authoritarian parent tends to be easygoing, overly agreeable, detached, and easily manipulated by the child or adolescent.

(Answers can be found on page 172.)

The previous chapter examined the concept of intelligence. The ways in which children develop the kinds of mental skills associated with reasoning and human intelligence are among the principal concerns of developmental psychology.

OBJECTIVES

After completing this chapter, you will be able to

- define developmental psychology;
- describe fetal development;
- explain Freud's theory of psychosexual development;
- specify key features of Erikson's theory of psychosocial development;
- identify the four stages in Piaget's theory of cognitive development;
- identify the three levels in Kohlberg's theory of moral development;
- describe the two basic dimensions of parental style.

A familiar proverb states, "As the twig is bent, so grows the tree." Meant to apply as a metaphor to the raising of children, this saying contains within it an entire justification for the study of developmental psychology. Every adult was once a child, and the adult was shaped and formed by experiences during childhood. Psychologists as far apart in many of their assumptions and conclusions as Sigmund Freud and John Watson subscribed to the general view that in order to understand adult behavior it is necessary to study child behavior.

The contemporary approach to developmental psychology expands the concept of development well past childhood and adolescence. There are also developmental stages associated with adulthood. This will be evident when Erik Erikson's theory of development is presented later in this chapter.

Developmental psychology is the study of the growth and maturation of the individual over an extended span of time. **Child psychology** is a subset of developmental psychology. It concerns itself primarily with the study of the individual from birth to the beginning of adolescence (usually around the age of twelve or thirteen). **Adolescent psychology** is also a subset of developmental psychology. It concerns itself primarily with the study of the individual from the beginning of adolescence to its end (usually around the age of eighteen). Sometimes child psychology refers loosely to both child and adolescent psychology.

(a) Developmental psychology is the study of the _____ and _____ of the individual over time.

(b) Child psychology is a _____ of developmental psychology.

(c) Adolescent psychology is also a _____ of developmental psychology.

   Answers: (a) growth; maturation; (b) subset; (c) subset.

Biological Aspects of Development: From Fertilized Egg to Infant

Freud said, "Biology is destiny." Although Freud is usually thought of as a psychologist, not a biologist, his early academic love was the study of biology. He was trained as a biologist before he became a medical doctor. Freud's statement recognizes that, although learning and experience shape behavior, much of our behavior is based on a foundation of genetic givens. For example, if a fertilized egg contains an XX chromosome pattern, the individual will become a female. If the fertilized egg contains an XY pattern, the individual will become a male. The fact that one is a female or a male will be an important determining factor in countless behaviors from birth to death. For a second example, let's say that a fertilized egg contains three chromosomes where normally there is a twenty-first pair of chromosomes. This is a chromosomal anomaly known as **trisomy 21.** The individual will suffer from **Down's syndrome,** a pattern characterized by mental retardation and poor health. Freud's view that biology is destiny has much to recommend it. (A **chromosomal anomaly** is an abnormal chromosome pattern.)

(a) Freud said, "Biology is _____."

(b) If a fertilized egg contains an XX chromosome pattern, the individual will become a _____.

(c) The chromosomal anomaly known as trisomy 21 is associated with what clinical pattern in the individual? _____

Answers: (a) destiny; (b) female; (c) Down's syndrome.

The individual begins when a given sperm and a given ovum unite. Provided by the father, the **sperm,** or more completely **spermatozoon,** is a highly mobile cell with a tail. Provided by the mother, the **ovum** is a single egg cell. Both the sperm and the ovum contain twenty-three single chromosomes. When the egg is fertilized, there will be twenty-three pairs of chromosomes. **Meiosis** is the process that reduces pairs of chromosomes to the individual chromosomes found in either the sperm or the ovum. **Mitosis,** on the other hand, is the process that allows a cell to reproduce itself. This process starts with twenty-three pairs of chromosomes, and all twenty-three pairs are replicated. It is mitosis that makes possible the growth of the individual from one cell, the fertilized egg, to billions of cells.

(a) A more complete name for the sperm is the _____.

(b) Provided by the mother, the _____ is a single egg cell.

(c) Both the sperm and the egg contain twenty-three _____ chromosomes.

(d) What is the process that reduces pairs of chromosomes to individual chromosomes? _____

(e) What is the process that allows a cell to reproduce itself? _____

Answers: (a) spermatozoon; (b) ovum; (c) single; (d) Meiosis; (e) Mitosis.

A **chromosome** is a rodlike structure that contains genes. A chromosome is so named because it is capable of picking up a dye, making the structure visible under a microscope. *Chromo* refers to color, and *soma* refers to body. Thus a chromosome is a "colored body."

A **gene** is the basic unit of heredity. It is made up of strands of **deoxyribonucleic acid (DNA),** a complex organic molecule with the unique ability to replicate itself. It is the genes that do all of the active work associated with hereditary influence. The relationship of a chromosome to a group of genes is similar to the relationship of a ship to its crew. The chromosome is the ship. The genes are the members of the crew.

(a) A rod-like structure containing genes is called what? _____

(b) A gene is the basic unit of _____.

(c) DNA stands for _____.

Answers: (a) A chromosome; (b) heredity; (c) deoxyribonucleic acid.

There are four stages associated with conception and birth: (1) zygote, (2) embryo, (3) fetus, and (4) neonate. When a sperm and an ovum unite to form a fertilized egg, the new being is called a **zygote.** The stage of the zygote lasts for one week. During this stage the zygote develops rapidly from a single cell to a large group of cells. A zygote may be imagined as a ball of cells without differentiation.

From one week to seven weeks, the new being is called an **embryo.** As the cells continue to divide and replicate themselves, some differentiation begins to take place. Three basic embryonic layers emerge: (1) ectoderm, (2) mesoderm, and (3) endoderm. The **ectoderm** is the outer layer of cells, and it will become the sense organs, skin, and nervous system. The **mesoderm** is the middle layer of cells, and it will become the heart, bones, and muscles. The **endoderm** is the internal layer of cells, and it will become the stomach, intestines, and lungs.

(a) When a sperm and an ovum unite to form a fertilized egg the new being is called a _____.

(b) From one week to seven weeks, the new being is called an _____.

(c) The _____ is the outer layer of embryonic cells.

(d) The _____ is the middle layer of embryonic cells.

(e) The _____ is the internal layer of embryonic cells.

     Answers: (a) zygote; (b) embryo; (c) ectoderm; (d) mesoderm; (e) endoderm.

From seven weeks to birth, the new being is called a **fetus.** Fetal development is rich and complex. The cells continue to divide, and they become specialized in their structures and functions. Brain cells (neurons), skin cells, hair cells, fat cells, and many other kinds of cells form. The head, limbs, fingers and toes, and other features of the body appear. In the typical case, the stage of the fetus lasts a little over seven months, making the total time from conception to birth about nine months.

At birth the new being is called a **neonate.** *Neo* means "new." And *nate* means "birth." Thus the word *neonate* simply means "newborn." If the neonate loses weight after birth, then he or she is not referred to as an infant until birth weight has been regained. The word **infant** is from Latin roots meaning "without speech."

(a) From seven weeks to birth, the new being is called a _____.

(b) At birth the new being is called a _____.

(c) The word _____ is from Latin roots meaning "without speech."

     Answers: (a) fetus; (b) neonate; (c) *infant.*

Freud's Theory of Psychosexual Development: From the Oral to the Genital Stage

The infant is on the threshold of continuing biological and psychological development. Our principal concern in this and future sections of this chapter is with psychological development. Freud's theory of development has been highly influential. First proposed about eighty years ago, it has had a large impact on the way in which both psychologists and parents have thought about sexual development in children. It has also influenced child-rearing practices.

According to Freud, there are five stages in psychosexual development. **Psychosexual development** refers to the development of a sexual identity, attitudes toward sexual behavior, and emotional reactions to sexual stimuli. Sexual development, in Freud's view, is much more than biological. Identity, attitudes, and emotional reactions are psychological in nature. That is why Freud used the term *psychosexual* instead of simply *sexual* to refer to the kind of development he wanted to study.

The five stages of psychosexual development are: (1) oral, (2) anal, (3) phallic, (4) latency, and (5) genital. In order to appreciate Freud's theory, it is necessary to introduce a concept he employed called **libido.** Libido is thought of as psychosexual energy, and Freud hypothesized that it is invested in different zones of the body during the various stages of psychosexual development. These zones, or areas, of the body are called the **erogenous zones,** and they are associated with sexual pleasure. The principal erogenous zones are the oral, anal, and genital areas of the body.

(a) The term _____ refers to the development of a sexual identity, attitudes toward sexual behavior, and emotional reactions to sexual stimuli.

(b) Freud thought of _____ as psychosexual energy.

(c) Zones of the body associated with sexual pleasure are called _____ zones.

   Answers: (a) psychosexual development; (b) libido; (c) erogenous.

The **oral stage** lasts for about two years (infancy). During this stage the infant obtains a substantial amount of pleasure from sucking, biting, chewing, and so forth.

The **anal stage** lasts for about one or two years (the stage of the toddler). During the anal stage the toddler obtains a substantial amount of pleasure from, at times, withholding fecal matter and, at other times, expelling it. Note that this stage coincides with the time at which most children are toilet trained.

The **phallic stage** lasts for about three years (the stage of the preschooler). During the phallic stage the preschooler, according to Freud, obtains a substantial amount of pleasure from self-stimulation of the phallus. The *phallus* in the male is the penis. In the female it is the clitoris. The phallic stage ends at about the age of six.

(a) What psychosexual stage is associated with infancy? _____

(b) What psychosexual stage coincides with the time at which most children are toilet trained? _____

(c) In the male, the phallus is the _____. In the female, the phallus is the _____.

   Answers: (a) The oral stage; (b) The anal stage; (c) penis; clitoris.

The **latency stage** lasts for about six years. It begins at age six or seven and ends at age twelve or thirteen. In effect, it ends when puberty begins. The libido has migrated from the oral to the anal to the phallic zone. Now it goes underground and becomes, to surface appearance, dormant. The libido goes underground not because of a lack of biological maturation, but because of psychological conflict. Freud suggested that the child has a certain amount of dawning sexual desire and tends to make the parent of the opposite sex the focus of this desire. However, due to moral development, guilt sets in and the libido goes into hiding. It is repressed to an unconscious level.

The emotional conflict associated with the child's forbidden wish to seek sexual expression with a parent is called the **Oedipus complex.** Freud was inspired to coin this term from his familiarity with the Greek tragedy *Oedipus Rex* (i.e., "Oedipus, the King") written by the dramatist Sophocles around 400 B.C. In the play, Oedipus inadvertently kills his own father and unknowingly marries his own mother. Writing in German in Austria, Freud used the term *Oedipus complex* to refer to either males or females. Later authors, writing in the United States, sometimes use the term *Oedipus complex* to refer to males and **Electra complex** to refer to females. (*Electra* is also a Greek play. Written by the dramatist Euripides, also around 400 B.C., it bears some resemblance to *Oedipus Rex*.)

(a) According to Freud, during the latency stage the libido is repressed to an _____ level.

(b) What name did Freud give to the emotional conflict associated with a child's forbidden sexual wish during the latency stage? _____

(c) What term, not coined by Freud, is sometimes used to describe a female child's sexual conflict during the latency stage? _____

Answers: (a) unconscious; (b) The Oedipus complex; (c) The Electra complex.

The **genital stage** begins at twelve or thirteen and continues throughout adulthood. With puberty, biological maturation can no longer be denied. The repression lifts and the individual becomes intensely conscious of sexual interest. Libido makes a final shift from the phallus to a more general interest in the opposite sex. In normal development, the individual transfers sexual interest away from the parent and toward potential partners who are not members of the family.

Freud's outline suggests that much can go wrong with sexual development. There can be too much excitation and arousal associated with one of the stages. Or, conversely, there can be too much inhibition, punishment, or emotional injury associated with one of the stages. Freud indicated that either too much excitation or too much inhibition can induce a **fixation of libido,** meaning the libido is to some extent "stuck" in one particular erogenous zone. According to Freud, such fixations may play a role in various problems and maladaptive behaviors, including overeating, constipation, pedophilia, exhibitionism, fetishism, and sexual dysfunctions.

Freud's theory is, as are all theories, a set of concepts, not a set of facts. Freud's theory has received its share of criticism. For example, research suggests that although self-stimulation of the phallus is relatively common in children, it is not, as Freud thought, a behavior pattern demonstrated by almost all children. The psychoanalyst Karen Horney, one of Freud's advocates, rejected the biological sexuality of the Oedipus complex. Instead, Horney suggested that, for example, a male child is often jealous of the position of power and importance the father has with the mother. The male child has a forbidden wish to take the father's place, not so much as a sexual rival, but as a psychological one.

(a) During what stage does the libido make a final shift from the phallus to a more general interest in the opposite sex? _____

(b) Freud indicated that either too much excitation or too much inhibition can induce a _____ of libido in one particular _____ zone.

(c) The psychoanalyst Karen Horney rejected Freud's emphasis on the _____ of the Oedipus complex.

Answers: (a) The genital stage; (b) fixation; erogenous zone; (c) biological sexuality.

Erikson's Theory of Psychosocial Development: From Trust to Integrity

Erik Erikson (1902–1994) was personally trained by Freud, and maintained respect for Freud's theory. However, he expanded Freud's concept of psychosexual development to include psychosocial development. **Psychosocial development** refers to the characteristic ways in which the individual learns to respond to other people. The term **social world** is often used to refer to the constellation of other human beings in our environment—parents, siblings, teachers, friends, sweethearts and lovers, husbands and wives, and coworkers. This is the world addressed by Erikson's theory.

According to Erikson, there are eight stages in psychosocial development: (1) trust versus mistrust, (2) autonomy versus shame and guilt, (3) initiative versus guilt, (4) industry versus inferiority, (5) identity versus role confusion, (6) intimacy versus isolation, (7) generativity versus self-absorption, and (8) integrity versus despair.

In each stage the first attribute mentioned is a positive, or desirable, personality trait. The second attribute is a negative, or undesirable, personality trait. Trust, for example, is positive. Mistrust is negative. At each stage of development, the individual is challenged by life to form the positive trait.

(a) The characteristic ways in which the individual learns to respond to other people is associated with what kind of development? _____

(b) The term _____ is often used to refer to the constellation of other human beings in our environment.

(c) In each stage described by Erikson, the first attribute mentioned is a _____, or desirable, personality trait.

   Answers: (a) Psychosocial development; (b) social world; (c) positive.

Trust versus mistrust is associated with infancy (birth to two years old). An infant with a sense of trust tends to thrive and expects good things to happen. Conversely, an infant with a sense of mistrust sometimes displays a failure to thrive syndrome. A lack of interest in the surrounding world and poor health, associated with mistrust, are characteristics of **infantile depression.** Affection, displayed in the form of loving attention, tends to foster the trait of trust. Lack of affection tends to foster the trait of mistrust. These last two statements concerning affection tend to apply to future stages as well. In general, affection and positive reinforcement tend to bring forth the positive traits.

Autonomy versus shame and doubt is associated with toddlerhood (two to three years old). A toddler with a sense of autonomy will be interested in exploring the immediate world and display an interest in novel stimulation. A certain amount of self-direction will emerge. Conversely, a toddler with a sense of shame and doubt will tend to hold back, to seem shy, and to lack self-confidence.

(a) An infant with a sense of _____ tends to thrive and expects good things to happen.

(b) A lack of interest in the surrounding world and poor health are characteristics of

   _____.

(c) A toddler with a sense of _____ and doubt will tend to hold back, to seem shy, and to lack _____.

   Answers: (a) trust; (b) infantile depression; (c) shame; self-confidence.

Initiative versus guilt is associated with the preschool period (three to six years old). A preschooler with a sense of initiative will be likely to start a project and see it through to completion. For example, four-year-old Rosalyn says, "I'm going to color all of the pictures in my coloring book." Conversely, a preschooler with a sense of guilt is hesitant, does not seek challenges, and holds back when an opportunity for self-expression presents itself.

Industry versus inferiority is associated with middle childhood (six to twelve years old). A child with a sense of industry will show an interest in school, study, complete homework, agree to do reasonable chores, and in general display responsible behavior. A child with a sense of inferiority will avoid studying, homework, and chores. The child obtains no satisfaction from these activities, particularly if the child often obtains poor grades or receives too much parental criticism.

(a) A preschooler with a sense of _____ will be likely to start a project and see it through to completion.

(b) A child with a sense of _____ will avoid studying, homework, and chores.

Answers: (a) initiative; (b) inferiority.

Identity versus role confusion is associated with adolescence (twelve to eighteen years old). An adolescent with an identity has a sense of direction in life. He or she already thinks in terms of a particular vocational area, has fairly well-defined plans for the future, and a high level of self-esteem. Although goals are not yet attained, they seem clearly desirable and possible. Conversely, an adolescent suffering from role confusion imagines no particular pathway in life and dreams of no well-shaped future. On the contrary, the future seems obscure and formless.

Intimacy versus isolation is associated with young adulthood. This starts when adolescence is over, usually around the age of eighteen. However, in practice, young adulthood may be deferred for a number of years until an identity has been attained. The present stage and the future stages to be discussed will not be identified with particular years. A young adult with the capacity for intimacy is able to form a close emotional bond with another person, often a marriage partner. Intimacy exists when two people genuinely recognize the importance of each other's thoughts and feelings. Informally, they can "be themselves" with each other, and do not have to put on an act. Conversely, isolation exists when an individual treats another individual like a thing, an object to be manipulated and taken advantage of. The term **I-thou relationship** is sometimes used to characterize intimacy; the term **I-it relationship** is used to characterize isolation.

(a) An adolescent with an _____ has a sense of direction in life.

(b) The term _____ relationship is sometimes used to characterize intimacy.

Answers: (a) identity; (b) I-thou.

Generativity versus self-absorption is associated with adulthood. An adult with the trait of generativity is capable of productive work. Usually he or she will spend many years employed in a vocation or a well-defined social role (e.g., parent). Generativity is linked to giving something of value to the world. The adult with this trait contributes in some way to the welfare of others. Conversely, an adult with the trait of self-absorption is concerned only with his or her own welfare. Taking, not giving, is the theme of the person's life. He or she is, in essence, a sort of parasite.

Integrity versus despair is associated with old age. An older person with the trait of integrity can face approaching death with a certain amount of acceptance. There is relative peace of mind because the individual is convinced that his or her life was spent well, that it had meaning. An older person in a state of despair has a sense of desperation as life draws to its inevitable end. There is very little peace of mind because the individual is thinking that he or she needs a second chance, an opportunity to get life right.

Although the individual has very little control over the first few stages of life, with adolescence and adulthood there is greater self-consciousness. There is a growth in the ability to reflect and think. Consequently, the individual bears some responsibility for the self-fashioning of the later stages.

(a) An adult with the trait of _____ is capable of productive work.

(b) An adult with the trait of _____ is concerned only with his or her own welfare.

(c) An older person with the trait of _____ can face approaching death with a certain amount of acceptance.

Answers: (a) generativity; (b) self-absorption; (c) integrity.

Piaget's Theory of Cognitive Development: From Magical Thinking to Logical Thinking

The section on Erikson's theory concluded with a comment on the ability to reflect and think. Jean Piaget (1896–1980), often recognized as the foremost child psychologist of the twentieth century, made the growth of the child's ability to think his particular domain of investigation.

Piaget, working primarily at Geneva University in Switzerland, began his investigations into the workings of the child's mind because of an interest in epistemology. **Epistemology,** a branch of philosophy, is the study of knowing. Piaget wanted to discover how we come to know what we know. Or, more accurately, he wanted to discover how we come to think we know what we think we know.

The method that Piaget used to study the child's mind is called the phenomenological method. The **phenomenological method** is characterized by asking a child a series of carefully worded questions that direct the child's attention to particular details of the child's immediate world. The child's responses reveal the way in which the he or she thinks about the world. Piaget's investigations suggest that there are four stages of **cognitive development,** the development of the way in which the child thinks. Informally, cognitive development may be thought of as the "growth of the mind."

(a) _____, a branch of philosophy, is the study of knowing.

(b) The _____ method, used by Piaget, is characterized by asking a child a series of carefully worded questions.

(c) _____ development refers to the development of the way in which the child thinks.

Answers: (a) Epistemology; (b) phenomenological; (c) Cognitive.

According to Piaget, there are four stages of cognitive development: (1) the sensorimotor stage, (2) the preoperational stage, (3) the concrete operations stage, and (4) the formal operations stage.

The **sensorimotor stage** is associated with infancy (birth to two years old). During this stage the infant has consciousness, but not self-consciousness. He or she is, of course, aware of the environment. There are reflexes. A stimulus induces a patterned, predictable motor response. This provides a clue to the term *sensorimotor* and why Piaget chose it. The infant senses the world and, without reflection or analysis, acts in response to his or her impressions.

In the older infant there is even a certain amount of intentional behavior. But the infant does not know that he or she exists in the same way that an older child or an adult knows that he or she exists. There is no way to establish these assertions beyond doubt, because a verbal interview with an infant is impossible. However, an infant acts as if self-consciousness is absent. For example, one-year-old James is shown his reflection in a mirror. He is curious, of course, and reaches out to touch the reflection. But he does not seem to know that he is seeing himself. There appears to be no sense of recognition. A postage stamp is lightly stuck to his forehead. He touches it in the mirror, but doesn't peel it off of his forehead. Tested again, when he is a little over two years old, James immediately recognizes that the stamp is on his own forehead, and, using the mirror, peels it off. He has developed self-consciousness, a characteristic not of infancy, but of the next stage.

(a) During the sensorimotor stage the infant senses the world and, without _____ or _____, acts in response to his or her impressions.

(b) During the sensorimotor stage the infant has consciousness, but not _____.

Answers: (a) reflection; analysis; (b) self-consciousness.

The **preoperational stage** is associated with toddlerhood and the preschool age (two to seven years old). The term *preoperational* is used to suggest that during this stage the child has not yet grasped the concept of cause and effect. Instead, the child tends to think in magical terms. **Magical thinking** is characterized by an absence of the recognition of the importance of the laws of nature. Four-year-old Daniel sees no problem when a magician instructs a carpet to fly.

Two additional characteristics of the preoperational stage are anthropomorphic thinking and egocentrism. **Anthropomorphic thinking** is characterized by a tendency to explain natural events in terms of human behavior. Consequently, leaves turn various colors in the fall because Jack Frost paints them. The huffing and puffing of an invisible giant is the cause of a windy day.

Egocentrism is a tendency to perceive oneself as existing at the center of the universe. Everything revolves around the self. Consequently, five-year-old Danielle, when riding in a car at night with her parents, asks, "Why is the Moon following us?" Two days later Danielle falls and scrapes her knee. She believes that her mother can feel the pain. Six-year-old Edward thinks that people in a foreign country on the other side of the world are upside down. He reasons that if the world is round, and we're right side up, then they have to be upside down. If an adult tells Edward that the people are right side up, he will be confused.

(a) The term *preoperational* is used to suggest that during this stage the child has not yet grasped the concept of _____ and _____.

(b) What kind of thinking is characterized by a tendency to explain natural events in terms of human behavior? _____

(c) _____ is a tendency to perceive oneself as existing at the center of the universe.

Answers: (a) cause; effect; (b) Anthropomorphic thinking; (c) Egocentrism.

The **concrete operations stage** is associated with middle childhood (seven to twelve years old). The child at this stage can think in terms of cause and effect. However, most of the thinking is "concrete," meaning that cognitive processes at this stage deal well with what can be seen or otherwise experienced, not with abstractions. For example, eight-year-old Jack can easily understand that $3 + 7 = 10$ because, if necessary, this can be demonstrated with physical objects such as pennies or chips. On the other hand, Jack can't grasp that $x + 8 = 11$ in problem 1, and that $x + 8 = 24$ in problem 2. If Jack is told that x is a variable, and that it can have more than one numerical value in different problems, he will have a hard time appreciating this fact. In brief, Jack can understand arithmetic, but he can't understand algebra.

During the stage of concrete operations, children are usually interested in how clocks work, how measurements are made, and why this causes that to happen. They often like to assemble things. A game such as Monopoly, with its play money, property deeds, and tokens, is attractive.

The **formal operations stage** is associated with adolescence and adulthood. (Adolescence begins at twelve or thirteen years old). The formal operations stage is characterized by the ability to think in abstract terms. The adolescent and adult can understand algebra. Subjects such as philosophy, with its various viewpoints on life, become accessible. Not only thinking, but thinking about thinking is possible. This is called **metathought.** It is what we are doing in this section of the book.

Formal operational thought makes it possible to use both inductive and deductive logic (discussed in chapter 9). The adult can reflect, analyze, and rethink ideas and viewpoints. This kind of thought opens up avenues of mental flexibility not available to children.

Piaget's theory presents a blueprint for cognitive development that captures the spectrum of thinking from its primitive beginning to its most sophisticated level.

(a) Cognitive processes associated with the concrete operations stage deal well with what can be seen or otherwise experienced, not with _____.

(b) A child functioning at the concrete operations stage can understand arithmetic, but will usually have a difficult time understanding _____.

(c) Associated with the formal operations stage, thinking about thinking is called _____.

(d) Formal operational thought makes it possible to use both _____ and _____ logic.

Answers: (a) abstractions; (b) algebra; (c) metathought; (d) inductive; deductive.

Kohlberg's Theory of Moral Development: From a Power Orientation to Living by Principles

Lawrence Kohlberg, a developmental psychologist associated with Harvard University, has drawn from Piaget's theory of cognitive development and applied it to moral development. **Moral development** is the development of the individual's sense of right and wrong. A high level of moral development is built on a foundation of cognitive development. But, of course, more is involved.

Prior to Kohlberg's actual research with subjects, theories of moral development were based largely on speculation. The philosophers Plato and Immanuel Kant believed that the moral sense is inborn, that it is a given of the human mind. On the other hand, the philosophers Aristotle and John Locke assumed that moral development requires learning and experience. Kohlberg's approach tends to favor the learning hypothesis. Human beings acquire a moral sense by learning to think clearly, by the example of role models, and by social reinforcement.

(a) Moral development is the development of the individual's sense of _____ and _____.

(b) The philosophers Plato and Immanuel Kant believed that the moral sense is
_____.

(c) The philosophers Aristotle and John Locke assumed that moral development
requires _____ and _____.

Answers: (a) right; wrong; (b) inborn; (c) learning; experience.

According to Kohlberg, there are three principal levels of moral development: (1) the premoral level, (2) the conventional level, and (3) the principled
level. (There are six stages associated with the three levels, two stages to
each level. The differences between the stages are subtle, and they will not be
specified.)

The **premoral level** is associated with early childhood (from about two to
seven years old). The theme of this level is **power orientation,** meaning that to
a child thinking at this level, "might makes right." The parents are seen as "right"
because they are bigger and stronger than the child. Five-year-old Kenneth is con-
sidering whether or not he should steal a one-dollar bill from his mother's purse.
His hesitation, if there is any, is based on the fear of being caught, not on guilt. He
is **amoral,** meaning that he has no actual moral sense, no internal feeling that he
is wrong to do something that is forbidden.

(a) According to Kohlberg, there are how many principal levels of moral development?

_____

(b) Thinking that "might makes right" is what kind of an orientation to morality?

_____

(c) The word _____ refers to a lack of a moral sense, an absence of an internal feeling of guilt.

Answers: (a) Three; (b) A power orientation; (c) *amoral.*

The **conventional level** is associated with late childhood and adolescence
(seven to eighteen years old). Also, many, probably most, adults continue to operate at the conventional level, never progressing to the principled level. The theme
of the conventional level is "law and order." Right is right because human beings
have codes of conduct and written laws. Fifteen-year-old Sally identifies with her
family. The family has a certain religion, certain attitudes, and well-defined
notions of what is and is not socially acceptable behavior. Sally doesn't question
the family's values. She doesn't examine or challenge them. She is operating at the
conventional level. Thirty-four-year-old Kelvin pays his taxes, has earned an hon-
orable discharge from the army, and thinks of himself as a "good citizen." Kelvin,
like Sally, is operating at the conventional level.

The **principled level** is associated with a relatively small percentage of adults. These are people who think for themselves about what is right and wrong. They are not chaotic in their thought processes. They are logical and clear sighted. In certain cases, they may decide that a law or a group of laws are unjust, and they may rebel. The founding fathers of the United States, men such as George Washington and Thomas Jefferson, fall in this last category. Saints, great leaders, and prophets also fall in the principled category.

It is clear that not all adults outgrow even the first level, the premoral level. Dictators who rule by brute force, who punish in accordance with their personal whims, operate at the premoral level.

(a) The theme of the conventional level of moral development is "_____ and _____."

(b) Saints, great leaders, and prophets are associated with what level of moral development? _____

Answers: (a) law; order; (b) The principled level.

Parental Style: Becoming an Effective Parent

Whether it be psychosexual, psychosocial, cognitive, or moral, development is greatly influenced what parents say and do. The general approach taken toward child rearing by a parent is called **parental style.** Research conducted by developmental psychologists such as Stanley Coopersmith and Diane Baumrind, both affiliated with the University of California, suggests that there are two primary dimensions of parental style. These are: (1) authoritarian-permissive and (2) accepting-rejecting.

The **authoritarian-permissive dimension** consists of bipolar opposites. At the one extreme, parents who manifest an **authoritarian style** are highly controlling, demanding, possessive, and overprotective. At the other extreme, parents who manifest a **permissive style** are easygoing, overly agreeable, detached, and easily manipulated by the child or adolescent. Such parents tend to avoid setting well-defined limits on behavior.

(a) There are how many primary dimensions of parental style? _____

(b) Parents who manifest an _____ style are highly controlling, demanding, possessive, and overprotective.

(c) Parents who manifest a _____ style are easygoing, overly agreeable, detached, and easily manipulated.

Answers: (a) Two; (b) authoritarian; (c) permissive.

The **accepting-rejecting dimension** also consists of bipolar opposites. At the one extreme, parents who manifest an **accepting style** provide the child with **unconditional love,** meaning that love is not withdrawn when a child's behavior is unacceptable. The child is loved for being himself or herself, and affection does not stop just because the parent is sometimes disappointed in something the child has done. There is much confusion about this particular point. Unconditional love does not mean unconditional acceptance of all behavior. It is possible to reject unacceptable behavior without rejecting the whole person.

Parents who manifest a **rejecting style** provide the child with either conditional love or no love at all. **Conditional love** is characterized by providing the tokens of love (e.g., kisses, hugs, and praise) only when they have been earned by certain behaviors such as getting good grades, doing chores, and being polite. A parent who provides no love seldom, if ever, brings forth demonstrations of love in either words or actions. The child acquires the impression that the parent wishes he or she had never been born.

(a) Love that is not withdrawn when a child's behavior is unacceptable is called _____ love.

(b) Parents who manifest a rejecting style provide the child with either _____ love or no love at all.

   Answers: (a) unconditional; (b) conditional.

The two dimensions generate five distinct categories of parental style: (1) authoritarian-accepting, (2) permissive-accepting, (3) authoritarian-rejecting,

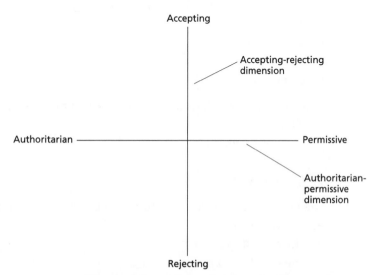

The two dimensions of parental style.

(4) permissive-rejecting, and (5) democratic-accepting. The first four styles are all flawed, and each of them is likely to generate difficulties in the child's adjustment to life. The fifth style is the optimal style. The word **democratic** is used to indicate an optimal midpoint on the authoritarian-permissive dimension. Parents who manifest a democratic style give a child real options. The child is allowed to make choices and important decisions. However, the democratic parent also sets realistic limits. If the child's choices are unacceptable and likely to create eventual problems for the child, then the democratic parent draws a line and is capable of being firm.

Research suggests that a parent who manifests a democratic-accepting style tends to induce optimal social behaviors in the child. This style tends to nurture the intelligence, creativity, emotional adjustment, and self-esteem of the child.

(a) The two dimensions of parental style generate how many distinct categories of parental style? _____

(b) The democratic-accepting style is the _____ parental style.

Answers: (a) Five; (b) optimal.

SELF-TEST

1. The basic unit of heredity is the
   a. chromosome
   b. gene
   c. trisomy 21 pattern
   d. ribonucleic acid (RNA) anomaly

2. From seven weeks to birth, the new being is called
   a. a fetus
   b. an embryo
   c. a zygote
   d. a neonate

3. According to Freud's usage, psychosexual energy is referred to as
   a. libido
   b. erotic ambivalence
   c. metabolism
   d. genital potency

4. The Oedipus complex is associated with what psychosexual stage?
   a. The oral stage
   b. The anal stage
   c. The genital stage
   d. The latency stage

5. A toddler with a particular positive psychosocial trait will be interested in exploring the immediate world and display an interest in novel stimulation. What is this trait?
   a. Autonomy
   b. Identity
   c. Intimacy
   d. Generativity

6. An older person with a particular positive psychosocial trait can face approaching death with a certain amount of acceptance. What is this trait?
   a. Generativity
   b. Isolation
   c. Identity
   d. Integrity

7. What method did Piaget use to study the child's mind?
   a. The experimental method
   b. The survey method
   c. The phenomenological method
   d. The correlational method

8. Magical thinking, anthropomorphic thinking, and egocentrism are associated with what stage of cognitive development?
   a. Trust versus mistrust
   b. The sensorimotor stage
   c. The formal operations stage
   d. The preoperational stage

9. What level of moral development is associated with a law and order orientation?
   a. The premoral level
   b. The preconventional level
   c. The conventional level
   d. The principled level

10. Research suggests that a parent who manifests what style tends to induce optimal social behaviors in the child?
    a. Authoritarian-accepting
    b. Democratic-accepting
    c. Permissive-accepting
    d. Authoritarian-rejecting

ANSWERS TO THE SELF-TEST

1-b   2-a   3-a   4-d   5-a   6-d   7-c   8-d   9-c   10-b

ANSWERS TO THE TRUE-OR-FALSE PREVIEW QUIZ

1. True.
2. True.
3. False. In psychosocial development, the stage of identity versus role confusion is associated with adolescence.
4. False. Cognitive development focuses primarily on the way the child thinks.
5. False. An authoritarian parent tends to be highly controlling, demanding, possessive, and overprotective.

KEY TERMS

accepting style

accepting-rejecting dimension

adolescent psychology

amoral

anal stage

anthropomorphic thinking

authoritarian style

authoritarian-permissive dimension

autonomy versus shame and doubt

child psychology

chromosomal anomaly

chromosome

cognitive development

concrete operations stage

conditional love

conventional level

democratic

deoxyribonucleic acid (DNA)

developmental psychology

Down's syndrome

ectoderm

egocentrism

Electra complex

embryo

endoderm

epistemology

erogenous zones

fetus

fixation of libido

formal operations stage

gene

generativity versus self-absorption

genital stage

I-it relationship

I-thou relationship

identity versus role confusion

industry versus inferiority

infant

infantile depression

initiative versus guilt

integrity versus despair

intimacy versus isolation

latency stage

libido

magical thinking

meiosis

mesoderm

metathought

mitosis

moral development

neonate

Oedipus complex

oral stage

ovum

parental style

permissive style

phallic stage

phenomenological method

power orientation

premoral level

preoperational stage

principled level

psychosexual development

psychosocial development

rejecting style

sensorimotor stage

social world

sperm (or spermatozoon)

trisomy 21

trust versus mistrust

unconditional love

zygote

12 Sex and Love: Are You in the Mood?

PREVIEW QUIZ

True or False

1. T F Some individuals are capable of multiple orgasms.
2. T F Sexual dysfunctions always have a biological basis.
3. T F *Impotence* is a somewhat out-of-date term for male erectile disorder.
4. T F Fetishism refers to sexual contact between a human being and an animal.
5. T F The concept of romantic love is an outgrowth of ancient Greek traditions associated with the teachings of the philosopher Plato.

(Answers can be found on page 189.)

Development, the subject matter of chapter 11, leads the individual to both biological and psychological maturation. And with maturation there arrives an interest in both sex and love. In this chapter we explore many aspects of these important topics.

Objectives

After completing this chapter, you will be able to

- describe the human four-stage sexual response cycle;
- identify the principal female sexual dysfunctions;
- identify the principal male sexual dysfunctions;
- identify dysfunctions that affect either sex;
- specify various kind of sexual variance;
- explain the concepts of intimacy and romantic love.

A popular song of the 1930s was titled "I'm in the Mood for Love." Although seventy years have elapsed since that particular song was a hit, the concept of "being in the mood" is still associated with sex and love. More often than not, it requires a receptive frame of mind as well as a particular attitude in order to be excited by a given partner.

The sexual drive, as we have seen in earlier chapters, has its roots in biological factors. However, it often interacts with romantic love, which is dominated by psychological factors. Together, sex and love play important roles in human behavior. Songwriters are aware of this point. Every other popular song is about either the wonderful aspects of being in love or the sadness associated with the loss of love.

The purpose of this chapter is to explore the psychology of sexual behavior. Unfortunately, although sexual behavior is a natural aspect of behavior in general, there are many ways in which sexual behavior can be both maladaptive and unsatisfying. Even "doing what comes naturally" requires a certain amount of learning and understanding.

(a) The concept of "being in the mood" is still associated with _____ and _____.

(b) Unfortunately, although sexual behavior is a natural aspect of behavior in general, there are many ways in which sexual behavior can be both _____ and _____.

Answers: (a) sex; love; (b) maladaptive; unsatisfying.

The Orgasm: The Peak of Sexual Pleasure

It is generally acknowledged that the orgasm is the peak of sexual pleasure. However, the orgasm itself is a part of a four-stage sexual response cycle. Using physiological recording devices and motion picture cameras, the physician William H. Masters and the psychologist Virginia E. Johnson studied the actual sexual responses of volunteer subjects. Their trailblazing book, *Human Sexual Response,* was published in 1966, and summarizes the results of their investigations. Until the publication of this book and associated articles by the same authors in scientific journals, very little factual information was available concerning the physiological facts associated with the sexual response cycle.

Here are the four stages of the sexual response cycle: (1) excitement, (2) plateau, (3) orgasm, and (4) resolution. **Excitement** is characterized by increases in blood pressure, pulse, and respiration rate. The individual is highly responsive to erotic stimulation. This varies greatly, of course, from person to person, and is largely a matter of individual differences, perception, and sexual preferences. In males, the penis becomes erect. In females, the clitoris swells in size. In general, there is an intensified flow of blood to the genital area.

During the stage of **plateau,** prior increases in physiological activity are maintained at a more or less constant level. In males, the penis becomes somewhat larger. In females, the clitoris retracts a little. The variation in the time associated with the plateau stage is considerable. The stage can last two minutes, twenty minutes, or more. Some of this is under the control of the individual. Plateau can be shortened or increased based on voluntary responses, responses that aim to diminish or amplify the momentary intensity of erotic stimulation.

(a) The first stage of the sexual response cycle is characterized by increases in blood pressure, pulse, and respiration rate. What is this stage called? _____

(b) In the second stage of the sexual response cycle, prior increases in physiological activity are maintained at a more or less constant level. What is this stage called? _____

Answers: (a) Excitement; (b) Plateau.

The **orgasm** is an involuntary response in both sexes. Although it can be induced by sexual behavior, it cannot be directly willed. Brief in duration, it is experienced as intensely pleasurable. Blood pressure and similar measures increase in intensity. In the male, there is an ejaculation accomplished by compressor muscles in the penis. In the female, there are waves of contractions in the **pubococcygeus (PC) muscle,** a muscle surrounding the channel of the vagina.

During the stage of **resolution** the individual becomes temporarily unresponsive to sexual stimulation. Stimulation that had erotic value only a few minutes ago has no capacity to induce excitement. Blood pressure and other physiological measures decline. The duration of the stage of resolution varies from individual to individual. For some individuals in some instances, it may last for only a few minutes. For others, the duration may be twenty minutes, an hour or two, or longer.

(a) The third stage of the sexual response cycle is associated with the peak of sexual pleasure. What is the third stage called? _____

(b) What muscle in the female surrounds the channel of the vagina? _____

(c) During the fourth stage of the sexual response cycle, the individual becomes temporarily unresponsive to sexual stimulation. What is the fourth stage called? _____

Answers: (a) Orgasm; (3) The pubococcygeus (PC) muscle; (3) Resolution.

One of the important findings associated with the Masters and Johnson research is that some individuals are capable of multiple orgasms. **Multiple orgasms** take place when a person has an orgasm, remains excited (or possibly experiences the resolution stage very briefly), and has at least one more orgasm. It is necessary to speak of the sexes separately when discussing multiple orgasms. Women have substantially greater multiorgasmic capacity than do men. Women who have second and even third orgasms report them to be more pleasurable than the first orgasm. It is estimated that about 15 percent of women sometimes have multiple orgasms.

Men who have a second orgasm within a brief span of time report it to be less pleasurable than the first orgasm. Unlike women, very few men will be capable of, or interested in seeking, a third orgasm without a well-defined resolution stage. It is estimated that about 7 percent of men sometimes have multiple orgasms. (In the case of multiple orgasms, the percentage estimates for both sexes are somewhat unreliable. The data are based primarily on the responses of subjects to questionnaires and interviews.)

Returning to the first and second stages, excitement and plateau, it is important to note that when sexual intercourse—without self-imposed delaying tactics—is the primary stimulus used to induce orgasm, the average male takes about two to four minutes to achieve an orgasm. Under similar conditions, the average female takes about ten to twenty minutes. This is an important difference in male and female sexual response, and it provides useful information to couples. In general, it is preferable for the female to attain orgasm before the male.

In the case of masturbation, both males and females can often attain orgasm within two to four minutes.

(a) Which sex has greater multiorgasmic capacity? _____

(b) Men who have a second orgasm within a brief span of time report it to be _____ pleasurable than the first orgasm.

(c) When sexual intercourse is the primary stimulus used to induce an orgasm, which sex usually takes longer to achieve an orgasm? _____

Answers: (a) Women; (b) less; (c) Women.

Female Sexual Dysfunctions: When Sex Is Not Satisfactory

A **sexual dysfunction** exists when the sexual response cycle manifests one of its stages in an abnormal, unsatisfactory manner. The word *dysfunction* means, loosely, "working wrong." The various sexual dysfunctions are characterized by such problems as lack of sexual desire, inability to become sexually excited, inability to attain an orgasm, and other related problems. Either sex can be troubled with a sexual dysfunction.

There are three sexual dysfunctions associated primarily with females: (1) female sexual arousal disorder, (2) female orgasmic disorder, and (3) vaginismus. **Female sexual arousal disorder** exists when the female does not respond to the kind of stimulation that is otherwise expected to induce excitement. An older term for this disorder, now considered to be obsolete, is **frigidity.** The female may herself be either surprised or distressed by the inability of her partner's efforts to bring forth the first stage of the sexual response cycle.

(a) A sexual dysfunction exists when the sexual response cycle manifests one of its stages in an _____, unsatisfactory manner.

(b) What disorder exists when the female does not respond to the kind of stimulation that is otherwise expected to induce excitement? _____

(c) What is an older, obsolete term for the above disorder? _____

Answers: (a) abnormal; (b) Female sexual arousal disorder; (b) Frigidity.

Female orgasmic disorder exists when the female is seldom, or never, able to attain an orgasm during sexual activity. A female suffering from the disorder often experiences a normal level of excitement. This leads to a prolonged plateau period, and then excitement subsides without the satisfaction of an orgasm. The individual feels she was on the verge of an orgasm, but it can't seem to be triggered. Females regularly report the experiences associated with the disorder to be frustrating and disconcerting.

Vaginismus exists when the muscle associated with the vaginal entrance cramps, making entry into the channel both difficult and painful.

The causal factors associated with the female disorders include poor health, chronic fatigue, hormonal imbalances, anxiety, feelings of guilt and shame, disgust with sexual activity, fear of pregnancy, an unresolved Oedipus complex, emotional conflicts, boredom with a particular partner, and hostility toward a particular partner. The factors both overlap and interact. When physicians and therapists treat a sexual disorder, the individual history of a particular patient must be taken into account. There is no one general, sweeping explanation for a particular person's suffering.

(a) What disorder exists when the female is seldom, or never, able to attain an orgasm during sexual activity? _____

(b) What disorder exists when the muscle associated with the vaginal entrance cramps, making entry into the channel both difficult and painful? _____

Answers: (a) Female orgasmic disorder; (b) Vaginismus.

Male Sexual Dysfunctions: Men Can Have Problems Too

From a cultural point of view, there has been a tendency to look upon men as sex machines. But men are not always smooth-running machines. They are not robots. Like women, they too have health problems and emotional conflicts. Consequently, it is possible to identify male sexual dysfunctions. There are three sexual dysfunctions associated primarily with males: (1) male erectile disorder, (2) premature ejaculation, and (3) male orgasmic disorder. **Male erectile disorder** exists when the male is either unable to attain an erection at all or is unable to attain an erection that is sufficient to complete an act of sexual intercourse. An older term for this disorder, now considered to be somewhat out of date, is **impotence,** meaning "lack of power."

(a) What disorder exists when the male is either unable to attain an erection at all or is unable to attain an erection sufficient to complete an act of sexual intercourse? _____

(b) What is an older, somewhat out-of-date term for the above disorder? _____

Answers: (a) Male erectile disorder; (b) Impotence.

Premature ejaculation exists when the span of time between excitement and orgasm is overly brief. There is no precise definition of "overly brief." In general, if a male attains his orgasm before a female is able to attain hers, both the duration and the outcome of sexual intercourse are considered to be unsatisfactory to both participants.

Male orgasmic disorder exists when the male is unable, after both excitement and a sustained period of plateau, to attain an orgasm. This dysfunction is also known as **retarded ejaculation.**

The causal factors listed earlier in connection with female dysfunctions also apply to male sexual dysfunctions.

(Although for convenience of exposition, heterosexual relations were assumed in the above presentation, the dysfunctions also apply to homosexual relations.)

(a) What male dysfunction exists when the span of time between excitement and orgasm is overly brief? _____

(b) Male orgasmic disorder is also known as _____.

Answers: (a) Premature ejaculation; (b) retarded ejaculation.

Dysfunctions Affecting Either Sex: When Desire Is Absent

There are three dysfunctions that affect either sex. These are: (1) hypoactive sexual desire disorder, (2) sexual aversion disorder, and (3) dyspareunia. **Hypoactive sexual desire disorder** exists when the individual's desire for sex is absent. He or she neither fantasizes about sexual relations nor seeks sexual contact as a goal. A term frequently used in psychoanalysis and psychiatry for this condition is **loss of libido.** Psychosexual energy is simply not present. In the vast majority of cases, hypoactive sexual desire disorder is preceded by a sustained period of normal sexual desire.

Sexual aversion disorder exists when the individual finds the thought of sexual relations revolting, disgusting, or nauseating. The individual may think of sexual intercourse as "dirty" or "messy." One woman in psychotherapy told her therapist, "I can't stand the thought of a man slobbering over me." Sexual aversion disorder may be present from early adolescence. Or, in other cases, it may follow a sustained period of normal sexual attraction.

Dyspareunia exists when sexual intercourse is painful. In the case of females, vaginismus, already noted, can be a factor in dyspareunia. In the case of males, thickening of the fibrous connective tissue within the penis, which induces the erect penis to bend at an angle, can be a cause of dyspareunia. In either sex, genital infections, often associated with sexually transmitted diseases, can play a role in dyspareunia.

Again, the set of causal factors already specified in association with specific female and male dysfunctions plays a role in general dysfunctions that affect either sex.

(a) What disorder exists when the individual's desire for sex is absent? _____

(b) What term frequently used in psychoanalysis and psychiatry is associated with absence of sexual desire? _____

(c) What disorder exists when the individual finds the thought of sexual relations revolting, disgusting, or nauseating? _____

(d) What dysfunction exists when sexual intercourse is painful? _____

Answers: (a) Hypoactive sexual desire disorder; (b) Loss of libido; (c) Sexual aversion disorder; (d) Dyspareunia.

Sexual Variance: Of Fetishes and Voyeurism

The term **sexual variance** is used to characterize sexual behaviors that are statistically deviant. This means only that these are behaviors that most people do not engage in. Statistical variance does not necessarily imply **pathology,** meaning sickness. A person who exhibits a form of sexual variance may be emotionally troubled or suffer from a mental disorder, but not necessarily.

The classical term for the behaviors identified in this section is **paraphilias.** This term comes from Greek roots meaning, roughly, "love on the edge" or "love on the borderline." This term is still employed widely in both psychiatry and general psychology. Here are the principal paraphilias, or kinds of sexual variance, that will be identified in this section: (1) bestiality, (2) exhibitionism, (3) fetishism, (4) incest, (5) masochism, (6) pederasty, (7) pedophilia, (8) sadism, (9) sodomy, (10) transsexualism, (11) transvestic fetishism (transvestism), and (12) voyeurism. A discussion of the relationship between homosexual behavior and sexual variance will be included toward the end of the section.

Bestiality refers to sexual contact between a human being and an animal. Another term for this kind of behavior is **zoophilia.** Although about 2 to 3 percent of females and about 6 to 8 percent of males report at least one sexual contact with an animal, overall sexual contact with animals tends to be low—probably less than 1 percent.

(a) The term _____ is used to characterize sexual behaviors that are statistically deviant.

(b) What is the classical term for behaviors that might be called "love on the edge" or "love on the borderline"? _____

(c) Name two terms that refer to sexual contact between a human being and an animal. _____ and _____

Answers: (a) sexual variance; (b) Paraphilias; (c) Bestiality; zoophilia.

Exhibitionism is characterized by sexual excitement associated with the voluntary exposure of one's body, including the genitals. The large majority of exhibitionism is associated with the self-exposure of a male to a female stranger. A common pattern is exhibition with simultaneous masturbation.

Fetishism is characterized by the use of an inanimate object such as a stocking, a pair of underwear, or a shoe as a sexual stimulus. A person who manifests fetishism finds the object capable of inducing sexual excitement. A relatively common practice is to masturbate in association with the object.

Incest refers to sexual relations with a close relative such as a parent or a sibling. The most common form of incest is between siblings. The next most common is father and daughter. The least common is mother and son. Although a sexual relationship between, for example, a stepfather and a stepdaughter does not qualify as biological incest, it may qualify as **psychological incest,** meaning that the emotional aspects of the behavior resemble those associated with incest in general. It is the forbidden aspect of incest that formed the core of Freud's concept of the Oedipus complex (see chapter 11).

(a) What paraphilia is characterized by sexual excitement associated with the voluntary exposure of one's body? _____

(b) _____ is characterized by the use of an inanimate object as a sexual stimulus.

(c) _____ refers to sexual relations with a close relative.

   Answers: (a) Exhibitionism; (b) Fetishism; (c) Incest.

Masochism refers to extracting sexual pleasure from physical or psychological pain. The term *masochism* is derived from the writings of the nineteenth-century Austrian novelist Leopold V. Sacher-Masoch. A person with masochistic tendencies sometimes requires physical pain or insults as a condition for reaching an orgasm. Masochism is somewhat more common in women than in men.

Pederasty refers to homosexual relations between an adult male and a prepubertal male. Sometimes the term us used to refer to male homosexual relations in general; however, this is not correct. Also, pederasty carries the implication that anal intercourse is a component of the sexual behavior. Pederasty is related to pedophilia (see below).

Pedophilia is characterized by the sexual attraction of an adult to a prepubertal child. Although the term can be used to apply to an adult who engages in fantasies containing children, it is more commonly applied to adults who act upon their desires. An adult who manifests pedophilia is sometimes referred to as a **pedophile.** The novel *Lolita* by Vladimir Nabokov takes pedophilia as its core element.

(a) Masochism refers to extracting sexual pleasure from physical or psychological _____.

(b) _____ refers to homosexual relations between an adult male and a prepubertal male.

(c) _____ is characterized by the sexual attraction of an adult to a prepubertal child.

   Answers: (a) pain; (b) Pederasty; (c) Pedophilia.

Sadism refers to inflicting psychological or physical pain on another person in association with sexual gratification. The term *sadism* is derived from the literary works of the eighteenth-century author Donatien Alphonse François, the Marquis de Sade. He described sexual relations that included general abuse of a partner, including insults, chaining, and whippings. It should be noted that a sexual relationship can be **sado-masochistic,** meaning that one partner manifests primarily sadistic tendencies and the other partner manifests primarily masochistic tendencies. Such a relationship is often relatively stable because each partner meets the other one's needs.

Sodomy refers to sexual practices thought by a given society or culture to be in violation of natural behavior patterns. The term comes from the biblical city Sodom, a community that was removed from the face of the Earth because of the wickedness of its inhabitants. In practice, the term *sodomy* is usually used to refer to the practice of anal intercourse. Less frequently, sodomy is used to make a reference to bestiality.

Transsexualism is characterized by a strong desire to become a person of the opposite sex. The individual is unhappy with his or her own biological gender, and often fantasizes about the emotional and sexual gratification that would be obtainable if only it were possible to experience a transformation of body and self. The American Psychiatric Association's diagnostic manual (see chapter 14) classifies transsexualism as a gender identity disorder. The term **gender identity disorder** refers to a state of dissatisfaction with one's own biological gender, and, consequently, has approximately the same meaning as transsexualism. The word *disorder* carries the somewhat stronger implication of mental or emotional pathology, because depression and suicidal tendencies are sometimes linked to a gender identity conflict. Transsexualism is relatively rare. It appears with somewhat greater frequency in males than in females. Treatment consists of psychotherapy and, more infrequently, sex reassignment surgery.

(a) _____ refers to inflicting psychological or physical pain on another person in association with sexual gratification.

(b) _____ refers to sexual practices thought by a given society or culture to be in violation of natural behavior patterns.

(c) _____ is characterized by a strong desire to become a person of the opposite sex.

Answers: (a) Sadism; (b) Sodomy; (c) Transsexualism.

Transvestic fetishism (transvestism) is characterized by dressing in the clothing of the opposite sex (i.e., cross-dressing). (The root "vest" refers to clothing.) A person who manifests transvestic fetishism finds cross-dressing to be sexually exciting. This kind of fetishism should not be confused with transsexualism. Transvestic fetishism usually has a heterosexual orientation, and the individual who practices it does not have a desire to become a member of the opposite sex.

Voyeurism is characterized by using a visual stimulus as a primary way to induce sexual excitement. Examples of visual stimuli include a photograph, a videotape, or an actual person. A common practice is to masturbate in association with the stimulus. If a partner is present, masturbation may take the place of sexual intercourse. A certain amount of gratification in connection with looking is standard sexual practice. However, if an individual usually prefers visual stimulation over physical contact, then the individual is manifesting voyeurism. Secret viewing is frequently a component of voyeurism.

A number of factors enter into explanations of the various kinds of sexual variance. These include the kind of biological and psychosocial factors earlier identified in connection with the sexual dysfunctions. There is no one general explanation for a particular individual's sexual variance. A general factor, or a set of general factors, has to be combined with the person's particular learning history. Individual differences in behavior are just that, *individual*.

(a) _____ is characterized by dressing in the clothing of the opposite sex.

(b) _____ is characterized by using a visual stimulus as a primary way to induce sexual excitement.

   Answers: (a) Transvestic fetishism (transvestism); (b) Voyeurism.

Homosexual behavior is no longer listed as a kind of sexual variance or paraphilia. In older editions of the American Psychiatric Association's diagnostic manual, it was listed. In the current manual, it is not.

Homosexual behavior is characterized by sexual relations with a member of the same sex. The term can be applied to both male and female behavior. However, **lesbianism** refers exclusively to female homosexual behavior. (The term is derived from Lesbos, a Greek island. It is legend that in the sixth century B.C. the writer Sappho and her followers, residents of the island, practiced homosexual behavior.)

Conservative estimates suggest that about 4 percent of males and about 2 percent of females are exclusively homosexual. A much larger percentage have had an occasional homosexual experience.

(a) _____ behavior is characterized by sexual relations with a member of the same sex.

(b) _____ refers exclusively to female homosexual behavior.

   Answers: (a) Homosexual; (b) Lesbianism.

Intimacy: What Is This Thing Called Love?

As indicated in chapter 11, intimacy is a psychosocial stage. It refers to emotional closeness between partners, an I-thou relationship in contrast to an I-it relationship. It is generally believed that in order to have intimacy in a marriage a prerequisite is to be in love with one's partner. Consequently, an examination of the concept of romantic love, and ideas related to it, will shed a certain amount of light on sexual behavior in a long-term relationship.

Unlike many of the world's cultures, our culture links sexual behavior, particularly within the institution of marriage, to romantic love. **Romantic love** is a mental and emotional state characterized by moments of joy and the idealization of one's partner. In her book *Love and Limerence,* the psychologist Dorothy Tennov uses the term **limerence** to identify the distinctive pattern of thoughts and emotions associated with being in love. These include daydreaming about the beloved one, the desire to have love returned, and the wish to spend a lot of time in the other person's presence. We use phrases such as "falling in love" to suggest that the state of being in love is somewhat involuntary.

The concept of romantic love is an outgrowth of the Middle Ages tradition of chivalry, a set of ideas and customs associated with knighthood. The knight was expected to pay **courtly love** to a noblewoman. This involved writing poems and jousting in tournaments with the fair lady's handkerchief tied to a lance. The lady was often unattainable, and sexual desire was unrequited. The present-day concept of courting a woman is obviously derived from the days when knighthood was in flower.

(a) Romantic love is a mental and emotional state characterized by moments of _____ and the _____ of one's partner.

(b) What term does the psychologist Dorothy Tennov use to identify the distinctive pattern of thoughts and emotions associated with being in love? _____

(c) The concept of romantic love is an outgrowth of the Middle Ages tradition of _____.

Answers: (a) joy; idealization; (b) Limerence; (b) chivalry.

It is only in relatively recent centuries, and primarily in the Western world, that the concept of romantic love has been tied to actual marriage. The problem is that romantic love has a certain tendency to fade after a marriage settles down and children become members of the family. True, there may be romantic moments, but one cannot expect a steady state of limerence to endure day after day for years. Romantic love is replaced with **conjugal love,** a state of deep affection, mutual respect, and shared responsibilities. The partner is loved and there is intimacy. And it is necessary to be more or less satisfied with conjugal love if one is to have a stable marriage. If there is a demand for romantic love, then this may play a role in a desire to have an affair or seek a divorce.

An increased understanding of the above point can be attained by referring to the idealization-frustration-demoralization syndrome. The syndrome was first identified about fifty years ago by the communication specialist Wendell Johnson in his book *People in Quandaries*. The **idealization-frustration-demoralization (IFD) syndrome** is a common interpersonal pattern, often destructive to marriages. The first stage, *idealization*, is characterized by a tendency to project on the partner, or potential partner, special attributes such as unusually good looks, great intelligence, outstanding creative ability, and so forth. She is a sort of Cinderella; he is a sort of Prince Charming. The stage of idealization is clearly linked to romantic love.

(a) In a stable marriage, romantic love is replaced with _____ love.

(b) What is the name of the IFD syndrome stage characterized by a tendency to project on the partner, or potential partner, special attributes? _____

Answers: (a) conjugal love; (b) Idealization.

The second stage of the IFD syndrome, *frustration*, emerges when the unrealistic expectations set up by the first stage cannot be met. One person lets the other one down in both big and small ways. Little by little illusions fall away and the partner is seen clearly, psychological warts and all.

The third stage, *demoralization*, is characterized by the conviction that the relationship is hopeless, that even valiant efforts to improve the relationship are doomed to failure. It is at this point that one member of a couple may seek an affair, a separation, or a divorce.

Johnson's basic message is clear. People should enter relationships with their eyes wide open. They should avoid idealization and an excessive attachment to the concept of romantic love. Granted, given our culture, a certain amount of romance is appropriate. However, idealization with its unrealistic expectations sets up the members of a couple for a fall.

(a) What is the name of the IFD syndrome stage that emerges when the unrealistic expectations set up by the first stage cannot be met? _____

(b) What is the name of the IFD syndrome stage characterized by the conviction that the relationship is hopeless? _____

Answers: (a) Frustration; (b) Demoralization.

The psychologist John Gottman has conducted a substantial amount of research into the interpersonal patterns associated with marriage. He has discovered four behavioral tendencies that tend to undermine the stability of a marriage, and he calls these the "Four Horsemen of the Apocalypse." The first horseman is **criticism.** The worst kind of criticism of a partner involves hostile remarks about the other person's personality. Statements such as "You're lazy," "You're inconsiderate," "You're dumb," "You're wasteful," and so forth sting and injure the target person's self-esteem. Instead, a criticism should be specific about a behavior. Instead of saying "You're lazy," a partner can say "You didn't throw out the trash" or "You haven't mowed the lawn."

Contempt exists when a partner is treated with little or no respect. If one person offers a thought or idea, the other one laughs at it or does not take it seriously. Sometimes scorn is conveyed in a nonverbal manner with a sneer or by turning one's eyes upward.

Defensiveness involves not accepting the value or correctness of a partner's complaints. The defensive partner can see no right in what the other person has said. Instead, extensive rationalizations are produced. These are designed to show that failures and lack of responsible behavior should be tolerated. An overly defensive partner cannot seem to simply say, when appropriate, "You're right. I was wrong. I made a mistake."

Withdrawal refers to emotional withdrawal. A partner manifesting withdrawal refuses to communicate in a meaningful fashion. He or she retreats into emotional isolation, placing a kind of psychological shell, an invisible barrier, around the self. A partner who is reaching out, who is trying to make contact, feels barred from entry into the other person's personal world.

Research suggests that individuals who make a conscious effort to avoid the four horsemen can improve both the quality and stability of a long-term relationship.

Intimacy is nurtured by understanding the concepts presented in this section. And, in turn, intimacy itself nurtures the positive aspects of a sexual relationship.

(a) Gottman identified four behavioral tendencies that tend to undermine the stability of a marriage. Name the tendency that exists when a partner is treated with little or no respect. _____

(b) Name the tendency identified by Gottman that exists when a partner retreats into emotional isolation. _____

Answers: (a) Contempt; (b) Withdrawal.

SELF-TEST

1. Which of the following is *not* a stage of the four-stage sexual response cycle?
   a. Excitement
   b. Plateau
   c. Orgasm
   d. Homeostasis

2. Which of the following is a correct statement?
   a. Women have substantially greater multi-orgasmic capacity than do men.
   b. Men have substantially greater multi-orgasmic capacity than do women.
   c. Neither sex is capable of multiple orgasms.
   d. Freud proved that the concept of multiple orgasms is a myth.

3. What dysfunction exists when the female does not respond to the kind of stimulation that is otherwise expected to induce excitement?
   a. Female orgasmic disorder
   b. Vaginismus
   c. Female sexual arousal disorder
   d. Sexual aversion disorder

4. What disorder exists when the female is seldom, or never, able to attain an orgasm during sexual activity?
   a. Inhibited orgasmic disorder
   b. Frigidity
   c. Female orgasmic disorder
   d. Dysfunctional orgasmic excitation

5. The older term *impotence* is associated with what disorder?
   a. Premature ejaculation
   b. Male erectile disorder
   c. Male orgasmic disorder
   d. Male resolution disorder

6. Male orgasmic disorder is also known as
   a. excitement disorder
   b. facilitated orgasmic response
   c. transvestic inhibition
   d. retarded ejaculation

7. What paraphilia is characterized by the use of an inanimate object such as a stocking or a shoe as a sexual stimulus?
   a. Fetishism
   b. Pedophilia
   c. Sadism
   d. Masochism

8. What paraphilia refers to extracting sexual pleasure from physical pain?
   a. Pederasty
   b. Masochism
   c. Pedophilia
   d. Transvestism

9. What term refers exclusively to female homosexual behavior?
   a. Gender identity disorder
   b. Transsexualism
   c. Lesbianism
   d. XX-oriented fetishism

10. What term does the psychologist Dorothy Tennov use to identify the distinctive pattern of thoughts and emotions associated with being in love?
   a. Conjugal love
   b. Limerence
   c. Idealization
   d. Transcendental ecstasy

ANSWERS TO THE SELF-TEST

1-d   2-a   3-c   4-c   5-b   6-d   7-a   8-b   9-c   10-b

ANSWERS TO THE TRUE-OR-FALSE PREVIEW QUIZ

1. True.
2. False. A sexual dysfunction *may* have a primarily biological basis or a primarily psychological basis.
3. True.
4. False. Fetishism is characterized by the use of an inanimate object as a sexual stimulus.
5. False. The concept of romantic love is an outgrowth of the Middle Ages tradition of chivalry.

KEY TERMS

bestiality

conjugal love

contempt

courtly love

criticism

defensiveness

dyspareunia

excitement

exhibitionism

female orgasmic disorder

female sexual arousal disorder

fetishism

Four Horsemen of the Apocalypse

frigidity

gender identity disorder

homosexual behavior

hypoactive sexual desire disorder

idealization-frustration-demoralization (IFD) syndrome

impotence

incest

lesbianism

limerence

loss of libido

male erectile disorder

male orgasmic disorder

masochism

multiple orgasms

orgasm

paraphilias

pathology

pederasty

pedophile

pedophilia

plateau

premature ejaculation

psychological incest

pubococcygeus (PC) muscle

resolution

retarded ejaculation

romantic love

sadism

sado-masochistic

sexual aversion disorder

sexual dysfunction

sexual variance

sodomy

transsexualism

transvestic fetishism (transvestism)

vaginismus

voyeurism

withdrawal

zoophilia

13 Personality: Psychological Factors That Make You an Individual

True or False

1. T F   Only you have your particular personality.
2. T F   Extraverts tend to be outgoing and friendly.
3. T F   According to Freud, there are four parts to the human personality: (1) the id, (2) the ego, (3) the superego, and (4) the collective unconscious.
4. T F   An inferiority complex is a group of highly realistic ideas about the self.
5. T F   The Rorschach test consists of ten inkblots.

(Answers can be found on page 210.)

Chapter 12 presented important aspects of sexual behavior. Sex plays a role in human identity and is an important part of any individual's personality. However, the human personality encompasses much more than sexual behavior. This chapter explores some of the important traits and processes that help us to describe and understand the human personality.

Objectives

After completing this chapter, you will be able to

- define personality;

- describe several type-trait theories;

- explain key aspects of Freud's theory of personality;

- explain key aspects of neo-Freudian theories of personality;

- specify how operant conditioning and observational learning affect the shaping of the personality;

- understand the role that consciousness plays in the self-shaping of the personality;

- describe three important personality tests.

How Does Your Personality Affect Your Behavior?

Your personality plays a role in almost everything that you do. If you are familiar with someone's personality, you can often predict how he or she will be likely to act in a particular situation. If, for example, you think of Alex as studious, then you will automatically predict that he will prepare conscientiously for his upcoming final examination in a college course.

A workable definition of **personality** is that it is the constellation of traits unique to the individual. Your personality is like a psychological fingerprint. Only you have your particular personality.

The word **trait,** as used above, refers to your relatively stable behavioral dispositions. However, your personality is somewhat more than your traits. Your personality also consists of the **ego,** the conscious "I" at the center of the personality. Also, your personality contains the **self,** the personality as viewed from within, as you yourself experience it. These points will be elaborated in later sections.

Although physical appearance can be a basis for interpersonal attraction, it is also true that one person will often want to get to know another person because of that person's personality. Like another's face or figure, we often find another's personality appealing or unappealing. Relationships, including marriages, often stand or fall on the basis of the way in which two people react to each other's personalities. These are some of the reasons why psychologists believe that the study of personality is important.

(a) A workable definition of personality is that it is the constellation of _____ unique to the individual.

(b) The _____ is the conscious "I" at the center of your personality.

Answers: (a) traits; (b) ego.

Your Traits: Are You Introverted or Extroverted?

The philosopher Aristotle was thought to have wisdom. The conqueror Attila the Hun is remembered for his aggressiveness. The physicist Marie Curie was recognized to be unusually persistent. In Charles Dickens's *A Christmas Carol,* the character Scrooge is known for being stingy. In Margaret Mitchell's *Gone With the Wind,* Scarlett O'Hara is admired for her courage.

Wisdom, aggressiveness, persistence, stinginess, and courage are all traits of personality. In psychology, **type-trait theories** are attempts to provide consistent descriptions of personality. Psychologists presenting these theories, theories based on observations and personality tests, are somewhat like mapmakers. Mapmakers may or may not understand the geological processes that create islands, continents, and mountains, but they try to present an accurate picture of what they find. Similarly, type-trait theorists may or may not comprehend the underlying processes that account for a trait or a set of traits, but they try to present an accurate picture of what they discover.

_____ theories are attempts to provide consistent descriptions of personality.

Answer: Type-trait.

A very early type-trait theory was the one presented by Hippocrates, who was often identified as the father of medicine, about 400 B.C. According to Hippocrates, there are four personality types: (1) sanguine, (2) choleric, (3) melancholic, and (4) phlegmatic. The dominant trait of a **sanguine** personality is optimism. The dominant trait of a **choleric** personality is irritability. The dominant trait of a **melancholic** personality is depression. The dominant trait of a **phlegmatic** personality is sluggishness.

Hippocrates believed that one's personality is influenced by the balance of humors in the body. In physiology, the word **humor** refers to any functioning fluid of the body. Hippocrates asserted that a person with a sanguine personality has a lot of the humor *blood.* A person with a choleric personality has a lot of the humor *yellow bile.* A person with a melancholic personality has a lot of the humor *black bile.* A person with a phlegmatic personality has a lot of the humor *phlegm.*

Hippocrates's humor theory of personality is not taken seriously today. However, he is credited for being a fairly astute observer of human behavior. The four types, if not entirely accurate, do have some interest and value. Present-day usage such as "being in a good humor" can be traced back to the thinking of Hippocrates.

(a) According to Hippocrates, what humor, or body fluid, is associated with the sangine personality? _____

(b) According to Hippocrates, what humor, or body fluid, is associated with the melancholic personality? _____

Answers: (a) Blood; (b) Black bile.

Another classical personality theory, one that bears some resemblance to Hippocrates's theory, was proposed about sixty years ago by the physiologist William H. Sheldon. Sheldon suggested that there are three basic body types: (1) endomorph, (2) mesomorph, and (3) ectomorph. The body types are innately determined during the stage of the embryo. The adult's body is shaped by varying amounts of endoderm, mesoderm, and ectoderm (see chapter 11). An **endomorph** tends to have a soft, flabby body. The endomorph will tend to be placid and lazy and to seek fun for fun's sake. A **mesomorph** tends to have a firm, muscular body. The mesomorph will tend to be assertive and ambitious and to seek action for action's sake. An **ectomorph** tends to have a thin, frail body. The ectomorph will tend to be shy, tense, and nervous.

Sheldon recognized that many, perhaps most, people are not pure types. Consequently, in his research he rated subjects on the three dimensions of the body and assigned them a somatotype. The **somatotype** is a profile that reflects an individual's particular pattern of body tissue. Although Sheldon collected quite a bit of data to support his approach to the study of personality, research by others has provided only weak support for his viewpoint.

(a) According to Sheldon, what body type tends to be thin and frail? _____

(b) According to Sheldon, what body type goes with such traits as placid and lazy?

_____

(c) The _____ is a profile that reflects an individual particular pattern of body tissue.

Answers: (a) The ectomorph; (b) The endomorph; (c) somatotype.

One of the most famous type-trait theories of personality is the one proposed in the early part of the twentieth century by the Swiss psychiatrist Carl Jung, one of Freud's early associates. Jung said that two basic personality types are the introvert and the extrovert. The **introvert** favors behaviors such as thinking, reading, reflecting, meditating, creative writing, remembering, composing music, day-dreaming, and spending time alone. These behaviors are associated with a general trait called introversion. As Jung explained it, *introversion* is characterized by a flow of libido toward the inner world. (Jung used the term *libido* to mean psychological energy.)

The **extravert** (also, **extrovert**) favors behaviors such as talking, going to motion pictures, taking trips, seeking financial success, exploration, being physically active, and spending time with a fairly large circle of friends. These behaviors are associated with a general trait called extraversion. *Extraversion* is characterized by a flow of libido toward the outer world.

Jung recognized that introverts and extraverts reflect a **bipolar trait,** a trait that exists on a continuum with logical opposites. The trait, correctly named, is **introversion–extraversion.**

A given person is not necessarily a pure type. The **ambivert** is an individual who displays a mixture of both introverted and extraverted behaviors.

Jung believed that the tendency to be an introvert or an extravert is primarily inborn, a part of one's biologically determined disposition. Jung himself was an introvert. This is reflected in the title of his autobiography, *Memories, Dreams, and Reflections.* By Jung's own admission, the inner life was more important to him than the outer life.

(a) According to Jung, the _____ favors behaviors such as thinking, reading, meditating, and daydreaming.

(b) Jung recognized that introverts and extraverts reflect a _____ trait, a trait that exists on a continuum with logical opposites.

(c) An _____ is an individual who displays a mixture of both introverted and extraverted behaviors.

Answers: (a) introvert; (b) bipolar; (c) ambivert.

A well-regarded, contemporary type-trait theory is the researcher Raymond B. Cattell's **sixteen personality factor theory.** Based on his statistical analysis of various personality tests, Cattell concluded that there are sixteen **factors,** or clusters of related bipolar traits, that describe the human personality. One of the bipolar traits, or factors, is **reserved–outgoing,** which corresponds closely to Jung's introversion-extraversion trait.

A second bipolar trait is **affected by feelings–emotionally stable.** A person manifesting the first extreme of the trait will tend to be deeply hurt by a criticism, become depressed easily, and experience emotional states vividly. A person manifesting the opposite extreme of the trait will seldom experience prolonged states of anger, anxiety, or depression. To such a person, life is lived in a relatively placid manner.

A third bipolar trait is **humble–assertive.** A person manifesting the first extreme of the trait will tend to be passive, easily controlled by others, and lack self-confidence in social relationships. A person manifesting the opposite extreme of the trait will tend to be a leader, influence others, and have quite a bit of self-confidence in social relationships. Cattell's map of the human personality continues in this manner until, as already indicated, sixteen bipolar traits are identified.

(a) According to Cattell's research, how many factors describe the human personality?
_____

(b) A person tends to be deeply hurt by a criticism and becomes depressed easily. Another person tends to seldom experience prolonged states of anxiety or depression. What bipolar trait is associated with these two extremes? _____

Answers: (a) Sixteen; (b) Affected by feelings–emotionally stable.

Freud's Theory: The Three Faces of You

As earlier noted, type-trait theories are of interest primarily because of their descriptive powers, not because of the explanations they offer for the existence of personality traits. On the other hand, Freud's theory of personality is of interest primarily because it focuses on the processes involved in the expression and shaping of the human personality. Freud's theory, proposed in the early part of the twentieth century, has been highly influential, particularly among psychotherapists.

According to Freud, there are three parts to the human personality: (1) the id, (2) the ego, and (3) the superego. The **id** is inborn, and it is present at birth. It is the psychological expression of the biological drives such as hunger, thirst, the need for sleep, and so forth. The word *id* is derived from Latin, and means simply "it." In other words, the "it" of the human personality is not uniquely individual. It is impersonal and roughly similar in all of us. The id is present in the infant, and Freud said it follows the **pleasure principle,** indicating that the id seeks relief from hunger, thirst, and other irritating states. Although the id is present at birth, it never departs. It is as much a part of the adult personality as the personality of the child.

The **ego** emerges with experience. It arises because of various frustrations and the need to cope with the world as it is, not as it is wished to be. The word *ego* is also derived from Latin, and means simply "I." The ego, or the "I" of the personality, follows the **reality principle,** suggesting that the ego helps the individual tolerate frustration and devise ways around obstacles to gratification. The ego takes form around the age of two or three. Like the id, it too will become a part of the adult personality.

(a) According to Freud, what part of the personality is inborn and present at birth?

_____

(b) The ego helps the individual tolerate frustration. The ego follows what principle?

_____

Answers: (a) The id; (b) The reality principle.

The **superego** emerges last. It reflects the influence of the family. The family is usually the agent that represents the values and norms of a larger culture to a growing child. This includes the family's religious beliefs and its participation in the rules and laws of a given nation. If a child identifies with the family, the superego will be **introjected,** meaning that it will become an integral part of the individual's personality.

Feelings of guilt arise when the demands of the superego are violated. This makes a reference to the **conscience,** one of the aspects of the superego. The conscience acts as a kind of inner police officer, guiding the individual in the direction of conforming to social expectations. The superego is relatively well established around the age of seven. Like the id and the ego, it is also a part of the adult personality.

Another aspect of the superego is the **ego ideal,** an image that sets forth what one should do with one's life in terms of a vocation, family responsibilities, and long-term goals. The ego ideal, being a part of the superego, reflects the wishes of the parents. It should be noted that Freud's concept of the ego ideal is not the same as Maslow's concept of self-actualization. When one actualizes the ego ideal, one becomes what the parents wish for. When one actualizes the self, one becomes what one was meant to be. Of course, these two goals are not necessarily in conflict. But sometimes they are.

(a) If a child identifies with the family, the superego will be _____.

(b) What aspect of the superego reflects the wishes of the parents and is associated with long-term goals? _____

Answers: (a) introjected; (b) The ego ideal.

Of particular importance in Freud's personality theory is the concept of ego defense mechanisms. **Ego defense mechanisms** are involuntary mental acts designed to protect the ego from the "slings and arrows of outrageous fortune." In other words, they act as shields, protecting us from some of the emotional pain and damage that can arise from coping with life. In view of the fact that it is necessary to have a strong, functional ego in order to deal with reality, it is understandable that the ego tends to develop a protective system.

Seven of the ego defense mechanisms are (1) denial of reality, (2) repression, (3) projection, (4) identification, (5) fantasy, (6) rationalization, and (7) reaction formation. **Denial of reality** takes place when the individual thinks, "This isn't

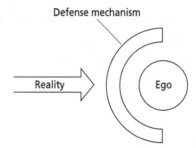

An ego defense mechanism acts like a shield.

so. This can't be happening." Examples include refusing to believe that the car is out of gas, that one has a serious illness, or that a cherished dream will never come true. Denial is a primitive mechanism, often used by toddlers and preschoolers. Four-year-old Oscar is told the family can't go on a picnic because it is raining. He looks out the window and says, "It's going to stop pretty soon." The observation may be made without any objective evidence that the sky is clearing.

Repression takes place when the ego pushes down unpleasant features of one's psychological world to an unconscious level. These typically consist of painful childhood memories and forbidden wishes associated with sexual and aggressive behavior. It is repression that defines the contents of the mind's unconscious domain (see chapter 1).

(a) Involuntary mental acts protecting us from some of the emotional pain and damage than can arise from coping with life are called _____.

(b) What mental process is involved when the ego pushes down unpleasant features of one's psychological world to an unconscious level? _____

Answers: (a) ego defense mechanisms; (b) Repression.

Projection takes place when the ego perceives in the outer world what is actually the reflection of the contents of the unconscious domain. For example, Edith has a substantial amount of repressed hostility toward others. Polite and highly moral, she is unable to acknowledge her aggressive impulses. Instead, she believes that others take advantage of her and that they have designed little plots against her.

Identification takes place when the ego attaches itself to a person perceived to have a desirable attribute such as power, status, or unusual ability. For example, forty-seven-year-old Percy is an English teacher in a high school. His ambition is to write and sell science-fiction novels. He has read and reread the autobiography of the famous science-fiction author Isaac Asimov, *In Memory Yet Green*. Percy draws inspiration from Asimov's life, and derives an impression that he himself is talented as a creative writer when he mentally associates himself with Asimov.

Fantasy takes place when the ego imagines successes or accomplishments that are not presently obtainable in actual day-to-day living. For example, nineteen-year-old Faith has a crush on a male coworker. She sometimes daydreams that she is his bride or that they are on a honeymoon cruise. The kind of emotional gratification associated with fantasy is called **vicarious gratification,** meaning substitute gratification.

Rationalization takes place when the ego provides a rational-sounding reason for a failure or a transgression. Diana receives an F on an algebra test. She rationalizes by thinking, "The questions were unfair. And the teacher didn't give us enough time to study." Grant is on a diet, and eats a candy bar one afternoon. He rationalizes by thinking, "I was feeling faint. My blood sugar must have been low. I needed something to keep going." A rationalization may have little or no basis in reality, and not be rational at all. However, its superficial logic is a balm to the threatened ego.

Reaction formation is characterized by converting a repressed wish into its psychological opposite at the conscious level. Prudence has a history of abusing food. Now on strict diet, she counts every calorie and seems to be afraid to eat. She has put herself temporarily into a kind of psychological prison in order to contain her desire to overeat. The desire is not gone. It is has been banished to an unconscious level. The reaction formation helps her to block off her forbidden impulse. Another example of reaction formation is associated with Conrad in chapter 7. Conrad is hostile toward his wife's sister. The hostility, a reaction formation, helps him to repress a forbidden sexual wish.

The defense mechanisms overlap to some extent. For example, identification, as explained above, contains elements of fantasy.

(a) _____ takes place when the ego attaches itself to a person perceived to have some particularly desirable attribute.

(b) The kind of emotional gratification associated with fantasy is called _____.

(c) _____ takes place when the ego provides a rational sounding reason for a failure or transgression.

Answers: (a) Identification; (b) vicarious gratification; (c) Rationalization.

Other Psychodynamic Theories: Is There a Collective Unconscious Mind?

Freud's general approach to the study of personality is said to be psychodynamic. A **psychodynamic theory** assumes that the personality is a field of forces that are sometimes in opposition. For example, the energy of the id is often opposed to the energy of the superego. The id may say, "Go. Do it!" The superego may say,

"Don't. That's not right." Also, as already indicated, the ego defense mechanism called repression populates the unconscious domain with forbidden wishes.

Freud's theory of personality is sweeping and addresses a broad spectrum of behavior. It was the first relatively modern theory of personality, and has had a great influence on most of the important theories generated during the twentieth century. **Neo-Freudians** are theorists who think along the lines of Freud's general tradition (*neo* means "new"). However, they may take issue with specific aspects of Freud's theory. Three eminent neo-Freudians identified in the next section are Carl Jung, Alfred Adler, and Karen Horney.

(a) A _____ theory assumes that the personality is a field of forces.

(b) Theorists who think along the lines of Freud's general tradition are called _____.

Answers: (a) psychodynamic; (b) neo-Freudians.

Carl Jung (1875–1961) was referred to in the context of type-trait theories. He was the one who proposed the introversion-extraversion dimension of personality. Jung was a Swiss psychiatrist, and in the early years of psychoanalysis was one of Freud's close associates. Jung agreed with Freud's concept of an unconscious domain, but asserted that Freud's way of looking at the unconscious aspects of the personality was limited. Jung theorized that there is a deeper unconscious layer than the one that Freud envisioned. Jung called this deeper layer the **collective unconscious.** According to Jung, the collective unconscious consists of the human race's stored experiences over the centuries. He called these stored experiences **archetypes,** meaning first, or early, patterns. Archetypes for human beings are similar to the concept of instincts in animals. Inborn, the archetypes determine and direct much of our behavior.

An example of an archetype is the **Hero.** (It is a convention of Jungian theory to capitalize an archetype.) If an individual tends to identify his or her ego with the Hero, then that person will tend to be courageous, have a spirit of adventure, be concerned for the welfare of unfortunate people, and so forth.

(a) According to Jung, the _____ consists of the human race's stored experiences over the centuries.

(b) Jung called first or early patterns _____.

(c) It is possible that a person who tends to be courageous and have a spirit of adventure identifies his or her ego with the inborn pattern that Jung called the _____.

Answers: (a) collective unconscious; (b) archetypes; (c) Hero.

Another example of an archetype is the **Martyr.** If an individual tends to identify his or her ego with the Martyr, then that person will be self-sacrificing and self-punishing, and tend to seek opportunities for others to be abusive to them. It is clear that in some cases identification with this archetype can have adverse consequences.

One of the important archetypes is the **Self.** If an individual tends to identify his her or ego with the Self, then that person will take a life pathway of personal discovery. Life will have a sense of purpose or mission. If successful, toward the end of life the individual will feel fulfilled, complete. Jung called this process **self-realization,** and it anticipated Maslow's concept of self-actualization (see chapter 7).

The notion of a collective unconscious mind is controversial. The belief that there can be inherited memories tends to be rejected by American psychology. Nonetheless, a number of personality theorists and psychotherapists have found it useful to think in terms of archetypes. Jung's concept of the collective unconscious mind is not dead in American psychology. However, it has been relegated to a borderline status.

(a) If an individual tends to identify his or her ego with the _____, then that person will take a life pathway of personal discovery.

(b) If an individual tends to identify his or her ego with the _____, then that person will be self-sacrificing.

(c) The existence of the collective unconscious is _____.

Answers: (a) Self; (b) Martyr; (c) controversial.

Alfred Adler (1870–1937), like Jung, was one of Freud's early coworkers. Both Freud and Adler lived in Vienna. Adler was working as an ophthalmologist when he read Freud's *The Interpretation of Dreams.* Inspired by Freud's book, he contacted Freud, and became a psychoanalyst. Eventually Adler broke with Freud and followed his own theoretical inclinations.

One of the main causes of the break with Freud was Adler's insistence that the will to power is just as influential in psychological development as the sexual drive. The **will to power** is an inborn drive to become effective and competent. (Adler obtained the concept of the will to power from the teachings of the philosopher Friedrich Nietzsche.) If the will to power is frustrated, as it often is, this sets up the conditions for an inferiority complex. An **inferiority complex** is a group of related ideas that may or may not be realistic about the self. An inferiority complex tends to contribute to feelings of inadequacy, incompetence, depression, anxiety, and chronic anger.

In order to cope with an inferiority complex, the individual often uses an ego defense mechanism called **compensation.** Compensation, as defined by Adler, is the capacity of the personality to convert a psychological minus into a sort of plus. For example, twenty-four-year-old Julian is five feet four inches tall. He has an inferiority complex about his stature. He was a champion runner in high school. He volunteers for hazardous duty in the Army. Using the defense mechanism of compensation, he is out to prove to himself and the world that he is just as big a man as men who are physically larger. The novel *What Makes Sammy Run?* by Budd Schulberg presents a powerful story based on what has been called the "little big man phenomenon."

Inferiority complexes tend to be specific. One can have an inferiority complex associated with mathematical ability, athletic capacity, social skills, musical talent, appearance, and so forth. It is possible to have more than one inferiority complex. It is important to realize that an inferiority complex does not mean that a person *is* inferior. It is a component of one's self-image. Inferiority complexes are, according to Adler, important features of the human personality.

(a) According to Adler, the _____ is an inborn drive to become effective and competent.

(b) An _____ is a group of related ideas that may or may not be realistic about the self.

(c) _____, as defined by Adler, is the capacity of the personality to convert a psychological minus into a sort of plus.

Answers: (a) will to power; (b) inferiority complex; (c) Compensation.

Karen Horney (1885–1952) was trained in psychoanalysis in Germany, and was one of the principal founders of psychoanalysis in the United States. Although she accepted the broad general outlines of Freudian theory, she revised certain aspects of it. She believed that Freud had been much too literal in his presentation of the Oedipus complex (see chapter 11). Her argument was that a child's wish to possess the parent of the opposite sex was psychological and emotional, not particularly sexual. For example, five-year-old Joel craves the same status and importance in his mother's eyes as that enjoyed by his father. Envious, he has the forbidden wish to take over the father's general position. He represses the wish to an unconscious level, and this is the basis of the Oedipus complex. In general, Horney replaced much of Freud's emphasis on the id and its biological foundations as central aspects of personality with an emphasis on the importance of learning and culture.

The overall impact of the theories of Jung, Adler, and Horney has been to enrich psychology's general understanding of important processes involved in the formation of the human personality.

(a) Horney believed that Freud had been much to literal in his presentation of the _____.

(b) Horney tended to place an emphasis not on biological factors, but on _____ and _____.

Answers: (a) Oedipus complex; (b) learning; culture.

Learned Aspects of Personality: The Effects of Experience

As already noted, Horney recognized the importance of learning in shaping the personality. Two learning processes of particular importance in personality development are operant conditioning and observational learning. The general importance of these processes was identified primarily by learning theorists such as B. F. Skinner and Albert Bandura (see chapter 6).

Operant conditioning takes place when behavior is shaped by reinforcers. **Reinforcers** increase the probability of occurrence of a given class of behavior. Applying the process of operant conditioning to the shaping of a personality, let's assume that Kimberly is raised in a show business family. Both of her parents are talkative and friendly. From an early age, they applaud Kimberly when she sings, dances, or acts. Later, they approve of most of her friends, and encourage her to have a rich social life. Kimberly is being reinforced for extraversion, and it is no surprise that this trait is dominant in her adult personality.

Conversely, let's assume that Leona is raised in a quiet, scholarly family. Both of her parents are reflective and people of few words. From an early age, they approve of Leona when she is quiet and doesn't interrupt adult activities. They sometimes say, "Children should be seen and not heard." Similar parental behaviors suggest that Leona is being reinforced for introversion, and, again, it is no surprise that the trait is dominant in her adult personality.

(a) _____ takes place when behavior is shaped by reinforcers.

(b) Reinforcers increase the _____ of occurrence of a given class of behavior.

   Answers: (a) Operant conditioning; (b) probability.

Of course, reinforcement interacts with inborn disposition. If introversion-extraversion is an inborn tendency, as Jung suggested, then this complicates the above picture. If an individual has in innate tendency to be an introvert, and introversion is reinforced, then the individual's adult personality is likely to be highly introverted. On the other hand, if an individual has an innate tendency to be an extravert, and extraversion is reinforced, then the individual's adult personality is likely to be highly extraverted.

But let's assume that an individual's innate tendency is to be an introvert and that extraversion is reinforced. Then development will be somewhat strained, and the adult personality is likely to be conflicted. He or she may be an extravert on the surface with a deeper yearning to express introverted tendencies. The actor John Barrymore, once known as "the great profile," appears to present such a case. Raised in a show business family and encouraged to be a performer, he dreamed of a quieter life and had a substantial talent for drawing and painting. His abuse of alcohol and self-destructive tendencies are detailed in the biography *Goodnight, Sweet Prince* by his friend, the author Gene Fowler.

Observational learning takes place when an individual imitates the behavior of a role model. For example, Martha admires her mother, a physician. Martha observes from childhood through adolescence her mother's dedication to medicine and her concern for patients. Wanting to be like her mother, Martha enters medical school when she is twenty-two years old. Her adult personality displays the traits of dedication and concern originally modeled by her mother.

As with operant conditioning, if one's innate disposition is in opposition to the behavior of a model, then there may be internal conflict.

It is clear that the learning process plays a significant role in the acquisition of a personality.

(a) Assume that an individual's innate tendency is to be an introvert and that extraversion is reinforced. Then development will be somewhat strained, and the adult personality is likely to be _____.

(b) _____ takes place when an individual imitates the behavior of a role model.

Answers: (a) conflicted; (b) Observational learning.

The Conscious Individual: The Self-Shaping of the Personality

The individual is, of course, shaped by powerful forces, the kinds of forces already described in this chapter. However, it is possible to shift the emphasis from a generally reactive process to a proactive one. A **proactive behavioral process** focuses on the role played by consciousness in the acquisition of personality. The **humanistic viewpoint** (see chapter 1) recognizes that the individual can think, reflect, and decide. Abraham Maslow and Carl Rogers, two of the principal advocates of the humanistic viewpoint, called attention to the idea that an adult does not have to be a pawn of fate, a plaything of genetic tendencies and childhood experiences. Instead, consciousness can be used as a self-shaping tool.

Maslow believed that the process of self-actualization was to some extent under the control of one's will. A person can choose to take the kinds of actions that will help him or her to maximize talents and potential. Maslow asserted that human beings have a great capacity for **autonomy,** the power to control and direct one's own life.

(a) A _____ behavioral process focuses on the role played by consciousness in the acquisition of personality.

(b) The _____ viewpoint recognizes that the individual can think, reflect, and decide.

(c) Maslow asserted that human beings have a great capacity for _____, the power to control and direct one's own life.

Answers: (a) proactive; (b) humanistic; (c) autonomy.

Rogers placed an emphasis on the **self-concept,** the way in which one perceives one's own personality. The self-concept exists in contrast to the **ideal self,** the way one would like to be. If the self-concept and the ideal self are far apart, then a state of **incongruence** exists. Incongruence tends to induce depression and anxiety. Like Maslow, Rogers believed that the individual has some control over the status of the self. Rogers employed these concepts as important aspects of his approach to psychotherapy (see client-centered therapy in chapter 15).

The humanistic viewpoint attempts to put the individual in the psychological driver's seat. It asserts that a human being's personality doesn't just happen. The individual, to some extent, creates his or her own personality.

(a) Rogers placed an emphasis on the _____, the way in which one perceives one's own personality.

(b) The self-concept exists in contrast to the _____, the way one would like to be.

(c) If the self-concept and the ideal self are far apart, then a state of _____ exists.

Answers: (a) self-concept; (b) ideal self; (c) incongruence.

Personality Tests: "Can That Silly Inkblot Test Really Tell You Anything about People?"

Personality tests are measuring instruments used primarily for two purposes: to conduct research on the nature of personality and to make evaluations of personality useful in counseling and clinical settings.

Three specific personality tests will be described in this section: (1) the Rorschach test, (2) the Thematic Apperception Test (TAT), and (3) the Minnesota Multiphasic Personality Inventory (MMPI).

The **Rorschach test** consists of ten inkblots with bilateral symmetry (i.e., the right half of each inkblot is the mirror image of the left half). There are ten cards, five in black and white and five with some color. The cards are always shown in the same order. The key instruction is, "Tell me what you see, or are able to imagine to be there, in each card." First published in 1921, the test was developed by the Swiss psychoanalyst Hermann Rorschach.

The Rorschach test is called a **projective test,** a test in which it is assumed that what the subject says he or she perceives the blots to be are in fact reflections of unconscious motives. The subject is "projecting" the unconscious on the inkblots. The fact that the inkblots are **ambiguous stimuli,** stimuli that can be perceived in two or more ways, suggests that whatever structure is given to the blots is provided by the subject.

The Rorschach test is able to measure such aspects of personality as introversion-extraversion, repressed motives, emotional stability, creativity, and even, to some extent, intelligence. A substantial amount of clinical data suggests that in fact the test *can* tell quite a bit about people.

(a) The _____ test consists of ten inkblots with bilateral symmetry.

(b) The Rorschach test is called a _____ test, a test in which it is assumed that what the subject says he or she perceives the blots to be are in fact reflections of unconscious motives.

(c) _____ stimuli are stimuli that can be perceived two or more ways.

Answers: (a) Rorschach; (b) projective; (c) Ambiguous.

The **Thematic Apperception Test (TAT)** also consists of a set of cards, nineteen with pictures and one blank. Like the Rorschach, the TAT is a projective test. The pictures portray people, sometimes in situations with others and sometimes alone. The pictures can be interpreted in two or more ways, and so are considered to be ambiguous stimuli. The key instructions are, "Tell me a story about what you see in this card. The story should have a beginning, a middle, and an end. Also, tell me what the person or people are thinking and feeling." In the case of the blank card, the subject is asked to first imagine a picture. First published in 1938, the TAT was developed by the Harvard psychologist Henry A. Murray.

The word **apperception** means "subconscious perception." You will recall that in psychoanalytical theory the subconscious, or preconscious, level is closer to actual consciousness than is the unconscious level.

An analysis of a subject's stories tends to reveal his or her primary motivational dispositions. A profile with highs and lows emerges, revealing motivational levels associated with such psychological needs as achievement, power, affiliation, and self-abasement (see chapter 7).

(a) What test consists of a set of nineteen cards with pictures and one blank card?

_____

(b) The word _____ means "subconscious perception."

Answers: (a) The Thematic Apperception Test (TAT); (b) *apperception.*

The **Minnesota Multiphasic Personality Inventory (MMPI)** is a self-reporting, paper-and-pencil test with a group of 550 statements. One of three responses can be given to the statements: True, False, or Cannot say. The MMPI is a standardized, objective test, not a projective test. It can be scored by machine, and is a highly reliable measuring instrument. First published in 1942, the MMPI was developed by research psychologists at the University of Minnesota.

The following statements are designed to convey an impression of what the items on the MMPI are like. However, they are not items on the actual test.

1. My mother and father were very kind and loving.
2. I suffer terribly from constipation.
3. If you don't use people, then they'll use you.
4. I've lost interest in sex.
5. I often have conversations with the living dead.
6. Everybody's out to get me.
7. In many ways I am an undiscovered genius.

As odd as the questions seem, research has shown similar questions to be valid and useful.

(a) What test is a self-reporting, paper-and-pencil test with a group of 550 statements?
_____

(b) The MMPI is a standardized, _____ test, not a projective test.

(c) As odd as the questions on the MMPI seem, research has shown them to be _____ and useful.

Answers: (a) The Minnesota Multiphasic Personality Inventory (MMPI); (b) objective; (c) valid.

The aim of the MMPI is to provide results in terms of **clinical scales,** measures of pathological (i.e., "sick") aspects of the personality. The instrument is highly useful to clinical psychologists and psychiatrists.

There are ten clinical scales associated with the MMPI. A subject can have a high or low score on each scale. Above a designated level, a high score on a given scale is considered to be sign of pathology.

The ten clinical scales yielded by the MMPI are listed below. Only brief descriptions of the scales are given because this material will be covered in more detail in chapter 14.

1. **Hypochondriasis.** This scale measures excessive preoccupation with one's health.
2. **Depression.** As its name indicates, this scale measures depression.

3. **Hysteria.** This scale measures a tendency to develop *conversion disorders* in which anxiety is converted into a physical symptom such as paralysis.
4. **Psychopathic deviation.** This scale measures a tendency to violate moral standards and codes of conduct without feelings of guilt.
5. **Masculinity–femininity.** This scale measures the subject's tendency to have interests generally associated the interests of members of the opposite sex.
6. **Paranoia.** This scale measures a tendency to mistrust other people.
7. **Psychasthenia.** This scale measures a tendency to develop neurotic reactions.
8. **Schizophrenia.** This scale measures a tendency to have delusions and distorted thoughts.
9. **Hypomania.** This scale measures a tendency to become overly emotional and excessively excited.
10. **Social introversion.** This scale measures a tendency to withdraw from other people.

The three personality tests presented in this section are published in current editions. Available to personality researchers and mental health professionals, they are standardized, and have been evaluated for both validity and reliability.

(a) The aim of the MMPI is to provide results in terms of _____ scales.

(b) What MMPI scale measures excessive preoccupation with one's health? _____

(c) What MMPI scale measures a tendency to develop conversion disorders? _____

(d) What MMPI scale measures a tendency to have delusions and distorted thoughts? _____

Answers: (a) clinical; (b) Hypochondriasis; (c) Hysteria; (d) Schizophrenia.

SELF-TEST

1. A workable definition of personality is that it is
   a. the synchronicity of the id and the ego
   b. the sum of the archetypes of the collective unconscious
   c. the interaction of the ego ideal and the superego
   d. the constellation of traits unique to the individual

2. Which one of the following is *not* a personality type identified by Hippocrates?
   a. Mesomorph
   b. Sanguine

   c. Choleric
   d. Melancholic

3. According to Jung, an extravert tends to favor which of the following behaviors?
   a. Meditating
   b. Daydreaming
   c. Exploration
   d. Spending time alone

4. According to Freud, what part of the personality follows the pleasure principle?
   a. The ego
   b. The id
   c. The superego
   d. The conscience

5. What ego defense mechanism is characterized by the ego pushing down unpleasant features of one's psychological world to an unconscious level?
   a. Projection
   b. Repression
   c. Fantasy
   d. Identification

6. According to Jung, the collective unconscious contains
   a. personal repressed memories
   b. the introjected superego
   c. archetypes
   d. the transcendental ego

7. According to Adler, if the will to power is frustrated, this sets up the conditions for
   a. an inferiority complex
   b. an Oedipus complex
   c. a martyr complex
   d. a perpetual youth complex

8. Let's say that Kimberly receives reinforcers in the form of praise and applause for extraverted behavior, and that a series of such reinforcers shapes her personality. What learning process is taking place in this case?
   a. Superego gratification
   b. Social inhibition
   c. Identification with an archetype
   d. Operant conditioning

9. Maslow believed that the process of self-actualization is to some extent under the control of one's will. He asserted that human beings have a great capacity for
   a. expressing the curiosity drive
   b. frustrating themselves
   c. autonomy
   d. letting the id control their lives

10. The Rorschach test is a test in which it is assumed that what the subject says he or she perceives the blots to be are in fact reflections of unconscious motives. Accordingly, the Rorschach is
    a. an objective test
    b. a machine-scored test
    c. an invalid test
    d. a projective test

ANSWERS TO THE SELF-TEST

1-d 2-a 3-c 4-b 5-b 6-c 7-a 8-d 9-c 10-d

ANSWERS TO THE TRUE-OR-FALSE PREVIEW QUIZ

1. True.
2. True.
3. False. According to Freud, there are three, not four, parts to the human personality: (1) the id, (2) the ego, and (3) the superego.
4. False. An inferiority complex is a group of related ideas that may or may not be realistic about the self.
5. True.

KEY TERMS

affected by feelings–emotionally stable	choleric
ambiguous stimuli	clinical scales
ambivert	collective unconscious
apperception	compensation
archetypes	conscience
autonomy	denial of reality
bipolar trait	depression

ectomorph

ego

ego defense mechanisms

ego ideal

endomorph

extravert (also, extrovert)

factors

fantasy

Hero

humanistic viewpoint

humble-assertive

humor

hypochondriasis

hypomania

hysteria

id

ideal self

identification

incongruence

inferiority complex

introjected

introversion-extraversion

introvert

Martyr

masculinity-femininity

melancholic

mesomorph

Minnesota Multiphasic Personality Inventory (MMPI)

neo-Freudians

observational learning

operant conditioning

paranoia

personality

personality tests

phlegmatic

pleasure principle

proactive behavioral process

projection

projective test

psychasthenia

psychodynamic theory

psychopathic deviation

rationalization

reaction formation

reality principle

reinforcers

repression

reserved-outgoing

Rorschach test

sanguine

schizophrenia

self

Self

self-concept

self-realization

sixteen personality factor theory

social introversion

somatotype

superego

Thematic Apperception Test (TAT)

trait

type-trait theories

vicarious gratification

will to power

14 Abnormal Psychology: Exploring Mental Disorders

True or False

1. T F Deviation from a given norm or standard is the only criterion needed in order to determine whether a behavior pattern is or is not pathological.
2. T F Psychiatrists and clinical psychologists classify and diagnose mental disorders with the aid of the *Diagnostic and Statistical Manual of Mental Disorders,* fourth edition.
3. T F Anxiety disorders are characterized by a core of delusions.
4. T F Schizophrenia is characterized by the presentation to others of two or more selves.
5. T F The antisocial personality disorder is characterized by a lack of guilt feelings.

(Answers can be found on page 228.)

As suggested by your study of the tests in the last chapter, the human personality is not always stable. People often display eccentricities and maladaptive traits. This chapter provides information that will help you recognize and understand abnormal behavior.

Objectives

After completing this chapter, you will be able to

• define abnormal behavior;

• specify the criteria associated with pathological aspects of abnormal behavior;

• explain how mental disorders are classified;

• describe the principal mental disorders;

• identify the various viewpoints used to explain abnormal behavior.

Such motion pictures as *Spellbound, The Snake Pit, One Flew Over the Cuckoo's Nest,* and *Girl, Interrupted* all focus on mental health problems. Almost every issue of a daily newspaper has an article on depression, anxiety, schizophrenia, and other disorders. There are many commercials on television for prescription drugs designed to treat these conditions. Clearly, a substantial amount of popular attention is directed toward mental disorders.

And abnormal behavior *is* a major public health problem. Depression is sometimes called the common cold of mental disability. Chronic anxiety in the form of persistent worry is approximately as common as depression. About 1 percent of adults suffer from schizophrenia, a severe mental disorder. This percentage translates into a figure approaching 2 million people in the United States alone. Conservatively, about one in ten adults have some kind of definable mental health problem.

The toll on job performance and family life is considerable. Consequently, it is of value to have some reliable information about abnormal behavior. This chapter defines abnormal behavior and describes some of the major pathological syndromes associated with it. The next chapter presents various kinds of therapy used to treat mental disorders.

(a) Depression is sometimes called the _____ of mental disability.

(b) Approximately what percent of adults suffer from schizophrenia? _____

Answers: (a) common cold; (b) 1 percent.

Defining Abnormal Behavior: It Takes More than Deviation

Abnormal behavior is behavior that deviates from a given norm or standard of behavior. If the average adult in the United States takes five baths or showers a week, and Tom takes twenty-one, then Tom's behavior is abnormal. The definition presented above is strictly statistical. It does *not* imply pathology (i.e., "sickness"). If Tom is a salesman, sweats a lot, and wants to be presentable to others, he may actually find it necessary to bathe twenty-one times a week. On the other hand, Tom may suffer from irrational anxiety about his body odor. The showers may represent compulsive behavior used to reduce anxiety. In this case, it is possible that Tom suffers from an obsessive–compulsive anxiety disorder.

Abnormal behavior is behavior that _____ from a given norm or standard of behavior.

   Answer: deviates.

It takes more than deviation alone for a behavior pattern to be considered pathological. Additional criteria help mental health professionals to identify the presence of a mental disorder. First, there is almost always *suffering* associated with a mental disorder. Often it is the *self* that suffers. Depression, anxiety, and confusion are miserable mental and emotional states. On the other hand, sometimes it is *others* that suffer. For example, a person with an antisocial personality disorder may, without feeling guilty, manipulate and use another person (see pp. 223–224, on personality disorders).

Second, pathological behavior is often self-defeating. **Self-defeating behavior** is behavior that provides momentary gratification with an excessive long-term cost. Examples include overspending, chronic procrastination, and compulsive gambling.

Third, pathological behavior is often self-destructive. **Self-destructive behavior** tends to injure the body. Examples include overeating, drug abuse, self-inflicted injuries, and irrational risk-taking.

Fourth, pathological behavior is salient. **Salient behavior** is behavior that stands out. It tends to be striking and conspicuous. Examples include a person wearing three sweaters on a summer day or someone holding a conversation with an invisible companion. Sometimes the word *vivid* is used for this particular criterion of pathology.

Fifth, pathological behavior is **illogical behavior.** An observer of the behavior thinks, "What this person is doing right now makes no sense." In some instances the victim of a mental disorder recognizes the nonsensical aspect of a thought or a behavior. The suffering individual thinks, "What I'm doing now is irrational. I know that saying magic words to myself won't protect me from injury, but I can't seem to control myself."

Other criteria of pathology could be specified. However, these five are sufficient to establish that it takes more than statistical abnormality to think of a behavior pattern as a sign of a mental disorder.

(a) Depression and anxiety are miserable mental and emotional states. This suggests that there is almost always _____ associated with a mental disorder.

(b) Chronic procrastination and compulsive gambling are examples of _____ behavior.

(c) Behavior that stands out is called either vivid or _____.

Answers: (a) suffering; (b) self-defeating; (c) salient.

Classifying Mental Disorders: Clusters of Signs and Symptoms

Although the term *mental disorder* was used earlier, it has not yet been defined. A **mental disorder** is a disorder characterized by both abnormal behavior and the presence of pathological signs and symptoms. This definition consolidates what has already been said. A distinction needs to be made between a sign and a symptom. A **sign** is something that is evident to others. It is external. For example, moping, making incomprehensible statements, and wearing filthy clothes are signs to others that a friend or relative may have a problem.

A **symptom** is something that the individual himself or herself experiences. It is internal. For example, feeling depressed, anxious, or confused are symptoms the self perceives as distressing. A cluster of signs and symptoms is called a **syndrome.** Psychiatrists and clinical psychologists use recognizable syndromes as the primary basis for classifying and diagnosing mental disorders.

(a) A mental disorder is a disorder characterized by both abnormal behavior and the presence of _____ signs and symptoms.

(b) A cluster of signs and symptoms is called a _____.

Answers: (a) pathological; (b) syndrome.

The handbook used in actual clinical practice is called the *Diagnostic and Statistical Manual of Mental Disorders,* fourth edition (DSM-IV), and it is published by the American Psychiatric Association. DSM-IV uses a five-axis system to classify disorders. (The word **axis** is used to mean a core area of importance and concern).

Axis 1 refers to *clinical syndromes.* As already indicated, these are clusters of signs and symptoms that allow a mental health professional to say that a given individual is suffering from a particular mental disorder. It is the most important of the five axes. The bulk of this chapter will identify these clinical syndromes. They include anxiety disorders, mood disorders, and others.

Axis 2 refers to *personality disorders*. A personality disorder may or may not be present. However, if one does exist, it often complicates the clinical syndrome.

Axis 3 refers to *medical conditions*. If a person's health is poor, this may complicate treatment. For example, a schizophrenic patient with diabetes needs a special diet along with psychiatric treatment.

Axis 4 refers to *psychosocial problems*. These are problems relating to others and the patient's life situation. An unhappy marriage, loss of a job, and similar difficulties need to be evaluated in connection with the clinical syndrome.

Axis 5 refers to a *global assessment*. This consists of a broad, general assessment of how well the patient had been functioning in everyday life before the appearance of a mental disorder. The mental health worker makes an appraisal on a 100-point scale. A score of 100 or 90 represents superior functioning. A score of 20 or 30 represents poor functioning.

The five axes provide mental health professionals with a comprehensive picture of the status of a given individual's mental disorder.

(a) DSM-IV uses a system with how many axes to classify mental disorders? _____

(b) Axis 1 in the DSM-IV system refers to _____.

(c) Axis 4 in the DSM-IV system refers to _____.

Answers: (a) Five; (b) clinical syndromes; (c) psychosocial problems.

Anxiety Disorders: Suffering from Chronic Worry

This section and several to follow identify mental disorders in terms of their major clinical syndromes (axis 1). The primary goal is to describe the principal signs and symptoms of these disorders. Explanations for these deviant actions will be reserved for the last section of the chapter.

Anxiety disorders are disorders characterized by a core of irrational fear. Anxiety itself is experienced as a kind of psychological fire alarm. The individual thinks, "Something terrible is going to happen!" Freud distinguished between neurotic anxiety and rational anxiety. **Neurotic anxiety** is irrational, and it is the kind of anxiety that plays a significant role in the anxiety disorders. **Rational anxiety** is identical to realistic fear.

Four types of anxiety disorders will be identified: (1) generalized anxiety disorder, (2) phobic disorders, (3) obsessive-compulsive disorder (OCD), and (4) post-traumatic stress disorder (PTSD).

Generalized anxiety disorder is characterized by vague feelings of apprehension. This is called **free-floating anxiety.** There are psychological storm clouds for no apparent reason, and there is **chronic worry** that goes on and on seemingly without end. The anxiety, or worry, seems to follow the person anywhere and everywhere without rhyme or reason. The victim feels powerless to escape from the anxiety.

(a) What disorders are characterized by a core of irrational fear? _____

(b) Associated with generalized anxiety disorder, vague feelings of apprehension are called _____ anxiety.

Answers: (a) Anxiety disorders; (b) free-floating.

Phobic disorders are characterized by feelings of apprehension with a relatively definable source. The principal kinds of phobic disorders are (1) specific phobias, (2) social phobia, and (3) agoraphobia. **Specific phobias** involve the fear of an object or situation. A fear of animals is called **zoophobia;** a fear of heights is called **acrophobia;** and a fear of confined places is called **claustrophobia.**

Social phobia is characterized by a fear of the opinions of other people. The victim does not want to be judged or overly visible. This phobia often manifests itself as **pathological shyness,** shyness that is so severe that it interferes with daily living.

Agoraphobia is characterized by a fear of leaving the home or a familiar territory. A person who will not venture out of the house has a severe case of agoraphobia. A person who is afraid to travel more than five or ten miles out of a small town has a moderate case of agoraphobia.

Obsessive-compulsive disorder (OCD) is characterized by ideas that induce anxiety, and rituals that in turn reduce that anxiety. For example, Abraham, a man who has no history of heart disease, may think, "Today I will die of a heart attack." Then he decides that if he mentally recites the word *abracadabra* three times, the feared event won't happen. Eventually he becomes psychologically addicted to the ritual, and it becomes a behavioral pattern that he finds difficult to give up.

Post-traumatic stress disorder (PTSD) is characterized by anxiety and related symptoms following a genuinely threatening experience. A person lives through an awful earthquake, a devastating fire, military combat, a rape, or other extremely upsetting event. This is followed by such symptoms as general fearfulness, nightmares, depression, an inability to relax, and so forth.

(a) _____ phobias involve the fear of an object or situation.

(b) _____ is characterized by a fear of leaving the home or a familiar territory.

(c) _____ is characterized by ideas that induce anxiety, and rituals that in turn reduce that anxiety.

Answers: (a) Specific; (b) Agoraphobia; (c) Obsessive-compulsive disorder (OCD).

Somatoform Disorders: When the Body Is Involved

Somatoform disorders are disorders in which anxiety is converted into a bodily symptom. *Soma* is a Greek root meaning "body." Consequently, in a somatoform disorder, anxiety takes a somatic, or bodily, form. Four types of somatoform disorders will be identified: (1) somatization disorder, (2) hypochondriacal disorder, (3) pain disorder, and (4) conversion disorder.

It is important to realize in all of the following disorders that the causal factors associated with the disorders are primarily psychological and emotional. The person does *not* have a physical illness. However, the person's symptoms *resemble* a physical illness.

Somatization disorder is characterized by various complaints. Opal says she suffers from diarrhea and bloating. Newton says his joints creak like old hinges. Ramona says her muscles twitch for no reason. Sometimes the individual has related sexual dysfunctions (see chapter 12).

Hypochondriacal disorder (or **hypochondriasis**) is characterized by irrational worry about one's health. Peggy has had two headaches in one week and starts to think she's getting cancer of the brain. Ivan for no particular reason fears that he has diabetes. People who suffer from hypochondriasis often take excessive numbers of vitamin pills or visit a string of physicians in a vain search for a nonexistent illness.

(a) Somatoform disorders are disorders in which anxiety is converted into a _____ symptom.

(b) Hypochondriacal disorder (or hypochondriasis) is characterized by irrational worry about one's _____.

Answers: (a) bodily; (b) health.

Pain disorder is characterized by sustained painful sensations. Kristen says that her back aches all the time. Ernest says that he suffers from frequent stomach cramps. Renee says her bones ache. Physicians can find no organic basis for the pain in any of these cases, and yet it cannot be said that the pain is not felt. Pain is personal and private, a symptom, and an outside observer is in no position to deny its subjective reality.

Conversion disorder is characterized, in most cases, by symptoms resembling a neurological problem such as paralysis, inability to control a limb or limbs, or loss of the capacity to see or hear. These are called **pseudoneurological symptoms,** symptoms that are false signs of a neurological disorder. The older term for conversion disorder is **hysteria,** and it is still sometimes used. Ancient

Greek physicians thought that the victim's symptoms were caused by a "wandering uterus" and that the condition affected only women. (*Hyster* is the Greek word for uterus.)

Conversion disorder occupies a unique place in the history of psychology. Anna O., the first psychoanalytic patient, suffered from it. You will recall from chapter 2 that Josef Breuer and Sigmund Freud published *Studies on Hysteria* in 1895.

(a) Symptoms that are false signs of a neurological disorder are called _____ symptoms.

(b) An older term for conversion disorder is _____.

Answers: (a) pseudoneurological; (b) hysteria.

Dissociative Disorders: Loss of Identity

Dissociative disorders are disorders in which the individual experiences either a loss of identity or a distortion in the sense of self. Four types of dissociative disorders will be specified: (1) psychogenic amnesia, (2) psychogenic fugue, (3) dissociative identity disorder, and (4) despersonalization disorder.

Psychogenic amnesia is characterized by a loss of personal memories. (The word *amnesia* means "without memory.") As a consequence, one's sense of identity is destroyed. Ambrose does not remember his name. He is unable to recall his date of birth, the fact that he is married, that he is the father of two children, that he is an accountant by profession, and so forth. The condition is called *psychogenic* because it has its origin, or genesis, in psychological and emotional factors.

Pyschogenic fugue is characterized by running away from a home territory. The individual with this condition suffers from amnesia and also takes flight. The word *fugue* has the same root as *fugitive*. The victim of psychogenic fugue is, in a sense, a fugitive from himself. Roberta, like Ambrose above, has lost her sense of identity. In addition, she finds herself in a strange city, wandering the streets in a confused state, not knowing how she arrived in this particular place.

(a) _____ disorders are disorders in which the individual experiences either a loss of identity or a distortion in the sense of self.

(b) _____ amnesia is characterized by a loss of personal memories.

(c) What disorder is characterized by running away from a home territory? _____

Answers: (a) Dissociative; (b) Psychogenic; (c) Psychogenic fugue.

Dissociative identity disorder (DID) is characterized by the presentation to others of two or more selves. The older name for this condition is **multiple**

personality disorder. In the book *The Three Faces of Eve,* and the film of the same name, Eve's original self splits into two selves, Eve White and Eve Black. Eve White is polite, organized, and moral. Eve Black is bratty, spoiled, and immoral. Eve White is called the **superior personality,** the personality that most closely resembles the normal, socialized one. Eve Black is called the **inferior personality,** the personality that is wild and carefree and resembles the Freudian id. Since the publication of this famous case history there have been a number of similar books published. Clinical psychology and psychiatry accept the reality of DID. Popular reports suggest, incorrectly, that the condition is common. Psychiatry looks upon the condition as rare.

Depersonalization disorder is characterized by a disturbance in the way in which the individual perceives the self. The troubled person may imagine that he or she is ugly, looks bloated, possesses legs that are too short, or has an excessively loud voice. These perceptions are unsettling. Sometimes victims of the disorder have an **out-of-body experience,** an experience in which it seems that the self is somehow walking or floating outside of the physical body.

(a) What is an older name for dissociative identity disorder (DID)? _____

(b) _____ disorder is characterized by a disturbance in the way in which the individual perceives the self.

Answers: (a) Multiple personality disorder; (b) Depersonalization.

The Mood Disorders: Emotional Ups and Downs

Mood disorders are characterized by significant variations in emotional states. *Mood* is experienced as positive or negative. A **positive mood** is associated with feeling well and optimistic thinking. A **negative mood** is associated with fatigue and pessimistic thinking. Mood is an involuntary reaction; it cannot be directly willed.

Four mood disorders will be identified: (1) dysthymia, (2) major depressive disorder, (3) cyclothymia, and (4) bipolar disorder.

Dysthymia is characterized by mild, relatively persistent depression. *Depression* refers to a negative mood state. As already indicated, such a state is associated with fatigue and pessimistic thinking. *Dys* means something is wrong or "bad." The root *thymia* means "mood" in Greek. An older term for dysthymia is **neurotic depression.**

Major depressive episode is characterized by severe, highly persistent depression. Lack of appetite, chronic fatigue, moving slowly, and sleep disturbances are symptoms of this disorder. The victim may think about suicide. The disorder is in fact associated with an increased risk of actual suicide.

Both dysthymia and major depressive episode are classified as **unipolar dis-**

orders, disorders that display only one emotional direction. In the case of these disorders, that direction is negative.

(a) What mood disorder is characterized by mild, relatively persistent depression?
_____

(b) What mood disorder is characterized by severe, highly persistent depression?
_____

    Answers: (a) Dysthymia; (b) Major depressive episode.

Cyclothymia is a characterized by excessive mood swings. The individual is "high" and then "low." The mood swings, although significant, are not overly striking. The high mood is called *hypomania,* a condition that is not as severe as out–and–out mania (see below).

Bipolar disorder is characterized by severe, highly disruptive mood swings. The individual is "higher than a kite" and then "lower than low." The mood swings are dramatic. The high mood is called mania. **Mania** is a state of unrealistic elation associated with wild, irrational ideas and a general loss of self-control. Errol, in a state of mania, tells all his friends that he is going to write a best-selling novel and discover a cure for cancer in the next month. An older term for bipolar disorder is **manic-depressive disorder.**

Both cyclothymia and bipolar disorder are classified as *bipolar disorders,* disorders that display first one and then a second emotional direction. Although positive moods are experienced in connection with these disorders, they are nonetheless basically kinds of depression. This is because the positive moods are not enduring. They are fragile and can be thought of as shams masking the underlying depression.

(a) What disorder is characterized by significant, but not overly striking, mood swings?
_____

(b) What is an older term for bipolar disorder? _____

    Answers: (a) Cyclothymia; (b) Manic-depressive disorder.

The Psychotic Disorders: Suffering from Delusions

Psychotic disorders are disorders characterized by a loss of touch with reality. The primary distinguishing features are the presence of delusions and cognitive distortions. **Delusions** are false beliefs, ideas about the world that most people think are impossible or absurd. A person with a delusion may think he or she is two centuries old, a visitor from an alien civilization, able to walk through walls, or possessed of incredible telepathic powers. **Cognitive distortions** are thoughts that are illogical or irrational. Frequently psychotic disorders are accompanied by hallucinations. **Hallucinations** are false perceptions. The victim may see someone who isn't there, hear voices, or smell nonexistent odors.

Two types of psychotic disorders will be identified: schizophrenia and delusional disorder.

Schizophrenia is a psychotic disorder that fits all of the criteria specified above. A schizophrenic patient suffers from delusions and cognitive distortions. The term *schizophrenia* was coined by Eugen Bleuler, the psychiatrist who trained Carl Jung. *Schiz* means "split"; *phrenia* refers to the head. Loosely, a schizophrenic condition refers to a "head" or "mind" that has split away from reality. (It does not mean two or more personalities.) An older term for schizophrenia is **dementia praecox,** meaning madness with an early, or youthful, onset. Indeed, signs and symptoms of schizophrenia often appear in adolescence.

Schizophrenia takes on several shapes. Consequently, it is possible to divide the disorder into categories: (1) paranoid type, (2) catatonic type, (3) disorganized type, and (4) undifferentiated type. The **paranoid type** is characterized by delusions or mistrust and suspicion. Kendra says her food has been poisoned. Clay says his thoughts are being recorded by the CIA.

The **catatonic type** is characterized by mutism and odd postures. *Mutism* refers to an unwillingness to speak. Clive has not spoken for ten days. He spends his time in a boxer's fighting stance.

(a) _____ disorders are disorders characterized by a loss of touch with reality.

(b) A schizophrenic patient suffers from _____ and _____ distortions.

(c) What type of schizophrenia is characterized by delusions of mistrust and suspicion? _____

Answers: (a) Psychotic; (b) delusions; cognitive; (c) The paranoid type.

The **disorganized type** is characterized by silliness and completely inappropriate behavior. Dorothy giggles whenever she is spoken too, eats all food with her hands, and urinates anywhere. An older term for this condition is **hebephrenic schizophrenia.** Hebes is the Greek god of youth. The general idea is that the individual has regressed to an infantile level.

The **undifferentiated type** is a diagnostic category used when the patient is schizophrenic, but displays behaviors that overlap with the earlier described categories. In other words, no clear pattern emerges.

Delusional disorder, not a kind of schizophrenia, is a psychotic disorder characterized by an organized, systematic delusional system. An older term for this disorder is **paranoia.** Delusional disorder is not to be confused with schizophrenia, paranoid type (see above). The difference between the two disorders is that in delusional disorder the false ideas form a coherent whole. In schizophrenia they do not. People with delusional disorder can be very convincing. Sometimes they can attract followers. Julius says that he is a visitor to the Earth from an alien world and has come to spread a message of peace. He has written pamphlets and a history of his world, and he has drawn detailed interstellar maps. Everything he says fits together. The points he makes are consistent. If his initial premise is granted, that he is an alien, then he seems to be rational.

(a) What is an older name for the disorganized type of schizophrenia? _____

(b) What disorder, not a kind of schizophrenia, is characterized by an organized, systematic delusional system? _____

Answers: (a) Hebephrenic schizophrenia; (b) Delusional disorder.

The Personality Disorders: Making Others Suffer

Personality disorders are characterized by maladaptive behavioral traits. The individual's persistent way of coping with the world is, in the long run, ineffective and self-defeating. It is important to understand that a personality disorder does not, on the surface, appear to be any kind of mental illness. The individual is not necessarily suffering from chronic anxiety or depression. Also, the individual is not psychotic. Often, there is not a great deal of personal suffering associated with these disorders. There is sometimes a tendency for the individual with a personality disorder to inflict suffering on others.

Three kinds of personality disorders will be identified: (1) narcissistic, (2) antisocial, and (3) obsessive-compulsive. A **narcissistic personality disorder** is characterized by self-absorption. The individual is in love with himself or herself. Such people are described as vain and selfish. They are often overly preoccupied with their appearance. They tend to be cold and lacking in sympathy.

(a) What disorders are characterized by maladaptive behavioral traits? _____

(b) What disorder is characterized by self-absorption? _____

Answers: (a) Personality disorders; (b) Narcissistic personality disorder.

The **antisocial personality disorder** is characterized by a lack of guilt feelings. People with this disorder can lie, cheat, steal, and manipulate others without remorse. The word *antisocial* doesn't mean they are unfriendly. Often, they have a superficial charm. They are antisocial in the sense that they refuse to conform to society's conventions, to its standards and norms of behavior.

The **obsessive-compulsive personality disorder** is characterized by perfectionism. People with this disorder want order in the environment. Everything must be in its place. Things must be done on schedule. Tasks must be completed without flaw or error. Such individuals find it difficult to just let up a little and enjoy life. The obsessive-compulsive personality disorder should not be confused with a disorder presented earlier, the obsessive-compulsive disorder. The personality disorder, as already indicated, is characterized by a need for perfection. On the other hand, the anxiety disorder is characterized by a need to reduce the anxiety generated by obsessive ideas.

(a) The _____ personality disorder is characterized by a lack of guilt feelings.

(b) The _____ personality disorder is characterized by perfectionism.

    Answers: (a) antisocial; (b) obsessive-compulsive.

The Organic Mental Disorders: When the Nervous System Itself Has Pathology

Organic mental disorders are characterized by constellations of signs and symptoms that suggest there is actual damage to the brain and nervous system. This damage may be caused by a genetic tendency, a toxic agent, a vitamin deficiency, or an infection. In brief, the nervous system itself has pathology (i.e., is "sick").

Three organic mental disorders will be identified: (1) alcohol amnestic disorder, (2) dementia of the Alzheimer's type, and (3) general paresis. In all three disorders a certain degree of dementia is present. The term *dementia* refers to loss of intellectual capacity.

Alcohol amnestic disorder is characterized primarily by memory difficulties. It was noted earlier that the word *amnesia* means "without memory." Unlike psychogenic amnesia, the memory problems associated with alcohol amnestic disorder are general, not specific to the individual's sense of identity. The disorder was first studied by the Russian neurologist Sergei Korsakoff over one hundred years ago. An older name for the condition is **Korsakoff's psychosis.** Alcohol abuse tends to induce a deficiency of **thiamine,** a B-complex vitamin. Some of the impairment associated with alcohol amnestic disorder is reversible with vitamin therapy. On the other hand, some of the impairment is due to the loss of neurons linked to the toxic effects of alcohol. Impairment associated with destroyed neurons is not reversible.

(a) _____ mental disorders are characterized by constellations of signs and symptoms that suggest there is actual damage to the brain and nervous system.

(b) What is an older name for alcohol amnestic disorder? _____

    Answers: (a) Organic; (b) Korsakoff's psychosis.

Dementia of the Alzheimer's type is characterized by a progressive decline in mental functioning. The ability to remember, learn, understand ideas, make decisions, and control one's muscles is lost. In the latter stages of the disorder the victim becomes weak and emaciated. In clinical work, the term *dementia of the Alzheimer's type* is somewhat preferred over the more popular term **Alzheimer's disease,** because an actual diagnosis based on signs and symptoms alone is difficult. On the other hand, a post-mortem examination can determine if the degeneration of neurons in the brain in fact follows the pattern of the actual disease. This pattern includes tangles of fibers within nerve cells, the loss of nerve cells within certain areas of the brain, and amyloid plaques. **Amyloid plaques** are excessive protein deposits between nerve cells. The syndrome was first studied by the German neurologist Alois Alzheimer in the early part of the twentieth century.

General paresis is characterized by both dementia and paralysis. It is linked to syphilis, a sexually transmitted disease. The primary cause of the disorder is destruction of the brain and nervous system by the corkscrew-shaped bacterium that causes syphilis.

(a) Dementia of the _____ type is characterized by a progressive decline in mental functioning.

(b) What organic mental disorder is linked to syphilis? _____

   Answers: (a) Alzheimer's; (b) General paresis.

Viewpoints: Ways to Explain Abnormal Behavior

When an individual's behavior is abnormal and pathological, as it is in the case of the mental disorders, one of the first questions that comes to mind is why. We are curious and want an explanation of the deviant actions.

For centuries, a popular explanation of aberrant behavior was **demonology,** the view that Satan's agents had taken possession of the troubled person's soul. This explanation is not the one favored by psychology and psychiatry. Instead, these fields of study tend to subscribe to viewpoints based on an understanding of natural law. Five such viewpoints will be identified: (1) biological, (2) psychodynamic, (3) learning, (4) humanistic, and (5) sociocultural.

The **biological viewpoint** assumes that pathological behavior is caused by an organic factor. A genetic tendency, a biochemical imbalance, a brain injury, or an infection can all play roles in mental disorders. For example, there is much evidence to support the hypothesis that schizophrenia is a **biogenetic disorder,** one that is strongly influenced by a genetic tendency. This genetic tendency is probably the principal cause of a difficulty in the way in which the brain employs **dopamine,** one of the nervous system's neurotransmitters (see chapter 3).

The **psychodynamic viewpoint** assumes that pathological behavior arises because of repressed emotional conflicts. For example, Theresa, a highly traditional, conventional woman, suffers from agoraphobia. Her conscious fear of leaving her home territory is a cover, a mask over a forbidden wish. She is angry with her husband and is filled with buried resentments. The forbidden wish is a desire to take flight from the marriage.

(a) The _____ viewpoint assumes that pathological behavior is caused by an organic factor.

(b) The _____ viewpoint assumes that pathological behavior arises because of repressed emotional conflicts.

Answers: (a) biological; (b) psychodynamic.

The **learning viewpoint** assumes that pathological behavior is a maladaptive response to an adverse experience (or a set of related experiences). For example, Quentin suffers from claustrophobia. When he was a preschooler, his mother used to punish him by locking him in a dark closet for an hour or two at a time. His phobia can be understood as a kind of conditioned reflex (see chapter 6).

The **humanistic viewpoint** assumes that pathological behavior is a response to an inability to become self-actualizing. For example, Joan suffers from chronic depression. When she was an adolescent she displayed talent in creative writing and won several high-school short story contests. She dreamed of a career as a novelist. Today, she is divorced with three children, and works as a checker in a discount store. One of the factors in her depression is the frustration associated with her inability to make the most of her talents.

The **sociocultural viewpoint** assumes that pathological behavior is a maladaptive response to large, inescapable forces and events arising from the social world, the world of other people. Such forces include war, economic depression, overcrowded housing, a totalitarian government, and so forth. For example, fifty-seven-year-old Lloyd is suffering from a major depressive episode and often thinks of suicide. Once he was worth more than two million dollars in stock. Major reverses in the economy, combined with some impulsive, ill-considered decisions on his part, wiped out his fortune.

It is not necessary to make a choice among the viewpoints and decide which viewpoint is *the* correct one. The viewpoints overlap and are not mutually exclusive. Often the factors associated with two or more viewpoints may interact. In appropriate cases, any of the viewpoints may be useful and applicable.

(a) The _____ viewpoint assumes that pathological behavior is a maladaptive response to an adverse experience (or a set or related experiences).

(b) The _____ viewpoint assumes that pathological behavior is a response to an inability to become self-actualizing.

Answers: (a) learning; (b) humanistic.

SELF-TEST

1. One of the following is *not* a criterion that helps mental health professionals to identify the presence of a mental disorder.
   a. Suffering
   b. Self-destructive behavior
   c. Creative behavior
   d. Illogical behavior

2. Axis 1 of DSM-IV refers to
   a. psychosocial problems
   b. medical conditions
   c. global assessment of functioning
   d. clinical syndromes

3. One of the chief features of a generalized anxiety disorder is
   a. highly specific fears
   b. free-floating anxiety
   c. magical rituals
   d. post-traumatic stress

4. Pseudoneurological symptoms tend to be associated with
   a. hypochondriacal disorders
   b. obsessive-compulsive disorder (OCD)
   c. pain disorder
   d. conversion disorder

5. The presentation of two or more selves is associated with
   a. psychogenic fugue
   b. dissociative identity disorder (DID)
   c. depersonalization disorder
   d. schizophrenia

6. Unrealistic elation associated with wild, irrational ideas and a general loss of self-control describes what state?
   a. The euphoria syndrome
   b. Blissful ecstasy
   c. Mania
   d. Dysthymia

7. Delusions are
   a. false beliefs
   b. false perceptions
   c. valid cognitive content
   d. reliable sensations

8. Self-absorption is a distinguishing feature of
   a. obsessive-compulsive disorder
   b. narcissistic personality disorder
   c. organic mental disorders
   d. anxiety disorders

9. An older name for alcohol amnestic disorder is
   a. dementia of the Alzheimer's type
   b. general paresis
   c. Korsakoff's psychosis
   d. Psychogenic dementia

10. The observation that a genetic tendency can play a part in a mental disorder is associated primarily with what viewpoint?
    a. The biological viewpoint
    b. The psychodynamic viewpoint
    c. The learning viewpoint
    d. The humanistic viewpoint

ANSWERS TO THE SELF-TEST

1-c   2-d   3-b   4-d   5-b   6-c   7-a   8-b   9-c   10-a

ANSWERS TO THE TRUE-OR-FALSE PREVIEW QUIZ

1. False. It takes more than deviation alone for a behavior pattern to be considered pathological. The chapter lists five additional criteria.
2. True.
3. False. Anxiety disorders are characterized by a core of irrational fear.
4. False. Dissociative identity disorder (DID), not schizophrenia, is characterized by the presentation to others of two or more selves.
5. True.

KEY TERMS

abnormal behavior

acrophobia

agoraphobia

alcohol amnestic disorder

Alzheimer's disease

amyloid plaques

antisocial personality disorder

anxiety disorders

axis

biogenetic disorder

biological viewpoint

bipolar disorder

catatonic type

chronic worry

claustrophobia

cognitive distortions

conversion disorder

cyclothymia

delusional disorder

delusions

dementia of the Alzheimer's type

dementia praecox

demonology

depersonalization disorder

disorganized type

dissociative disorders

dissociative identity disorder (DID)

dopamine

dysthymia

free-floating anxiety

general paresis

generalized anxiety disorder

hallucinations

hebephrenic schizophrenia

humanistic viewpoint

hypochondriacal disorder
(or hypochondriasis)

hysteria

illogical behavior

inferior personality

Korsakoff's psychosis

learning viewpoint

major depressive episode

mania

manic-depressive disorder

mental disorder

mood disorders

multiple personality disorder

narcissistic personality disorder

negative mood

neurotic anxiety

neurotic depression

obsessive-compulsive disorder (OCD)

obsessive-compulsive personality
disorder

organic mental disorders

out-of-body experience

pain disorder

paranoia

paranoid type

pathological shyness

personality disorders

phobic disorders

positive mood

post-traumatic stress disorder (PTSD)

psuedoneurological symptoms

psychodynamic viewpoint

psychogenic amnesia

psychogenic fugue

psychotic disorders

rational anxiety

salient behavior

schizophrenia

self-defeating behavior

self-destructive behavior

sign

social phobia

sociocultural viewpoint

somatization disorder

somatoform disorders

specific phobias

superior personality

symptom

syndrome

thiamine

undifferentiated type

unipolar disorders

zoophobia

<u>15</u> Therapy: Helping Troubled People

PREVIEW QUIZ

True or False

1. **T F**   The literal meaning of the term *psychotherapy* is "healing of the mind" or "healing of the self."
2. **T F**   The main way that Freud explored the unconscious roots of mental-emotional problems was with the "digging" tool of operant conditioning.
3. **T F**   Client-centered therapy is based on the assumption that the troubled person has powerful inner resources, resources that will help the individual think and feel better.
4. **T F**   Behavior therapy is based on the assumption that mental and emotional problems often arise because of repressed memories and forbidden wishes.
5. **T F**   Antipsychotic agents are drugs that treat mental disorders characterized by chronic anxiety.

(Answers can be found on page 245.)

As you learned in chapter 14, suffering is usually associated with various mental disorders. Mental health professionals seek ways to alleviate this suffering. This chapter presents ways in which therapy—both psychological and biological—can help troubled people cope with life.

Objectives

After completing this chapter, you will be able to

- define therapy;

- distinguish between psychologically based therapies and biologically based therapies;

- specify some principal features of psychoanalysis;

- describe key aspects of client-centered therapy;

- identify central concepts associated with behavior therapy;

- explain the basic assumption underlying cognitive-behavior therapy;

- state the value of group therapy;

- list basic kinds of psychiatric drugs.

Mental disorders are far from hopeless conditions. Gone are the days when mental patients were written off as outcasts and lost members of the human race. Today there are treatments. The treatments have varying degrees of effectiveness. Sometimes a given treatment provides dramatic relief. More often, a particular patient will recover slowly, and treatment becomes a prolonged process.

Treatment for mental disorders is given in the form of various kinds of therapy. **Therapy** consists of procedures that aim to either cure sick people or alleviate their suffering. The term is applied to general medicine as well as to clinical psychology and psychiatry. In the mental health field there are two basic categories of therapy: psychologically based therapies and biologically based therapies. **Psychologically based therapies** begin with the assumption that mental disorders are caused by emotional conflicts, maladaptive learning, cognitive errors, or similar behavioral processes. These therapies recognize that the suffering individual may be free of organic pathology, that there is often nothing objectively wrong with the brain and nervous system.

Psychotherapy is the general term applied to any kind of psychologically based therapy. A presentation of various kinds of psychotherapy constitutes a principal portion of this chapter. The literal meaning of the term *psychotherapy* is "healing of the mind" or "healing of the self."

Biologically based therapies begin with the assumption that mental disorders are caused by actual pathology of the brain and nervous system. These therapies recognize that the suffering individual often has a genetic tendency toward a disorder, an imbalance in neurotransmitters, a hormone problem, an infection, or similar difficulties at a biological level.

Drug therapy is the most common form of biologically based therapy. It is characterized by the prescription of certain chemical agents that have been shown to either eliminate or reduce the severity of symptoms associated with various mental disorders.

(a) What therapies are based on the assumption that mental disorders are caused by emotional conflicts, maladaptive learning, cognitive errors, or similar behavioral processes? _____

(b) What therapies are based on the assumption that mental disorders are caused by actual pathology of the brain and nervous system? _____

Answers: (a) Psychologically based therapies; (b) Biologically based therapies.

Psychodynamic Therapy: Exploring Unconscious Roots

Psychodynamic therapy is any kind of psychotherapy that attempts to reduce suffering by exploring the unconscious roots of a mental-emotional problem. Psychodynamic therapy has its origins in Freud's psychoanalysis. Accordingly, a description of the psychoanalytic process follows.

Free association is the principal "digging" tool used by psychoanalysis. Free association consists of saying anything that comes to mind without a concern for logic or the appropriateness of the content. In classical psychoanalysis, this is accomplished while reclining on a couch. The aim of free association is to dredge up from the unconscious level a fund of information that can be discussed and understood, with the help of the therapist, at a conscious level. In the last fifteen or twenty minutes of a fifty-minute session, the patient sits up and interpretations are made of the memories and ideas obtained by free association.

An **interpretation** consists of making sense of content that has been repressed at the unconscious level. Usually the therapist makes the interpretation, but there is room for discussion. The patient should play an active role in modifying the interpretation. If a patient accepts an interpretation that has important meaning, then the patient often experiences an *insight,* a sudden burst of understanding. It is believed that insights into the self have therapeutic power.

Interpretations are also made of slips of the tongue, dreams, and various kinds of transference. **Slips of the tongue** are speech errors that reveal a forbidden wish. According to Freud, there are no "innocent" errors. They all have unconscious meaning. For example, a wife says to her husband, just before retiring to bed, "I want to kill you." The husband is taken aback. The wife, abashed, says, "Honey, I don't know why I said that. I meant to say I want to kiss you." The interpretation in this case is that, at the level of the id, there is substantial hostility toward the husband. Slips of the tongue are sometimes called **Freudian slips.** (Not all psychologists agree that every slip of the tongue has an unconscious meaning. There are probably so-called **Watsonian slips** also, errors made because of a conflict of speech habits.)

(a) What kind of therapy attempts to reduce suffering by exploring the unconscious roots of a mental-emotional problem? _____

(b) What is the principal "digging" tool used by psychoanalysis? _____

(c) An _____ consists of making sense of content that has been repressed at the unconscious level.

(d) According to Freud, _____ are speech errors that reveal a forbidden wish.

Answers: (a) Psychodynamic therapy; (b) Free association; (c) interpretation; (d) slips of the tongue.

The interpretation of dreams is a central feature of psychoanalytic therapy. Freud said that dreams are "the royal road to the unconscious." He asserted that a dream has two levels. The **manifest level** is the surface of the dream. It is what is presented to the dreaming subject and what is remembered when the individual wakes up. The **latent level** is the concealed aspect of the dream, its meaning. This contains a forbidden wish. The manifest level is often cast in symbolic form. The symbols cloak or disguise the hidden content of the dream. Like slips of the tongue, the interpretation of a dream is likely to reveal either repressed hostility or a repressed sexual impulse. For example, a fifty-year-old married man dreams that a young man meets a beautiful stranger in an unfamiliar city and has sexual relations with her. An interpretation might suggest that the young man symbolizes the dreamer's youthful nature. The forbidden wish is perhaps a desire to have sex outside of the marriage.

Patient-initiated **transference** exists when the patient projects onto the therapist feelings obtained from an unconscious level. There are two kinds of patient-initiated transference. A **positive transference** occurs when the patient sees the therapist in glowing, magical terms. The therapist is a wonder worker; he or she can do no wrong. Sometimes that patient develops a crush on the therapist and thinks he or she is in love.

A **negative transference** occurs when the patient sees the therapist in negative, derogatory terms. The therapist is a jerk; his or her interpretations are stupid. A negative transference often forms toward the completion of therapy when the patient is trying to become autonomous and less dependent on the therapist. In both of the above kinds of transference, the therapist needs to interpret the transference in terms of unconscious desires. The therapist's aim should be to help the patient attain greater self-understanding.

Therapist-initiated transference is called **countertransference.** This takes place when the therapist develops a crush on the patient and thinks that he or she is in love. In such an instance, it is the therapist's ethical responsibility to avoid acting on his or her feelings. Often the therapist needs to reassign to case to a different professional person.

The general aim of psychoanalysis is to make accessible and comprehensible to the conscious mind information that has been creating emotional problems at an unconscious level.

(a) The _____ level of a dream is its concealed aspect, its meaning.

(b) A _____ occurs when the patient sees the therapist in glowing, magical terms.

Answers: (a) latent; (b) positive transference.

Client-Centered Therapy: A Humanistic Approach

Client-centered therapy is based on the assumption that the troubled person has powerful inner resources, resources that will help the individual think and feel better. Note that the word *patient* is avoided, and instead the word *client* is used. This is done in order to downplay the identification of a therapy-seeker as a sick person. The originator of client-centered therapy is Carl Rogers, a former president of the American Psychological Association. Rogers believed, in common with Maslow, that human beings have an inborn tendency to be self-actualizing. It is this tendency that must be tapped in order for the client to improve.

Unlike psychodynamic therapy, client-centered therapy does not attempt to explore the unconscious level. Instead, all work is done in face-to-face interviews at a conscious level. The therapy is a sort of intelligent discussion between the therapist and the client.

Rogers believed that most of us have an **ideal self,** a person we would like to become. We also have a **self-concept,** an image of the way we are. In the case of troubled people, the self-concept is unsatisfactory in relation to the ideal self. This state is known as **incongruence.** Client-centered therapy helps the client resolve the gap between the self-concept and the ideal self. When the gap is largely closed, there is a state of **congruence.** In such a state an individual is less likely to suffer from depression and anxiety.

In order to nurture a personal growth process, client-centered therapy employs a number of well-defined techniques and principles. Five of these will be identified below.

First, the therapy should be **non-directive.** The therapist should not tell the client what to do or try to make decisions for him or her. Indeed, an older name for client-centered therapy was **non-directive therapy.** Assume that Agatha is thinking of leaving her husband. She says, "He's been cheating on me again. What do you think? Do you think I should leave him?" The therapist does not answer, "Yes, I think so. He's no good for you." Nor does the therapist answer, "No, I don't think so. I believe you need to keep your marriage intact." Instead, the therapist might say something such as, "Let's explore the pros and cons together. Maybe I can help you evaluate your feelings. Then you can make a decision that is right for you."

(a) According to Rogers, in the case of troubled people, the self-concept is unsatisfactory in relation to the ideal self. This state is known as _____.

(b) An older name for client-centered therapy was _____ therapy.

Answers: (a) incongruence; (b) non-directive.

Second, the therapy should create a condition of **unconditional positive regard.** This means that the client needs to be respected as a person even if he or she speaks of moral lapses or irresponsible behavior. The aim of the therapy is to help, not to judge, the client.

Third, the therapy should employ **active listening.** The therapist gives the client high-quality verbal feedback. The therapist needs, from time to time, to summarize what the client has been saying. The therapist's remarks should help the client to recognize powerful feelings and persistent attitudes. Nodding and being agreeable is not active listening; it is passive listening. Although the therapist should not give direction, he or she should assist the client in his or her process of greater self-understanding.

Fourth, the therapist should be capable of **empathy.** Empathy exists when the therapist can readily imagine what it would be like to experience life as the client experiences it. The therapist, to some extent, shares the perceptual and emotional world of the troubled person. When empathy exists, the client tends to feel understood, that he or she and the therapist are "on the same wavelength."

Fifth, the therapist must be **genuine.** He or she should not be merely doing a job. Instead, the therapist must see the practice of psychotherapy as a high calling and really care about the client's long-run welfare.

(a) What three-word term does client-centered therapy use to indicate that a client should be respected even if he or she speaks of moral lapses or irresponsible behavior?

_____

(b) High-quality verbal feedback is called _____ listening.

(c) What exists when a therapist can readily imagine what it would be like to experience life as the client experiences it? _____

Answers: (a) Unconditional positive regard; (b) active; (c) Empathy.

Behavior Therapy: A "Bad" Habit Can Be Modified

Behavior therapy is based on the assumption that mental and emotional problems often consist of learned maladaptive responses. The key word here is *learned.* Behavior therapy is inspired by the work of such researchers as Ivan Pavlov, John Watson, and B. F. Skinner (see chapter 6). Informally, learned maladaptive responses are what people call bad habits. They are "bad" in the sense that they do not serve the long-run interests of the individual.

Let's examine two kinds of behavior therapy. First, **systematic desensitization** is based on principles of classical conditioning. It takes advantage of the process that Pavlov called **extinction,** the unlearning of a conditioned reflex. Systematic desensitization is of particular value in the treatment of phobic disorders. Originated by Joseph Wolpe, a psychiatrist, systematic desensitization assumes that irrational fears tend to decrease little by little with continued exposure to a fearful stimulus. Of course, the fearful stimulus needs to be presented in a safe environment, helping the patient to learn that there is nothing in reality to fear, that the fear is in fact nothing more than a "fear of fear itself."

For example, Gabrielle is a thirty-two-year-old married woman who is afraid to drive a car. She has never operated a motor vehicle and is so fearful that she won't even take a driver training class. She and the therapist draw up a list of fearful situations associated with driving. A "weak" situation is sitting in the driver's seat of a parked car with the motor running. A "strong" situation is driving on a freeway. When they are rank ordered, such a list is called a **hierarchy of fears.** Starting with the weak situation, the therapist presents a series of **guided fantasies,** word pictures that induce anxiety. Repeated exposure to the imagined situations reduces actual fear. In time, Gabrielle takes a driver training class and eventually obtains a driver's license.

Fearful stimuli can also be presented, when safe, in real life. This is called *in vivo* desensitization.

(a) Behavior therapy is based on the assumption that mental and emotional problems often consist of _____ maladaptive responses.

(b) Systematic desensitization takes advantage of the process that Pavlov called _____, the unlearning of a conditioned reflex.

(c) In systematic desensitization, word pictures that induce anxiety are called _____ fantasies.

Answers: (a) learned; (b) extinction; (c) guided.

Second, **behavior modification** is based on principles of operant conditioning. Behavior modification is of particular value in the treatment of maladaptive behaviors that involve actions with consequences. Examples of such behaviors are alcohol abuse, other drug abuse, frequent overeating, chronic procrastination, and self-destructive behaviors. Behavior modification is also used in mental hospitals to shape the behavior of difficult, disturbing patients in more cooperative directions. A **token economy** exists when patents can exchange tokens, earned for desirable behavior, for something of greater value such as a piece of pie or an opportunity to do something particularly interesting.

The basic idea of behavior modification is to reinforce desirable, adaptive behavior and to withhold reinforcement for undesirable, maladaptive behavior.

When behavior modification is used in voluntary, self-referred therapy, the patient and the therapist discuss **self-control strategies,** strategies that help the patient take control of his or her personal environment in such a manner that maladaptive behavior is in time extinguished.

The principles involved in behavior therapy are identical to those presented in the context of chapter 6, the chapter on learning. The behavior therapist makes a practical application of these principles to the problems of both mildly troubled people and people with mental disorders.

(a) Behavior modification is based on principles of _____ conditioning.

(b) The basic idea of behavior modification is to _____ desirable, adaptive behavior.

Answers: (a) operant; (b) reinforce.

Cognitive-Behavior Therapy: How Thinking Affects Emotions and Actions

Cognitive-behavior therapy refers to any approach to therapy that helps the patient to think more rationally in order to bring emotional states under better control. Two kinds of cognitive-behavior therapy will be identified.

Rational-emotive behavior therapy (REBT) operates on the assumption that irrational thoughts induce inappropriate anxiety, depression, and anger. Albert Ellis, a New York psychologist, originated REBT. He explicitly credits the ancient philosophy of **stoicism** for some of his inspiration. Stoicism taught that it is not events in themselves that make us suffer but the way we evaluate them.

REBT teaches patients an **A-B-C-D system** of emotional self-control. For example, Patrick is prone to chronic anxiety. He is driving in his car and hears a knocking sound. According to Ellis, this is point A, or the **activating event.** It is not the actual sound (A), but what Patrick thinks about A that induces anxiety. He thinks, "The engine is going to explode!" This is point B, the *belief.* In this case the belief is irrational because it is an overgeneralization. Patrick is jumping to an unwarranted conclusion. Patrick feels apprehensive. His heart is pounding. His mouth is dry. This is point C, the *consequence* of the belief. Point C in the system always refers to an emotional consequence. At this point, without therapy, Patrick usually stops. He suffers.

However, with therapy Patrick learns to introduce point D, a *dispute* of his belief. He says to himself, "I'm overgeneralizing. It's ridiculous to think that the engine is going to explode just because it's knocking. There are all kinds of things that make an engine knock. I'll just slow down and pull into the next gas station to check things out." Although disputing his irrational belief may not eliminate all of Patrick's anxiety, it will modulate it and place it within acceptable bounds.

As indicated above, the same A-B-C-D system can also be applied to depression and anger.

(a) Cognitive-behavior therapy refers to any approach to therapy that helps the patient to think more _____ in order to bring emotional states under better control.

(b) Rational-emotive behavior therapy (REBT) teaches patients an _____ system of emotional self-control.

Answers: (a) rationally; (b) A-B-C-D.

Cognitive therapy takes the same view of the relationship between thought and emotion as does REBT. Aaron Beck, a psychiatrist, originated cognitive therapy. Beck speaks of **automatic thoughts,** thoughts that appear at a conscious level without intention or the use of will. They are just a part of our thinking, and they are unbidden. As described by Beck, they are very similar to Ellis's concept of irrational thoughts.

Automatic thoughts tend to be illogical. They are said to be **cognitive distortions,** ways of thinking that tend to make the suffering person look upon the world incorrectly and unrealistically. As in REBT, the patient is encouraged to reflect on automatic thoughts and find ways to bring them under voluntary control. This is done primarily by an analysis of the thoughts themselves. Often, such an analysis reveals their absurdity.

In both REBT and cognitive therapy the therapist coaches the patient in ways to improve the quality of his or her thought processes.

It is not necessary to decide which kind of therapy is the best one. Many psychotherapists use **multi-modal therapy,** a general approach recognizing that all of the approaches have their use and place in the treatment of troubled people. In multi-modal therapy, the specific kind of therapy employed depends on the needs of the patient and the type of mental or emotional problem presented to the therapist.

(a) Beck speaks of _____ thoughts, thoughts that appear at a conscious level without intention or the use of will.

(b) Many psychotherapists use _____ therapy, a general approach recognizing that all of the approaches have their use and place in the treatment of troubled people.

Answers: (a) automatic; (b) multi-modal.

Group Therapy: Encountering Others

Group therapy, as its name clearly suggests, is therapy conducted in group settings. A typical group ranges from five to seven in number. The therapist acts as a **facilitator,** an individual who mediates between members of the group, allows everyone a chance to participate, and keeps the group on track. Any of the prior kinds of therapy specified can be conducted in a group setting.

Group therapy arose during World War II, over fifty years ago. There was a need to treat large numbers of patients suffering from **battle fatigue,** an inability to continue active service because of adverse emotional reactions to the stress of combat. (This same condition was called **shell shock** in World War I and *post-traumatic stress disorder [PTSD]* in the Vietnam War and later conflicts.) Trained psychotherapists were in short supply in military psychiatric wards. Out of necessity, clinical psychologists and psychiatrists began to see patients in groups. Group therapy was found to be highly effective. The patients learned from each other, shared feelings, and helped each other heal. Group therapy remains a principal way in which to make psychotherapy accessible to a large number of sufferers. It is used frequently in both mental hospitals and private practice settings.

In the 1960s a trend arose called the **human potential movement.** The basic idea of the movement was to go beyond using a group approach to heal the sick. Instead, the group structure was used to help a relatively normal person exceed his or her present level of mental and emotional development. To a large extent, the movement was based on Maslow's principle of self-actualization. Groups that aim at fostering one's potentialities and personal growth are called **encounter groups.** In an **encounter,** one human being meets another human being in an authentic manner without sham or pretense. At an informal level, members of the group "get real" with each other. The atmosphere of the group creates a kind of psychological mirror that allows the individual to see the self in a more reality-oriented way. Encounter groups were very popular in the 1960s and 1970s. Their popularity has ebbed, but they are still used.

(a) In group therapy, the therapist acts as a _____, an individual who mediates between members of the group, allows everyone a chance to participate, and keeps the group on track.

(b) Group therapy during World War II was often used to treat what condition related to the stress of combat? _____

(c) Groups that aim at fostering one's potentialities and personal growth are called _____ groups.

Answers: (a) facilitator; (b) Battle fatigue; (c) encounter.

Drug Therapy: A Revolution in Psychiatry

Drug therapy has revolutionized psychiatry in the past forty years. Before the advent of effective psychiatric drugs in the 1960s, one of the principal treatments used with severely disturbed mental patients—patients with disorders such as schizophrenia or major depressive episode—was electroconvulsive therapy. **Electroconvulsive therapy (ECT)** passes a mild electric current through the frontal lobes of the brain, inducing a seizure similar to a **grand mal seizure** in epilepsy. The therapy is sometimes effective; research suggests that it temporarily increases the level of certain of the nervous system's neurotransmitters, particularly norepinephrine. Although ECT is still sometimes employed, it has by and large given way to drug therapy.

Four categories of psychiatric drugs are: (1) antipsychotic agents, (2) antianxiety agents, (3) antidepressent agents, and (4) mood-stabilizing agents.

Antipsychotic agents are drugs that treat mental disorders characterized by a loss of touch with reality. The principal disorder treated with antipsychotic agents is schizophrenia. Delusions, hallucinations, and agitation tend to be either eliminated or reduced in intensity when patients use antipsychotic agents. The term **major tranquilizers** is sometimes also employed to classify these drugs. One of the ways in which antipsychotic agents work is by regulating the activity of the neurotransmitter dopamine.

Psychiatric drugs, like drugs in general, have a generic name and a trade name. Only the trade name of the drug is capitalized. A trade name for chlorpromazine is Thorazine. A trade name for haloperidol is Haldol. A trade name for clozapine is Clozaril. There are a number of other antipsychotic agents.

Antianxiety agents are used to treat the irrational anxiety associated with such disorders as generalized anxiety disorder, phobic disorder, and obsessive-compulsive disorder (OCD). Patients who take the agents usually report that they have fewer problems with chronic worry and related symptoms. These drugs have a sedative-hypnotic action. They lower central nervous system arousal. The term **minor tranquilizers** is sometimes employed to classify these drugs.

One of the ways in which some of the antianxiety agents work is by inducing muscle relaxation. Such relaxation has been found to be antagonistic to anxiety.

A trade name for diazepam is Valium. A trade name for meprobamate is Miltown. A trade name for alprazolam is Xanax. There are a number of other antianxiety agents.

(a) What kind of therapy passes a mild electric current through the frontal lobes of the brain? _____

(b) _____ agents are drugs that treat mental disorders characterized by a loss of touch with reality.

(c) What is another term used to classify antianxiety agents? _____

Answers: (a) Electroconvulsive therapy (ECT); (b) Antipsychotic; (c) Minor tranquilizers.

Antidepressant agents are used to treat such mental disorders as dysthymia and major depressive disorder. The three basic types of antidepressants are (1) tricyclic agents, (2) monoamine oxidase (MAO) inhibitors, and (3) selective serotonin reuptake inhibitors (SSRIs). The three types work in somewhat different ways. The tricyclic agents and the MAO inhibitors regulate the activity of the neurotransmitter norephinephrine, and to some extent serotonin. The SSRIs, as their name indicates, selectively regulate the activity of the neurotransmitter serotonin.

A trade name for imipramine, a tricyclic agent, is Tofranil. A trade name for phenelzine, an MAO inhibitor, is Nardil. A trade name for fluoxetine, an SSRI, is Prozac.

Mood-stabilizing agents are used primarily to treat cyclothymia and bipolar disorder. Strictly speaking, antidepressant agents also have the effect of stabilizing mood. However, the term *mood-stabilizing agents* is reserved for drugs that treat disorders in which emotional states such as mania alternate with emotional states such as depression.

Lithium carbonate, a natural mineral salt, is the best known mood-stabilizing agent. Its way of working is not completely understood. However, it does appear to regulate the activity of certain neurotransmitters and promote desirable changes in the ways in which some neurons function.

Trade names for lithium carbonate include Carbolith and Lithotabs.

Psychiatric drugs are treatments, not cures, for mental disorders. They help a troubled person live with a chronic problem. The principal aim associated with their use is long-term management of a mental disorder.

Also, psychiatric drugs have potentially toxic side effects. That is why all of them are prescription drugs and should be administered under the watchful eye of a medical doctor familiar with their various actions. All psychiatrists are medical doctors. Clinical psychologists have doctoral degrees in psychology, not medicine. Consequently, in most states they cannot prescribe drugs of any kind.

(a) The three basic kinds of antidepressant agents are tricyclic agents, monoamine oxidase (MAO) inhibitors, and _____.

(b) Mood-stabilizing agents are used primarily to treat cyclothymia and _____ disorder.

(c) _____, a natural mineral salt, is the best known mood-stabilizing agent.

> *Answers:* (a) selective serotonin reuptake inhibitors (SSRIs); (b) bipolar; (c) Lithium carbonate.

SELF-TEST

1. What therapies are based on the assumption that mental disorders are caused by emotional conflicts, maladaptive learning, cognitive errors, or similar behavioral processes?
   a. Psychologically based therapies
   b. Biologically based therapies
   c. Drug therapies
   d. Hormone therapies

2. What is the principal "digging" tool used by psychoanalysis?
   a. The interpretation of dreams
   b. The interpretation of slips of the tongue
   c. Unmasking of the ego defense mechanisms
   d. Free association

3. According to Freud, what aspect of a dream contains a forbidden wish?
   a. The manifest level
   b. The latent level
   c. The conscious content
   d. Its ego-oriented features

4. What feature of client-centered therapy is associated with the concept that the client needs to be respected as a person even if he or she speaks of moral lapses or irresponsible behavior?
   a. Empathy
   b. Congruence of the two selves
   c. Unconditional positive regard
   d. Active listening

5. Behavior modification is based on
   a. biological assumptions
   b. principles of operant conditioning
   c. Freudian theory
   d. the recovery of repressed information

6. Albert Ellis originated rational-emotive behavior therapy (REBT). He explicitly credits what ancient philosophy for some of his inspiration?
   a. Stoicism
   b. Empiricism
   c. Hedonism
   d. Determinism

7. Aaron Beck speaks of automatic thoughts. These are very similar to Ellis's concept of
   a. repressed memories
   b. activating events
   c. irrational thoughts
   d. involuntary perceptions

8. Groups that aim at fostering one's potentialities and personal growth are called
   a. Jungian self-realization groups
   b. encounter groups
   c. psychoanalytic groups
   d. actualization-orientation groups

9. What drugs treat mental disorders characterized by a loss of touch with reality?
   a. Antianxiety agents
   b. Antidepressent agents
   c. Mood-stabilizing agents
   d. Antipsychotic agents

10. Which of the following drugs is associated primarily with the treatment of bipolar disorder?
    a. Lithium carbonate
    b. Haloperidol
    c. Chlorpromazine
    d. Diazepam

ANSWERS TO THE SELF-TEST

1-a 2-d 3-b 4-c 5-b 6-a 7-c 8-b 9-d 10-a

ANSWERS TO THE TRUE-OR-FALSE PREVIEW QUIZ

1. True.
2. False. The main way that Freud explored the unconscious roots of mental-emotional problems was with the "digging" tool of free association.
3. True.
4. False. Behavior therapy is based on the assumption that mental and emotional problems often arise because of learned maladaptive responses.
5. False. Antipsychotic agents are drugs that treat mental disorders characterized by a loss of touch with reality.

KEY TERMS

A-B-C-D system
activating event
active listening
antianxiety agents
antidepressant agents
antipsychotic agents
automatic thoughts
battle fatigue
behavior modification
behavior therapy
biologically based therapies
client-centered therapy
cognitive distortions
cognitive therapy
cognitive-behavior therapy
congruence
countertransference
drug therapy
electroconvulsive therapy (ECT)
empathy
encounter
encounter groups
extinction

facilitator
free association
Freudian slips
genuine
grand mal seizure
group therapy
guided fantasies
hierarchy of fears
human potential movement
ideal self
incongruence
interpretation
in vivo desensitization
latent level
lithium carbonate
major tranquilizers
manifest level
minor tranquilizers
mood-stabilizing agents
multi-modal therapy
negative transference
non-directive
non-directive therapy

positive transference

post-traumatic stress disorder (PTSD)

psychodynamic therapy

psychologically based therapies

psychotherapy

rational-emotive behavior therapy (REBT)

self-concept

self-control strategies

shell shock

slips of the tongue

stoicism

systematic desensitization

therapy

token economy

transference

unconditional positive regard

Watsonian slips

16 Social Psychology: Interacting with Other People

True or False

1. **T F** Social psychology is the systematic study of how exchanges with other people in our environment influence our thoughts, feelings, and actions.
2. **T F** Personality traits play almost no role in interpersonal attraction.
3. **T F** In the art of persuasion, a one-sided argument is usually more effective than a two-sided argument.
4. **T F** The social phenomenon known as bystander apathy suggests that people in the city are cold and unfeeling and that people in a small town are warm and understanding.
5. **T F** Cognitive dissonance is a mental state created when opposed ideas exist simultaneously at a conscious level.

(Answers can be found on page 260.)

Psychology is to a large extent the study of thoughts, feelings, and actions. Nonetheless, much of our behavior takes place in the context of either a relationship or a reaction to other people. Social psychology, the subject of this chapter, recognizes the importance that others play in determining our behavior.

Objectives

After completing this chapter, you will be able to

- define social psychology;
- identify six important aspects of interpersonal attraction;
- describe the four key components making up an attitude;
- discuss the factors involved in the art of persuasion;
- specify the processes that induce conformity;
- explain the three ways in which human beings reduce cognitive dissonance.

You will recall from chapter 9 that Aristotle called the human being the thinking animal. The human being could just as well be called the *social animal*. (*The Social Animal* is, indeed, the title of a book by the research psychologist Elliot Aaronson.)

A moment's reflection reveals that much human behavior occurs in group settings: the family, school, club, church, military unit, and so forth. These group settings automatically imply interactions with other people. The way in which we interact with others such as our friends, parents, siblings, and coworkers affects our moods and much of what we do.

All of us are immersed in a sort of sea of other human beings. This is what was referred to in the context of Erik Erikson's developmental theory as the **social world** (see chapter 11). And although we all seek isolation and escape from the social world from time to time, few of us would want to become permanent hermits.

In order to examine the full spectrum of human behavior it is essential to explore **social behavior,** behavior that involves interactions with other people. **Social psychology,** the subject matter of this chapter, is the systematic study of how exchanges with these others in our environment influence our thoughts, feelings, and actions.

(a) Social behavior is behavior that involves _____ with other people.

(b) Social psychology is the systematic study of how exchanges with others in our environment influence our _____, feelings, and _____.

Answers: (a) interactions; (b) thoughts; actions.

Interpersonal Attraction: Who Likes Whom, and Why?

The **social dyad** is a group consisting of two people. It is the basic unit of social behavior. The dyad is a common element in dating behavior, marriage, and the formation of friendships. Consequently a study of the dyad and the factors involved in its formation is an important aspect of social psychology. **Interpersonal attraction** exists between two people when they make, or wish to make, more approach responses than avoidance responses to each other. It is this, the presence of an interpersonal attraction, that leads to the spontaneous formation of dyads. Informally, we say that two people are "drawn" to each other or that some kind of "magnetism" exists.

It should be noted that attraction is not necessarily interpersonal. It is interpersonal only if the attraction is mutual. If Gerald has a crush on Lauren, and if Lauren does not share Gerald's feelings, then the attraction is **unilateral,** not interpersonal. The concepts presented below can be understood in the framework of either unilateral or interpersonal attraction. Six aspects of interpersonal attraction will be explored.

First, *physical appearance* plays an important role in interpersonal attraction. Beverly thinks, "Gilbert is so good-looking." Gilbert thinks, "Beverly is so beautiful." Obviously, these perceptions play an important part in their interpersonal attraction. The word *perception* needs to be stressed. Females other than Beverly may not perceive Gilbert as good-looking. Males other than Gilbert may not perceive Beverly as beautiful. An old saying states, "Beauty is in the eye of the beholder." The perception of physical appearance itself is affected by a number of factors, including the ones identified below.

Second, *personality traits* are a set of factors. It is sometimes said that opposites attract. In the case of personality, there seems to be an element of truth in the assertion. There is likely to be an interpersonal attraction between an extravert and an introvert. The extravert has an audience, and the introvert is more comfortable listening than talking. There is also likely to be an interpersonal attraction between a dominating person and a submissive one. The dominating person has someone to boss, and the submissive person wants to be told what to do. The principle at work here is called **reciprocity,** which consists of an exchange that has value for both individuals.

(a) The social dyad is a group consisting of _____ people.

(b) _____ attraction exists between two people when they make, or wish to make, more approach responses than avoidance responses to each other.

(c) Beverly thinks, "Gilbert is so good-looking." In this case, what factor is playing a role in her attraction to him? _____

(d) When it appears under certain circumstances that opposites in personality do in fact seem to attract each other, what principle appears to be at work? _____

Answers: (a) two; (b) Interpersonal; (c) Physical appearance; (d) Reciprocity.

Third, *interests* are sets of factors. If Arthur is interested in reading science-fiction novels, and if Herman is also interested in reading such novels, this may form a partial basis for a friendship. Mutual interests that people have in music, movies, decorating, travel, sports, and cooking provide additional examples of subjects that may bring people together. Does this contradict the observation that opposites attract? No, not if this observation is limited, as it was above, to personality traits. In the case of interests, it seems that another saying is applicable: "Birds of a feather flock together."

Fourth, the **matching hypothesis** states that interpersonal attraction is fostered when two people see themselves as relatively similar in intelligence, stature, ambition, and other personal characteristics. A woman who perceives herself as very bright will look for a very bright male. A man who is short will generally be attracted to a relatively short woman, not to a statuesque one. An individual who wants to become a big financial success will tend to be attracted to similarly ambitious people, not those with a low level of financial aspiration.

(a) Both Arthur and Herman like to read science-fiction novels. They like each other. In this case, what factor appears to be playing a role in interpersonal attraction? _____

(b) The _____ hypothesis states that interpersonal attraction is fostered when two people see themselves as relatively similar in personal characteristics.

Answers: (a) Interests; (b) matching.

Fifth, the ratio of *gains* to *losses* is a factor. Elliot Aronson, referred to earlier, developed the **gain-loss theory of interpersonal attraction.** A *gain* is a perceived benefit; for example, one's self-esteem might rise after receiving a compliment. A *loss* is a perceived detriment; for example, one's self-esteem might fall after receiving a criticism. Let's say that Rebecca gives compliments freely and frequently to Sophia. Rebecca is never critical. A different friend, Susan, gives compliments to Sophia somewhat less frequently and with more restraint. Sometimes she gives a little negative feedback. Who will Sophia be more attracted to? According to the gain-loss theory, she will tend to be more attracted to Susan. Sophia places more value on Susan's compliments than on Rebecca's. Susan's statements of praise seem thoughtful, and, consequently, when given they tend to raise Sophia's self-esteem more than the ones given by Rebecca. Sophia tends to think of Susan as genuine and authentic. Sophia suspects that Rebecca is an insincere fake.

Sixth, according to **attribution theory,** we are prone to explain the behavior of other human beings by attributing motives to them. We don't know for sure that these motives exist. We infer them from behavior, and then project them into the other person's inner world. For example, Murphy sits next to Trudy in a college class. Whenever Murphy speaks to Trudy, she is friendly and responsive. He begins to make attributions. "She likes me." Or, "She wants me to ask her out." Murphy's attraction to Trudy is intensified by these attributions. The attributions may or may not be correct. If they are correct, then asking Trudy for a date will be a rewarding experience. If they are incorrect, then asking Trudy for a date will be an embarrassing experience.

There are, of course, other factors involved in interpersonal attraction. However, the ones identified account for much of the variability in who likes whom.

(a) What theory of interpersonal attraction suggests that under certain conditions we might perceive another person as an insincere fake? _____

(b) When we infer motives from behavior, we are making an _____.

Answers: (a) The gain-loss theory; (b) attribution.

Attitudes: Exploring Psychological Positions

President Franklin Delano Roosevelt said, "I hate war." Mary, a mother says, "I'm pro-life. I can't stand the idea of abortion." Ralph says, "I think it's great that I can make business calls from my cell phone when I'm eating lunch."

All of the above statements reveal the presence of attitudes. An **attitude** is a relatively stable disposition to think, feel, or act in either a positive or negative manner in response to certain kinds of situations, people, or objects. When an attitude reflects in any way on the behavior of other individuals or groups, it is called a **social attitude.** The way in which we think about war, abortion, and the use of cell phones in public places provide examples of social attitudes.

There are four components to an attitude: (1) evaluative, (2) cognitive, (3) affective, and (4) behavioral.

The **evaluative component** refers to the fact that an attitude is said to be either positive or negative. Ralph has a positive attitude toward the use of cell phones in public places. Someone else may have a negative attitude toward the same behavior.

(a) When an attitude reflects in any way on the behavior of other individuals or groups it is called a _____ attitude.

(b) The _____ component of an attitude refers to the fact that an attitude is said to be either positive or negative.

Answers: (a) social; (b) evaluative.

The **cognitive component** refers to what an individual thinks *in association* with a particular attitude. Amanda has a positive attitude toward the use of nuclear reactors to generate electricity. She thinks, "If we want to live in the modern world, we need plenty of power. Nuclear reactors provide it." Preston has a negative attitude toward nuclear reactors. He thinks, "If we want to live in a safer world, a world without radioactive fallout, we should start generating more electricity with wind turbines."

The **affective component** refers to whatever emotions are triggered by a particular attitude. Richard has a positive attitude toward the potential entry of his nation into a particular war. When he hears a military band, his heart begins to race. He gets goose bumps. He is filled with pride in his country. John has a negative attitude toward the same war. When he hears military music or sees a parade, he sometimes feels depressed, and sometimes he feels angry.

The **behavioral component** refers to the action that an individual takes in connection with a particular attitude. Returning to Amanda, when she hears that a new nuclear plant is being proposed in her county of residence, she writes to the members of the board of supervisors encouraging them to vote in favor of zoning changes that will make construction possible. On the other hand, Preston carries signs in a protest march designed to block the building of a new nuclear power plant. He writes letters to the governor of the state begging him to interfere with the construction of the plant.

(a) The _____ component of an attitude refers to what an individual thinks in association with a particular attitude.

(b) The _____ component of an attitude refers to whatever emotions are triggered by a particular attitude.

(c) The _____ component of an attitude refers to the action that an individual takes in connection with a particular attitude.

   Answers: (a) cognitive; (b) affective; (c) behavioral.

The Art of Persuasion: Toward the Changing of Attitudes

Special interest groups, political parties, certain corporations, lobbying organizations, advertising agencies, and powerful individuals often have an interest in changing widely held attitudes. Consequently, a great deal of thought has been given to the **art of persuasion,** an application of the factors that can to some extent induce a change of attitude in either a target individual or a target audience.

It is often effective to make an **appeal to authority.** A reference can be made to a physician, scientist, attorney, psychologist, or other professional person. The authority, in order to be effective, should be *credible*. What he or she says should be easy to believe. This is why the authority figure often has a degree and or a lot of experience in a field of study associated with the attitude.

(a) The art of _____ refers to an application of the factors that can to some extent induce a change in attitude.

(b) Let's say that a speechmaker quotes a famous scientist in order to support a point being made in the presentation. This approach represents an appeal to _____.

Answers: (a) persuasion; (b) authority.

An **appeal to reason** is also often used. The agent of persuasion sets forth facts and makes a logical, rational appeal. A speechmaker says, "If we don't raise taxes, then we won't be able to repair roads and bridges." This is an appeal based on deductive logic (see chapter 9 and the section on logic.)

An appeal to reason can be made in the form of a one-sided or a two-sided argument. A **one-sided argument** sets forth only the favorable aspects of a given attitude. For example, a speechmaker states some of the reasons to raise taxes, but offers no reasons for keeping them at current levels.

A **two-sided argument** sets forth both the favorable and unfavorable aspects of a given attitude. For example, a speechmaker states some of the reasons to raise taxes. Then he or she offers a few reasons to keep them at current levels, and concludes with reasons to raise them. A certain appearance of balance and fairness has been given. However, the speechmaker has given primary emphasis to reasons to raise taxes. A two-sided argument is generally more persuasive than a one-sided argument.

Third, an **emotional appeal** is often persuasive. Such an appeal bypasses reason and logic. Lester has a negative attitude toward organized charities. He says, "They're a bunch of rip-off artists." Then he sees a television presentation featuring a child named Gloria in a wheelchair. Gloria, only seven, speaks of the pain and suffering associated with a specific disease. Lester finds himself writing a check to the charity that sponsored her appearance. His attitude toward one particular organized charity has moved, perhaps only temporarily, from negative to positive.

Fourth, the **mood** of the target person or audience is a factor in attitude change. Flora, a retired schoolteacher, has a negative attitude toward health maintenance organizations (HMOs). She is invited to a free brunch for senior citizens given by a particular HMO. After Flora and the group are well fed, a speaker warms up the audience with jokes. Finally, the speaker gets down to brass tacks and begins to use some of the methods of persuasion already identified above. Flora finds herself wavering. She begins to find the thought of joining this particular HMO appealing. Flora's good mood helps to induce an attitude change.

(a) A _____ argument sets forth only the favorable aspects of a given attitude.

(b) An _____ appeal bypasses reason and logic.

(c) Food and jokes sometimes facilitate attitude change by influencing the _____ of an audience.

Answers: (a) one-sided; (b) emotional; (c) mood.

Conformity and Social Influence: Reacting to Other People

If you are invited to a formal dinner party, how do you know which fork to pick up for the shrimp cocktail and which fork to use for the green salad? One way to find out is to wait until two or three people have started eating. Then simply do what they do. It is safe in this situation to conform to what others do.

A familiar proverb recommends: "When in Rome do as the Romans do." Again, the basic idea is that there is safety in conformity.

Conformity in social behavior exists when one individual makes an effort to match his or her behavior to the behavior of other members of a reference group. Conformity is at odds with the need for autonomy. **Autonomy** exists when one individual takes voluntary action that may or may not conform to group behavior. Autonomy is represented in expressions such as: "I'm going to do it my way," "I've got to take my own pathway," or "I'm determined to think for myself."

In order to have law and order as well as an organized society, it appears necessary to have some degree of social conformity. Total lack of conformity suggests public chaos. From the point of view of the family, school, religious organization, military organization, and similar groups, it is necessary that individuals display **prosocial behavior,** behavior that fosters the long-run interests of a given group. **Antisocial behavior,** on the other hand, undermines the long-run interests of a group.

(a) _____ in social behavior exists when one individual makes an effort to match his or her behavior to the behavior of other members of a reference group.

(b) _____ behavior fosters the long-run interests of a given group.

Answers: (a) Conformity; (b) Prosocial.

Certain factors play a significant role in determining behavior that encourages an individual to conform to the behavior of a given group. First, the perceived **ambiguity** of a situation makes social influence more effective. **Social influence** is the impact on one person's thinking and perception that arises from the behavior and opinions of one or more other people. Velma is an eighteen-year-old high-school graduate. She's thinking of taking a full-time clerical job with a local insurance broker. Alternatively, she's thinking of going full-time to the local community college while working part time. Both options seem equally attractive to her. The situation is ambiguous because she can easily see her near-future activity in two ways. Velma's best friend, Wanda, tells Velma all of the reasons why she thinks it's a good idea to go to a community college instead of taking on a regular job. The social influence exerted by Wanda resolves Velma's doubts, and she decides to go to the community college.

The social psychologist Muzafer Sherif did a series of experiments on social influence over sixty years ago. In a typical experiment, Maxwell, a subject, is brought alone into a dark room. There is a pinpoint of light. It is stationary. However, with no frame of reference, it appears to be moving. This is called the **autokinetic effect,** and it is due to slight involuntary movements of the eyeballs. The movements are random. The subject is allowed to believe that the perceived movement is in fact objective, actual movement, though he is unable to identify any particular pattern of motion.

Two additional people are brought into the room. They seem to be subjects, but they are not; they are working with the researcher. They engage Maxwell in discussion. The discussion leads the two new "subjects" to say, "The light is moving in a clockwise circle." This is not their perception, it's just what they have already agreed to say. Soon Maxwell perceives the light to be moving in a clockwise circle.

When Maxwell is interviewed later, he seems to be convinced that he actually saw the light moving clockwise. It appears that social influence affected his actual perception. Again, it is the ambiguity of a situation that makes social influence particularly powerful.

(a) The perceived _____ of a situation makes social influence more effective.

(b) A stationary pinpoint of light in a dark room, without a frame of reference, appears to be moving. This is called the _____ effect.

Answers: (a) ambiguity; (b) autokinetic.

Second, **obedience,** a tendency to conform to the requests of an authority figure, plays a role in conformity. If a nurse asks you to undress for a medical examination, you usually do. If a teacher asks you to sit in a particular place, you probably will. If a judge pounds a gavel and requests order, the courtroom generally quiets down.

A series of important experiments on obedience was reported by the psychologist Stanley Milgram in his book *Obedience to Authority.* Here is a description of a typical experiment. Sylvia believes that she is an assistant to a research psychologist. The research psychologist, an impressive authority with a Ph.D. and a white coat, explains that a subject will be administered electric shocks as a part of a learning experiment. When the subject makes a mistake, he or she will be given increasing levels of painful shock. The subject is not actually being shocked; he or she is acting. The whole setup is a sham. Nonetheless, Sylvia is convinced that she is turning dials that cause pain. Reluctantly, she is willing, with the encouragement of the researcher, to administer very high levels of shock.

Milgram found that a majority of subjects were willing to inflict high levels of shock on protesting "learners." The interpretation of the subjects' behavior was not that they were latent sadists or had excessive repressed hostility. No, they were conforming, responding to an authority figure. The key factor was, as indicated, simply obedience.

(a) _____ is a tendency to conform to the requests of an authority figure.

(b) Milgram found that subjects, when requested to do so by an authority figure, are often willing to administer high levels of _____ to another person.

Answers: (a) Obedience; (b) shock.

Third, **balance theory** suggests that human beings have a need for balance, a state of equilibrium, in their relationships to both objects and other people. For example, three female friends want to select a motion picture to see. Alice wants to go see picture A. Becky and Carla want to go see picture B. A state of imbalance exists, and there is a certain amount of social discomfort. A state of balance will be restored among the friends only if they all agree to go see or to avoid a certain picture.

It is most likely that Alice, in order to restore balance, will agree to go see picture B. However, if Alice is very stubborn, balance can also be restored if both Becky and Carla agree to go see picture A. Because of a psychological need for balance, human beings often conform to the wishes of others.

_____ theory suggests that human beings have a need for a state of equilibrium in their relationships to both objects and other people.

Answer: Balance.

Fourth, the **diffusion hypothesis** suggests that we are less likely to conform to social expectations if we perceive ourselves as carrying only an insignificant portion of an overall responsibility to act. Let's say that among eight brothers and sisters one sister, Janna, dies. A single mother, she leaves a three-year-old child, Luke. Who will take Luke in and give him a home? If none of the siblings really want to take on the responsibility of raising Luke, each of them will expect one of the others to do it. Perhaps no one will act, or they will be very slow to do so.

On the other hand, let's imagine a different scenario. Janna has only a sister and no brothers. Now Janna's sister feels the entire responsibility to raise Luke. She experiences tremendous pressure to come through and do the socially expected thing. Consequently, she responds and takes Luke into her home.

The diffusion hypothesis is usually used to explain **bystander apathy,** a tendency of individuals to do nothing to help out in a crisis if there are a lot of other people around. For example, if someone collapses and seems to be having a heart attack on a busy city street, many people will walk by and glance at the victim without doing anything. On the other hand, if the same thing happens in a small town, the witnesses to the person's plight are much more likely to come forward and render aid. The interpretation of this behavior is not that people in the city are cold and unfeeling and that people in a small town are warm and understanding. The explanation is in terms of the diffusion hypothesis. A person in the city may think, "Someone else will help. And I'm already late for work." A person in a small town may think, "I better give a hand. There's no one else to help." Bystander apathy represents a failure to conform to social expectations. But the logic of the diffusion hypothesis lends itself to also explaining, as indicated above, conformity.

(a) The _____ hypothesis suggests that we are less likely to conform to social expectations if we perceive ourselves as carrying only an insignificant portion of an overall responsibility to act.

(b) _____ is a tendency of individuals to do nothing to help out in a crisis if there are a lot of other people around.

Answers: (a) diffusion; (b) Bystander apathy.

Cognitive Dissonance Theory: The Square Peg Can't Fit in the Round Hole

Social behavior can often be explained in terms of a need to reduce cognitive dissonance. **Cognitive dissonance** is a mental state created when opposed ideas exist simultaneously at a conscious level. Idea A is, so to speak, like a square peg. Idea B is like a round hole. The two ideas are mutually exclusive and can't be fit together. Nonetheless, they coexist, at least for a time. And this produces a state of mental and emotional discomfort. The concept of cognitive dissonance was proposed by the social psychologist Leon Festinger.

Let us say that Louise is embroiled in a tumultuous love affair with Harry. Idea A is, "I can't live without Harry." Louise genuinely sees a future without Harry as meaningless. Idea B is, "I don't think he's good for me." Louise is convinced that Harry is selfish and abusive. There is a basic need to reduce cognitive dissonance. As long as dissonance is allowed to continue, she is in a state of misery.

According to Festinger, there are three ways in which human beings reduce dissonance: (1) a change in behavior, (2) a change in one of the ideas, and (3) the addition of a new idea.

In the case of Louise, a *change in behavior* can take place in one of several ways. She may begin to date other men in order to prove to herself that she *can* live without Harry. Or she may impulsively move to a new area, miles away from Harry, again trying to prove she isn't completely dependent. Or she may take a complete opposite tack. She may impulsively marry Harry, trying to set aside her misgivings about him.

Louise can *change one of her ideas.* She does a lot of thinking and makes lengthy entries in a personal journal. She changes idea A and concludes that "there are a lot of fish in the sea" and that Harry is just one of many potential partners. Or, conversely, she changes idea B and concludes that Harry isn't selfish and abusive at all. She has been misinterpreting his behavior. It is she that is wrong in her evaluations and perceptions.

Louise can *add a new idea.* She decides that what Harry needs is the right kind of nurturing. He is like a little boy waiting to grow up. If they were to marry, she would guide him and help him grow toward maturity and responsibility. With this new idea in mind, she can proceed to either marry Harry or continue the relationship.

Any one of the three approaches described above can be used to reduce dissonance. The theory of cognitive dissonance can be generalized to many situations. Gavin believes in the Commandment that says "Thou shalt not kill." He also believes that he should defend his country during time of war, and this may require the killing of others. Denise believes that in order to be a good mother to her children, she needs to devote all of her time to homemaking. She also believes that she wants to have a career as a magazine editor. As is evident, we often face situations that induce cognitive dissonance.

(a) _____ is a mental state created when opposed ideas exist simultaneously at a conscious level.

(b) Let's say that Louise begins to date other men in order to prove to herself that she *can* live without Harry. She is attempting to reduce dissonance by a _____.

Answers: (a) Cognitive dissonance; (b) change in behavior.

SELF-TEST

1. What exists between two people when they make, or wish to make, more approach responses than avoidance responses to each other?
   a. Bilateral attention
   b. Unilateral attraction
   c. Interpersonal attraction
   d. Narcissistic attraction

2. According to the matching hypothesis, one of the following is correct.
   a. A woman who perceives herself as very bright will look for a bright male.
   b. A man who is short will generally be attracted to statuesque women.
   c. An individual who wants to become a big financial success will tend to be attracted to people without ambition.
   d. A man who perceives himself as very bright will look for a woman of slightly below average intelligence.

3. Sophia is more attracted to her friend Susan than to her friend Rebecca. Susan gives compliments to Sophia sparingly and with restraint. Rebecca gives compliments to Sophia freely and frequently. What theory explains Sophia's greater attraction to Susan?
   a. The paradoxical theory of interpersonal attraction
   b. The gain-gain theory of interpersonal attraction
   c. The gain-loss theory of interpersonal attraction
   d. The win-win theory of interpersonal attraction

4. What component of an attitude refers to the fact that an attitude is said to be either positive or negative?
   a. The reactive component
   b. The variability component
   c. The polarization component
   d. The evaluative component

5. An appeal to authority, in order to be effective, should be
   a. information oriented
   b. credible
   c. scientific
   d. statistical

6. An emotional appeal is often persuasive. Such an appeal
   a. bypasses reason and logic
   b. is effective because it uses metalogic
   c. is said to be "cognitive" in its effects
   d. trades on the self-actualization process

7. Which of the following is at odds with conformity?
   a. The need for achievement
   b. The need for autonomy
   c. The need for order
   d. The need for affiliation

8. The autokinetic effect, associated with ambiguity in perception, has been used to study
   a. psychopathic deviation
   b. antisocial behavior
   c. the structure of social dyads
   d. social influence

9. What hypothesis suggests that we are less likely to conform to social expectations if we perceive ourselves carrying only an insignificant portion of an overall responsibility to act?
   a. The diffusion hypothesis
   b. The exclusion hypothesis
   c. The density hypothesis
   d. The credibility hypothesis

10. What mental state is created when opposed ideas exist simultaneously at a conscious level?
    a. Affective helplessness
    b. Cognitive dissonance
    c. Affective congruence
    d. Cognitive congruence

ANSWERS TO THE SELF-TEST

1-c 2-a 3-c 4-d 5-b 6-a 7-b 8-d 9-a 10-b

ANSWERS TO THE TRUE-OR-FALSE PREVIEW QUIZ

1. True.
2. False. Personality traits play an important role in interpersonal attraction.
3. False. In the art of persuasion, a two-sided argument is usually more effective than a one-sided argument.
4. False. The social phenomenon known as bystander apathy is explained by the diffusion hypothesis. This hypothesis suggests that we are less likely to conform to social expectations if we perceive ourselves as carrying only an insignificant portion of an overall responsibility to act.
5. True.

KEY TERMS

affective component

ambiguity

antisocial behavior

appeal to authority

appeal to reason

art of persuasion

attitude

attribution theory

autokinetic effect

autonomy

balance theory

behavioral component

bystander apathy

cognitive component

cognitive dissonance

conformity

diffusion hypothesis

emotional appeal

evaluative component

gain-loss theory of interpersonal attraction

interpersonal attraction

matching hypothesis

mood

obedience

one-sided argument

prosocial behavior

reciprocity

social attitude

social behavior

social dyad

social influence

social psychology

social world

two-sided argument

unilateral attraction

INDEX